Global Trafficking in Women and Children

Edited by Obi N. I. Ebbe and Dilip K. Das

CRC Press
Taylor & Francis Group
Boca Raton London New York

CRC Press is an imprint of the
Taylor & Francis Group, an **informa** business

CRC Press
Taylor & Francis Group
6000 Broken Sound Parkway NW, Suite 300
Boca Raton, FL 33487-2742

© 2008 by Taylor & Francis Group, LLC
CRC Press is an imprint of Taylor & Francis Group, an Informa business

Library of Congress Cataloging-in-Publication Data

Ebbe, Obi N. Ignatius.
    Global trafficking in women and children / Obi N.I. Ebbe and Dilip K. Das.
        p. cm.
    Includes bibliographical references and index.
    ISBN 978-1-4200-5943-4 (alk. paper)
    1. Human trafficking. 2. Prostitution. 3. Child prostitution. 4. Women--Crimes against. 5. Children--Crimes against. I. Das, Dilip K., 1941- II. Title.

HQ281.E18 2008
364.15--dc22   2007024601

Visit the Taylor & Francis Web site at
http://www.taylorandfrancis.com

and the CRC Press Web site at
http://www.crcpress.com

Contents

Part II

CASE STUDIES IN TRAFFICKING IN WOMEN AND CHILDREN

Foreword

"Every so often, we catch a glimpse of ourselves. Maybe a moment comes in a quiet conversation with a friend or as we look in the mirror to check how we are dressed. But once in a rare while, we take a moment to notice the woman staring back at us, to notice all the things going on internally that may not be noticeable to the outside world. Who is that we see?"

This quotation is taken from another contemporary publication that is no less powerful than this one: *Imagining Ourselves: Global Voices from a New Generation of Women*, by Paula Goldman (2006).

The quotation is very much true about us. Our society, our world order. And the book you are about to read, *Global Trafficking in Women and Children*, is the mirror that reflects worldwide processes in our society on both micro and macro levels. It is what the governments and the police see, and it is also what abused women and children around the world would see if they had a quiet moment to forget about their sufferings and the unfairness of the world they ended up in and look at themselves in the mirror, seeing the beautiful, dignified human being inside them.

Human trafficking is a global disease of our time in which the scope, prevalence, diversity, and complexity in human trading has been transformed, this change coinciding with the change of the millennium. This disease has historical parallels with the movement of people as commodities during the colonial slave trade. It is, as Obi N.I. Ebbe has put it so powerfully and evocatively in the second chapter of this book, "an attack on the dignity of the human race." It is a horrifying phenomenon that damages lives and burns out souls, and awareness about it has to be spread across oceans and continents every day, every hour, every minute.

This book, however, is much more than just a reflection. Although a mirror could provide us with a glimpse of something we might have not seen or might have forgotten, the depiction of things might be rather flat and one-sided. *Global Trafficking in Women and Children* acts as a kaleidoscope: it gathers knowledge and experience from 43 countries on several continents, allowing us to analyze the similarities and differences of the countries' history and current events that would predetermine the conditions for the trafficking phenomenon in each particular area. This international collection of works offers the readers a multifaceted approach to the problem, drawing on the practice of the countries that have a longer history of battling trafficking as an organized crime activity.

The work also acts as a magnifying glass, looking at particular case studies and the lives of individuals affected by the system, which bring about the sense of immediate tragic reality. It demonstrates clearly the scale and the spread of the problem of global trafficking in women and children, and it provides a powerful analysis of the circumstances that contribute to the abuse and victimization of women and children as well as of the international policies and strategies used to combat these crimes.

Readers looking for a structured and detailed overview of the problem of trafficking in women and children on the global cross-border level or who are dealing with present and future challenges will find many insights into their questions in this book. The material is a comprehensive portfolio of documents focusing on causes of human trafficking, prostitution and slavery, types of trafficking, its definitions, and debate around these issues. Political, economic, and social changes—processes happening on the area and country levels—including wars, poverty, famine, and similar factors of great scope combined with views and rituals rooted in the country's history and traditions affect the most vulnerable citizens. They affect these people's individual and family circumstances and draw them to what they see as safety or security—personal or financial—hope, and a better life. More developed countries and the ones belonging to the Third World might have a different history with the crime, but they are facing similar problems.

This book provides a broad and consistent compilation of the controls and prevention tools needed for combating this 21st-century crime, from providing international to country-specific laws and mechanisms to drawing comparisons and identifying the solutions that proved to be most successful in circumstances, some of which are simple, as evidenced within, and others less so. All in all, this book serves as an essential manual for practitioners from both government and nongovernmental sectors, researchers, students, and anybody who would like to have an insight into this subject.

Human trafficking and exploitation are not legal anywhere, yet they happen everywhere. The trafficked women and children are real slaves—they cannot just get up and walk away from their abusers holding them hostage, as they are made to believe this is the way for them to be. According to the nongovernmental organization Free the Slaves, there are over 27 million people with no freedom in the world today—more than at any other time in the history of mankind.

It would be naïve of us to think that the problems of abuse, slavery, and trafficking will go away tomorrow, especially as the powerful law of supply and demand is so voracious, as others have previously argued (e.g., Kempadoo & Doezema, 1998). More likely is that more countries and governments will wake up tomorrow and defeat the stigmas and taboos that today do not allow them to join the rest of the world in the battle for human rights and freedom. Cooperation at all levels, from local and regional to intercountry and from multiagency to truly global, seems to be the way forward—this is also the most proactive and self-sustaining approach. We are all members of the same human family, and our problems are not unique—they are shared. And so should be the solutions.

The work is shrinking metaphorically. As we know, via globalization, boundaries are vanishing, which, although unfortunately useful for the traffickers, also allows governments and police all over the world to unite and multiply their effect. A major cooperative effort is needed to tackle this corporeal globalization and organized crime (Pentinnen, 2004); this is where *Global Trafficking in Women and Children* is very well placed, bringing together international knowledge and allowing practitioners to move forward faster based on shared practice.

David Barrett
Maria Kukheueva
University of Bedfordshire
United Kingdom

References

P. Goldman, *Imagining Ourselves: Global Voices from a New Generation Of Women*, New World Library, 2006.

Global Sex Workers: Rights, Resistance, and Redefinition, ed. K. Kempadoo and J. Doezema, Routledge, London, 1998.

E. Pentinnen. *Corporeal Globalization: Narratives of Embodied Subjectivity and Otherness in the Sexscapes of Globalization*, Tampere Peace Research Institute, University of Tampere, Finland, 2004.

Preface

Trafficking in Women and Children: The Role of the Police

Structurally, this book is dichotomized. Part I focuses on the definition, nature, causes, control, and prevention of global trafficking in women and children. Part II presents case studies on trafficking in women and children. These case studies are selected from high-quality papers written by eminent scholars and criminal justice practitioners from all over the world and presented at the 11th annual meeting of the International Police Executive Symposium, held in Vancouver, Canada.

I am using the Executive Summary of the meeting prepared by the official reporter, Peter Kratcoski, as the basis of our discussion. I hope this will give the reader a sense of how trafficking in women and children is an enormous challenge for the police in every part of the world and of the role they must be ready to play.

Complex Problems

What police practitioners, government officials, academicians, and researchers from 43 countries involving six continents (Africa, Asia, Australia, Europe, North America, and South America) spoke about trafficking in women and children at the meeting made it crystal clear that this was not a menace that the police can tackle alone: It is a very complex phenomenon that is baffling to the police. Some of the complex issues include

- Other crimes involved in the trafficking: organized crime, drug trafficking and abuse, violation of immigration laws, extortion, trafficking in human beings, and various forms of violent crime.
- Solutions to the trafficking: short-term and long-range strategies required.
- The degree of trafficking victimizations: the actual amount of crime relating to the victimization of women and children occurring in each country is unknown, but it is believed to be far more than official statistics.

The police must note that criminal exploitation of women and children occurs in all countries. Nevertheless, the scope and nature of the problems differ and are directly related to the characteristics of the various countries or specific circumstances. These included

- Economic conditions (poverty, employment);
- Cultural traditions;
- Catastrophic events (war, famine, floods);
- Government tolerance for the violation of human rights and exploitation of women and children;
- Corruption within the government and the police;
- Lack of resources to combat the criminal organizations involved in these victimizations;
- Acceptance of victimization and a fatalistic view of the future;
- Discrimination against minorities and lower socioeconomic groups;
- Government and police administrative policies that tend to give these problems a low priority and offer few resources or options for victim assistance;
- Lack of communication and cooperation among government agencies, the police, and social agencies for developing strategies to assist these victims;
- The existence of sophisticated criminal networks that use technological tools to avoid detection;
- Weak legislation that made prosecution and conviction of the traffickers very difficult, or legislation with adequate provisions for prosecution that is not enforced; and
- Lack of cooperation from victims caused by fear of the police, distrust of the justice system, fear of being arrested and prosecuted, fear of retaliation from their traffickers or other persons involved in illegal activity related to the victimization, economic dependence of the victims' families on the proceeds of the illegal activity, or a fatalistic attitude that nothing will be done to change their lives.

Existing policies and strategies or future actions recommended at the meeting in Canada were closely related to the specific forms of victimization that were the most troublesome in specific countries. These responses to the problem can be categorized in terms of those that were set up to address a specific internal problem and those that were designed to combat problems that were seen as being international or even global in scope. The approaches can also be categorized as short-term programs that address immediate concerns, such as providing assistance to victims, and long-term responses that may require new legislation, development of international agreements and multiagency cooperation, or programming that addresses the root causes of the malaise.

For both the short-term and long-term solutions, all of the participants in the Canada IPES meeting agreed that the operational response had to be multiagency and that it should include both government and nongovernment agencies. They reported that experience has shown that the role of nongovernment organizations cannot be overemphasized. These organizations can provide assistance to the victims in situations where government appears unconcerned, and through pressure groups, they can be instrumental in drafting and enactment of new legislation or in the development of new policies within government and law enforcement agencies.

For more effective short-term responses, it was recommended that the police become more focused on the criminal and less focused on the unlawful activities of those who are victimized, which might involve prostitution, illegal immigration, or involvement in violations of child labor laws. Cooperation of citizens, the police, the judiciary, health agencies, and labor regulatory agencies gradually leads to an increase in the willingness of those who are victimized to cooperate with the police and provide valuable information that can lead to the arrest and prosecution of kingpins within the criminal organizations. The development and utilization of modern, sophisticated technological equipments, coupled with the use of highly trained practitioners, enhance the likelihood of apprehension and prosecution of perpetrators.

Long-term solutions are beyond the scope of the police agencies. For some countries, it may take several generations before economic and political stability reach the point at which all citizens are provided a reasonable standard of living. Until this occurs, the problems will continue.

The specific crime problems with regard to women and children that are experienced by each country and the mechanisms used to address the problems are related to the country's role in the exploitation process. In "push" countries, the authorities—including the police—must be aware that undesirable economic and social conditions may enhance the opportunities for victimization and induce the victims to cooperate with their victimizers in the initial stages of the victimization process. Programs in these countries must focus on improving the quality of life and educating citizens regarding the methods used to entrap women and children into lives of servitude. Transit countries face a different set of problems. These countries must give special attention to border controls and the enforcement of legislation designed to target organized crime. In origination countries, the law enforcement agents must concentrate on enforcing existing laws and develop new policies to curtail the actual criminal activity (child pornography, prostitution, violations of child labor laws, smuggling, and violence against women and children).

It was reported that the problem of criminal victimization of women and children has been addressed in numerous countries through enactment of new laws and cooperative agreements with other countries. The effectiveness of this legislation is highly dependent on several factors. These include the will of the government and the police to enforce the laws, the resources available, and the appropriate training of the police.

Long-term strategies must be based on sound intelligence and on the demonstration of some understanding of the causes of trafficking in women and children. A prevailing view emphasized the importance of having research data and theory to guide legislation changes and the implementation of crime prevention policies. It is here that academics and police practitioners have a common ground for cooperative ventures. Other opinions suggested that police priorities and the deployment of resources must be changed and that existing legislation designed to eliminate discrimination against women and children must be enforced.

The two parts of this book are organized as follows: Part I consists of four chapters on "Definition, Nature, Causes, Control, and Prevention of Global Trafficking in Women and Children." The chapters are:

- Introduction: An Overview of Trafficking in Women and Children (Chapter 1)
- The Nature and Scope of Trafficking in Women and Children (Chapter 2)
- Causes of Trafficking in Women and Children (Chapter 3)
- Control and Prevention of Global Trafficking in Women and Children (Chapter 4)

In Chapter 1 are definitions of trafficking in persons, child trafficking, child labor, slavery, trafficking in underage persons, and so on. These definitions are derived from the United Nations instruments as well as several countries' legislations, including those of the Union of Myanmar, the Republic of Georgia, and the United States.

In Chapter 2, "The Nature and Scope of Trafficking in Women and Children," Ebbe asserts that trafficking in women and children is growing "fastest in Central and Eastern Europe and the former Soviet Union." However, he also says that exploitation of these vulnerable segments in the society occurs everywhere. In certain parts of the world like Nepal, Bangladesh, India, Thailand, the Philippines, and Nigeria, and in numerous other poor countries in Africa, South America, and so on, trafficking is a result of abject poverty. Trafficking in women and children occurs in war zones because the victims are tempted to move to safer locations. Inside the same country, as in Nigeria and Indonesia, for example, trafficking victims are women and children from poor rural areas who are being moved to less poverty-stricken urban centers.

In addition, according to Ebbe, "Australia is a sex industry and like the Middle East, a center of sex slavery." Traffickers prey on poor parents in underdeveloped countries who have many children to feed. These trusting parents hand over their children to fraudulent traffickers in the hope of gaining a better future for their young ones. Some trafficked women become rich and free, but they then fly back to their countries again to bring women and children for prostitution. In effect, they become a new wave of traffickers.

In Chapter 3, "Causes of Trafficking in Women and Children," Ebbe explains trafficking and criminal exploitation of women and children using various sociological theories. Conflicts between the "haves" and "have nots," weak social controls, greed, poverty, anomie, globalization, hedonism, social conflict, prostitution, illegal house servants, child pornography, sexual slavery, and various other needs explain why there is trafficking in women and children.

The final chapter in Part I is Chapter 4, "Control and Prevention of Trafficking in Women and Children." In this chapter, Ebbe explains that the United Nations, governments, humanitarian nongovernment organizations, Amnesty International, and some religious organizations are determined to control and prevent trafficking in women and children. In addition, several countries have adopted stricter measures to control and prevent human trafficking. Apart from providing monetary aid to antitrafficking programs, the United States, for example, has passed a law making trafficking in women and children a felony. Ebbe also adds that trafficking in women and children involves enormous amounts of money, and that therefore it cannot be eliminated, but only reduced to a minimum.

Case Studies in Trafficking in Women and Children

Part II of this book consists of "Case Studies in Trafficking in Women and Children." This part of the text has 13 chapters, beginning with Chapter 5. Chapter 5 is "Trafficking in Women and Children in Japan." In this chapter, Haruhiko Higuchi explains the evil phenomenon of child prostitution, child pornography, and "fashion wealth" shops, which provide sexual services and the like. In addition, Japan is a country of destination. In Chapter 6, "Trafficking in Women and Children in China," Gu Minkang mentions that in China, the most serious criminal exploitation of women and children is the crime of abduction and trafficking in them. Minkang suggests that the combined efforts of various domestic agencies, international cooperation, and experience sharing can be effective measures against human trafficking.

In Chapter 7, "Child Labor and the Trafficking Industry in India," Chandrika Kelso refers to the abominable practice when, in India, a family, is unable to pay its debts. When this occurs, the family can then be forced to submit a child to the lender as a bonded laborer. Such child laborers are mistreated, abused, and made to work all day without any breaks. The situation in Nigeria, as seen in Chapter 8, "Trafficking Children for Child Labor and Prostitution in Nigeria," as described by Olakunle Michael Folami, is equally grim. According to him, the barbaric phenomenon of child labor involving children between the ages of 7 and 16 years has frightening dimensions. He adds that associated crimes are sexual labor, women trafficking, child soldiering, and drug trafficking.

Chapter 9 is the "Plight of Trafficked Women in Nepal." In this chapter, Govind Prasad Thapa mentions that in Nepal, victims are vulnerable and helpless. He asserts that trafficked women are "poor, semi-literate and illiterates." According to him, trafficking is a slow, continuous, creeping, organized, lucrative, and silent activity.

Chapter 10 is "The Emergence of Trafficking in Women and Children in Bosnia and Herzegovina: A Case Study." In this chapter, Velibor Lalić argues that the disintegration of society and the creation of a constitutional vacuum have formed free maneuvering space for criminal groups to take advantage of institutional weakness and the legal vacuum for realization of their criminal objectives.

In Chapter 11, D. Scharie Tavcer presents "Trafficking in Women for the Sex Industry in Moldova." Tavcer claims that the largest number of women trafficked to Western Europe through and from the Balkans are Moldovan, Albanian, Romanian, and Ukrainian. According to an estimate in 2001, there were 10,000 Moldovan women rescued from various European countries. She notes that "war in the Balkans, powerful and integrated organized crime networks in Asia, and the cultural practices in West Africa of sending young girls to be reared elsewhere may all be considered factors that facilitate or sustain trafficking." She adds that such factors can either push people into the hands of exploitative traffickers or pull them toward certain countries.

In Chapter 12, "Trafficking in Human Beings: Training and Services in American Law Enforcement Agencies," Deborah G. Wilson, William F. Walsh, and Sherilyn Kleuber note that "Trafficking is a global issue, . . . local law enforcement needs to join the global community and actively participate in the control and prevention of trafficking in human beings." In Chapter 13, "The Challenges of Trafficking in Women and Children in Sierra Leone," Brima Acha Kamara says that the steps taken against trafficking in this country are rather basic, and that the Sierra Leone Police community relations department is presently focused on child labor.

Kemi Asiwaju presents in Chapter 14 "The Challenges of Combating Trafficking in Women and Children in Nigeria." She mentions some basic steps taken by the Nigerian Police Force against trafficking. She says that the police have set up antitrafficking units in different states in Nigeria. Their main purpose is to investigate cases of trafficking and to ensure the effective prosecution of human trafficking cases.

In Chapter 15, "Operational Perspective on Trafficking in Women and Children in the United Kingdom," William Hughes presents the United Kingdom's multiagency and multilateral approach to trafficking. The country has been pursuing various actions "to ensure that victims of trafficking are properly supported " and is currently "working with the International Organization for Migration."

In Chapter 16, "The Role of Community Policing in Trafficking of Women and Children in Australia," John Murray mentions that "successful prosecution depends on information." In support of the role of community policing in combating trafficking, he says that "A community-police relationship that is based on mutual trust is more likely to uncover matters that are helpful in identifying sexual exploitation." In the final chapter, "Trafficking and Exploitation of Women and Children in Croatia," Marijo Rošić mentions that in Croatia, the national plan of action includes bilateral cooperation, regional cooperation, cooperation within the countries, and cooperation with international agencies (such as Europol and Interpol).

Dilip K. Das

Acknowledgements

We are profoundly indebted to the international scholars and practitioners who contributed to this book. The Royal Canadian Mounted Police, British Columbia Institute of Justice, Office of the Solicitor General of British Columbia, Vancouver and Abbotsford Police Departments (British Columbia) and, last but not the least, University College of the Fraser Valley made it possible to gather all these experts under the auspices of the International Police Executive Symposium (www.ipes.info) in its annual meeting in Canada. We convey our heartfelt gratitude to all of them for their generous hospitality and excellent arrangement for the meeting.

Daphne McGhee of Grambling State University (Grambling, Louisiana, USA) was of tremendous assistance. Also we are very much obliged to April Matthews of the Human Resources Office of the University of Tennessee at Chattanooga whose professional typing skills shaped the look of the manuscript. Furthermore, thanks to Professor Craig Laing, who helped to map out the global routes of trafficking in women and children. Mintie Das of IPES deserves our sincere thanks for her preliminary editing of all the papers included in the book. Dr. Ana Mijovic-Das traveled to Canada to help with the annual meeting of the IPES which generated the chapters for the book. We acknowledge her worthy contribution with a deep sense of appreciation.

Carolyn Spence has been more than just an editor to us. She has been an inspiration as she most enthusiastically and selflessly went beyond her call of duty to render all forms of assistance, solicited as well as unsolicited, in order to make it possible to bring this project to fruition. We thank her from the bottom of our hearts.

Obi N. I. Ebbe
University of Tennessee, Chattanooga

Dilip K. Das
International Police Executive Symposium

Part I

Definition, Nature, Control, and Prevention of Global Trafficking in Women and Children

Introduction: An Overview of Trafficking in Women and Children

1

OBI N.I. EBBE

Contents

The movement of women and children from one city to another and from one country to another for the purpose of employing them in criminal activities, keeping them in legal or illegal brothels, or using them as slaves is a crime against humanity and a violation of the civil rights of the individuals. Unmistakably, the illegal trafficking in women and children for purposes of slave labor, child labor, pornography, and forced prostitution has become a modern day social problem. A social problem is a condition that adversely affects a significant number of people and about which something can be done (Clinard, 1958; Campbell, 1981). Enormous hardship, pain, and suffering are created for women and children who are illegally transported and employed against their will in illegal and legal businesses. In addition, their relatives, who think that their loved ones have been taken away for meaningful employment and will return soon, wait at their homes of origin in vain. They later discover that their loved ones were living in perpetual servitude or were even dead.

Some families are disorganized when one of their members is fraudulently taken away for several months or years without hearing anything about or from him or her. Very often we read about women and children illegally transported out of their homelands for slave labor, pornography, child labor, or forced prostitution. Some of the women and children trafficked are even killed for their body parts (Ebbe, 1999, 2003: 151–152).

There has been little systematic study of the criminal exploitations of women and children through trafficking that has been documented in one text. This is an attempt to fill the void. Every now and again, we hear about missing children or missing adults. The question is, where are they? What happened to them? The answer is, they are killed for their body parts, sold into slavery, deployed in pornographic activities, forced into prostitution, or made into sex slaves for the rich. Undoubtedly, illegally transported women and children very often end up as being described as "missing persons."

Given the global nature—both intra- and intercontinental—of the trafficking in women and children, it is very hard to estimate the number of women and children trafficked each year. Both national and international crises have led to the proliferation of illegal transportation of women and children since the 1960s. From the Congo Kinshasa crisis of the 1960s to the Nigeria-Biafra war (1967–1970), the Eritrea–Ethiopia war of the 1970s, the Mozambique war of independence and its Marxist regime crisis of the 1970s and the 1980s, Ian Smith's white minority unilateral declaration of independence in Northern Rhodesia (Zimbabwe) in the 1960s and 1970s, the Angola civil war of the 1970s, 1980s, and 1990s, the South African white minority apartheid regime crisis from the 1960s to 1994, the Liberian civil war of the 1980s and 1990s, the Sierra Leone civil war of the 1990s, the Rwanda genocide of the 1970s and 1980s, Idi Amin's crisis of ethnic cleansing in Uganda in the 1970s and 1980s, the Nicaraguan contra crisis of the 1980s and 1990s, the Argentine crisis of the 1970s and 1980s, the Bosnia-Herzegovina crisis of ethnic cleansing of the 1990s, the Afghanistan–Soviet Union war of the 1970s and 1980s, the Al Qaida crisis in Afghanistan and the current American intervention, the American–Iraqi war that began in 2001, and the Palestinian–Israeli crisis of 1948 to the present, more than 3 million women and children have been illegally transported. However, to date, the global effect of all of the above crises on illegal transportation of refugees has not been studied in depth.

Civil wars and political crises have been the legacy of imperialism in developing countries. War displaces women and children, and some criminal-minded and greedy individuals find these individuals to be easy targets for exploitation and a good, quick money-making source. Most of the recent wars and political crises occurred in developing countries in Africa, Asia, Latin America, and the Middle East. As a consequence, the trafficking in women and children has emanated from the developing countries that were once colonial dependencies, and the recipients of the transported women and children have been the former colonial nations and their industrialized allies. Unmistakably, most of the women and children illegally transported internationally from Africa, South America, the Middle East, and Asia ended up in Western Europe, Canada, and the United States. Put in a nutshell, the trafficking in women and children is known to occur in both developing countries and in all major industrialized nations of the world.

Since the collapse of the Soviet Union, the picture of the origination regions has changed—they have become larger than ever before. Although the trafficked women have different characteristics, the motivating factors are the same in all regions.

There are various discussions of the characteristics of the women who are trafficked. Some studies describe the trafficked women as victims (Bertone, 2000; Doezema, 2000; Gushulak and Macpherson, 2000; Bales and Robbins, 2001; Hyland, 2001; Adepoju, 2005; Bales, 2002; Brennan, 2005; Laczko and Gozdziak, 2005). However, not all trafficked women are victims (Tyldum and Brunovskis, 2005). Undoubtedly, studies show that most trafficked women, both voluntarily and involuntarily recruited, are victimized by their traffickers.

Although studies of trafficking in women and children are fragmented, there is a need for researchers to continue to draw samples from trafficked women, prostitutes, law enforcement agencies, nongovernment organizations (NGOs), and Human Rights Watch groups in different parts of the globe and interview them to get information on the scope of such trafficking. Such studies, using data from United Nations (UN) agency records, can inform the international community of the scope of the problem.

1.1   Previous Studies

Most studies of trafficking in persons have concentrated on Asia, Eastern and Central Europe, Australia, and South and Central America. Very few studies on the subject have, so far, concentrated on North America, Africa, or the Middle East. The studies done so far were conducted, in the main, by the UN agencies responsible for crime prevention and criminal justice programmes (e.g., the International Scientific and Professional Advisory Council, the UN Office on Drugs and Crime, the UN Interregional Crime and Justice Research Institute, the UN Children's Fund, the International Organization for Migration, and the International Labour Organization), some social scientists (Ebbe, 1997, 1999, 2003; Bales, 1999, 2000, 2002; Bertone, 2000; Doezema, 2000; Hughes, 2000; Aronowitz, 2001, 2002; Shelley, 2001, 2003a, 2003b; Agbu, 2003; Zhang and Chin, 2003; Okereke, 2005), NGOs (Global Survival Network, 1997; Human Rights Watch, 2000, 2001, 2002a, 2002b, 2002c, 2002d, 2003), the North Atlantic Treaty Organisation (2003), and the U.S. Department of State (2001, 2002, 2003, 2004).

A great number of these studies and agency reports examined the whole process of human trafficking, looking at the causes and processes of the recruitment, transportation, and exploitation of the victims (Bales, 1999;

Ebbe, 1999; Bertone, 2000; Gushulak and MacPherson, 2000; UN, 2000a, 2001a, 2001b; Aronowitz, 2001; International Organization for Migration, 2001, 2002; Shelley, 2001, 2003a, 2003b; Australian Crime Commission, 2005; Laczko and Gozdziak, 2005; Adepoju, 2005). Some of the studies try to provide approaches to countertrafficking strategies and the rehabilitation of victims (Ivey and Kramer, 1998; Gushulak and MacPherson, 2000; Popoola, 2001; and Heyzer, 2002; Horn, 2003), whereas others concentrated, in the main, on the characteristics of the traffickers (Heikkinen and Lohrmann, 1998; International Organization for Migration, 1998, 2001; Global Alliance Against Trafficking in Women, 1999).

Furthermore, most of the studies are based on small samples of female survivors of trafficking, who have been identified by law enforcement agencies, NGOs, and some religious organizations. These studies show that very few victims are located, and very few are assisted. Research on the subject, however, is growing by leaps and bounds and spans through historical, political, humanitarian, legal, and social economic dimensions (Laczko and Gozdziak, 2005). Since 1995, the International Organization for Migration has published over forty studies on trafficking in human beings. Most of them were made after the UN responded in 2000 to the calls from NGOs for a convention on the trafficking problem. The International Organization for Migration studies took an action-oriented approach, preparing the ground for countertrafficking interventions.

This text presents twelve (model) case studies involving, in the main, seven of the most used originating countries (India, Nigeria, Moldova, Bosnia-Herzegovina, Croatia, Nepal, and Sierra Leone) and three destination countries (the United States, Japan, and China) of the trafficking in women and children. Suffice it to say that the United States, Japan, and China are among the major destination countries of trafficked women and children, and they are also exporters on a smaller scale than developing countries. This text uses selected case studies to exemplify the nature, scope, and etiological factors of the human trafficking problem.

The practice of transporting women and children from one region to another is not of recent origin, but its global criminal overtones have become inhuman and mind-boggling. After series of reports from NGOs and religious groups to the UN General Assembly on the toll of trafficking in women and children on many families and individuals in both the originating and destination countries, an international action was taken. On December 15, 2000, in Palermo, Italy, the "Protocol to Prevent, Suppress and Punish Trafficking in Persons, Especially Women and Children, Supplementing the United Nations Convention against Transnational Organized Crime" was adopted (UN, 2000).

Article 2 of the UN Protocol on Trafficking has three purposes:

1. To prevent and combat trafficking in persons paying particular attention to women and children;
2. To protect and assist the victims of such trafficking, with full respect for their human rights; and
3. To promote cooperation among state parties in order to meet those objectives.

1.1.1   Trafficking in Persons

The UN Protocol Article 3(a) defined trafficking in persons to mean "the recruitment, transportation, transfer, harbouring or receipt of persons, by means of the threat of use of force or other forms of coercion, of abduction, of fraud, of deception, of the abuse of power or of a position of vulnerability or of the giving or receiving of payments or benefits to achieve the consent of a person having control over another person, for the purpose of exploitation." Exploitation is defined as "the exploitation of the prostitution of others or other forms of sexual exploitation, forced labor or services, slavery or practices similar to slavery, servitude or the removal of organs."

Article 3(b) states that "the consent of a victim of trafficking in persons to the intended exploitation set forth in subparagraph (a) of this article shall be irrelevant where any of the means set forth in subparagraph (a) have been used."

In addition, Article 3(c) states that "the recruitment, transportation, transfer, harboring or receipt of a child for the purpose of exploitation shall be considered 'trafficking in persons' even if this does not involve any of the means set forth in subparagraph (a) of this article," and Article 3(d) states that "'Child' shall mean any person under eighteen years of age" (UN, 2000).

The protocol intentionally decided not to define "exploitation of prostitution of others and other forms of sexual exploitations," because there was no consensus among government delegates to the negotiations on the common meaning of the phrase. The government delegates to the Palermo Convention agreed that involuntary forced participation in prostitution would constitute trafficking, but most of the government delegates rejected the idea that voluntary, noncoercive participation by adults in prostitution is tantamount to trafficking. States' parties therefore, are allowed to define voluntary prostitution of adults according to their own customs and laws. On the whole, the trafficking protocol, in unequivocal terms, permits states to focus only on forced prostitution and other crimes involving force and coercion, and states should not treat all adult participation in prostitution as trafficking.

1.1.2   Child Trafficking

Studies and commentators have put women and children in a single group, but in fact, the law against trafficking in women and children had to differentiate the two classes and treat them as two separate categories. For instance, although there are arguments both for and against the boundaries of forced adult prostitution, there are no such arguments that prostitution of a child is not coercive and an evil act. Unmistakably, by international law, a person under 18 years of age is a child and has not reached the age of consent: A child under 18 years of age cannot consent.

By the definition of the UN Protocol (2000), that a 17-year-old young woman agrees or chooses to be a prostitute and follows the trafficker to another city or country for the purpose of prostitution or engaging in a lucrative employment does not exculpate the trafficker from criminal liability for the charge of child trafficking. Therefore, coercion or duress are not necessary components of trafficking in children (Esadze, 2004). Furthermore, it should be noted that parental consent is irrelevant in the defense to a charge of trafficking in children.

The UN Protocol defines child trafficking thus: "the recruitment, transportation, transfer, harbouring or receipt of a child for the purpose of exploitation shall be considered 'trafficking in persons' even if this does not involve any of the means set out in subparagraph (a) [coercion, fraud, deception, etc.] of this article" (UN, 2000).

Another concept for definition in this study is "child labor" exploitation. There was no consensus among states delegates about what form of labor constitutes exploitation of the child. It was agreed, however, that a form of labor that would constitute exploitation of the child should be left to domestic regulation (2001). Este defines trafficking in children as "the movement of children for the purpose of financial gain as 'sex workers' across borders or within countries, across state lines, from city to city, or from rural to urban setting. The use of force is often, but not always, a feature of trafficking in children for sex" (Este, 2001). Captive Daughters International defines "sex trafficking" to include all acts involved in the recruitment and/or transport of a person within and across national borders to gratify the sexual desires of others. Further, sex trafficking is accomplished by means of direct or indirect violence or threat of violence, abuse of authority or dominant position, debt-bondage, deception, or other forms of coercion."[1]

In international child trafficking, the form of labor is irrelevant. What is required is that the child be transported out of his or her country. Once again, his or her consent or that of his or her parent or guardian is irrelevant: Children under 18 cannot give valid consent, and any recruitment, transportation, transfer, harboring, or receipt of children for the purpose of exploitation is a form of trafficking, regardless of the means used.

In the case of adults, consent can be a factor in some nations. In some countries, where the consent of the adult female could be a mitigating circumstance considered in the case of trafficking, it may be difficult to establish a *bona fide* consent of the victim. Trafficking prosecutions are sometimes lost, because the evidence needed to establish the true nature of the consent is not available. At the same time, constitutional and other human rights protections in many countries require that those accused of trafficking be able to raise the possibility of consent as a defense. The protocol, therefore, states that if any of the improper means set out in the definition (i.e., coercion, fraud, or deception) have been used, any alleged consent to the subsequent exploitation is irrelevant.[2]

Another concept that needs to be defined is that of slavery. The most widely used definition is provided by the Committee Against Modern Slavery and has five criteria:

1. Confiscation of identification papers;
2. Taking advantage of the vulnerability of a person to make him or her supply a service (or work) without payment or against a very small payment that has no correlation to the amount of work provided, and providing lodging and working conditions contrary to human dignity (15–18-hour working days, 7 days a week, no holidays or vacation, insufficient food, squalid housing, etc.);
3. Sequestration or "self-sequestration": the person is conditioned by the employer, who says things like, "You are in an irregular situation, if the police stop you in the street, you will go to prison and will be deported";
4. Rupture of family links: prohibition against receiving or sending mail and making phone calls; and
5. Cultural isolation: The people subject to slavery come from Southeast Asia, Madagascar, West or East Africa, the Maghreb, and so on—they do not know the language and the laws of the destination country, or the rights that protect them, and they are thus in a vulnerable situation.[3]

Human trafficking has been described as a modern-day form of slavery. The Trafficking in Persons (PIT) Report of 2005 emphasizes that the defining element of the definition of trafficking is the force, fraud, or coercion exercised on the person by another to perform or remain in service to the master. There is also internal trafficking that occurs that does not require movement. The Trafficking Victims Protection Act of 2000 (TVPA) eliminates the element of physical transportation and defines "severe forms of trafficking" as

1. Sex trafficking in which a commercial sex act is induced by force, fraud, or coercion, or in which the person induced to perform such an act has not attained 18 years of age; or
2. The recruitment, harboring, transportation, provision, or obtaining of a person for labor or services, through the use of force, fraud, or coercion for the purpose of subjection to involuntary servitude, peonage, debt bondage, or slavery. [4]

States' parties are required to ratify the UN Protocol and to enact laws against trafficking in women and children. They also may add more controlling laws to suit domestic needs without detracting from the UN Protocol. Here we provide two examples of national legislations against trafficking in women and children.

The Republic of Georgia on June 6, 2003, has its Criminal Code article 143, "Trafficking in Persons," (Esadze, 2004):

1. Selling or buying of persons, or subjecting them to other illegal deals, also recruiting, transporting, harboring, or taking them on for purposes of exploitation, with the use of force, blackmail or deception;
   —Is punishable by imprisonment from 5 to 12 years.
2. The same offense, committed:
   a. Repeatedly;
   b. Against two or more persons;
   c. Against a pregnant woman, knowing about her pregnancy;
   d. With the abuse of official authority;
   e. By taking a victim abroad;
   f. With the use of life threatening or health threatening coercion, or threatening to use such force;
   g. Knowingly, against a vulnerable person, or against a person who is financially or otherwise dependent on the offender;
   —Is punishable by imprisonment from 8 to 15 years.
3. Offense, stipulated by first and second paragraphs of this article:
   a. Committed by an organized group;
   b. Which resulted in a death of a victim or caused other serious consequences;
   —Is punishable by imprisonment from 12 to 20 years.

Furthermore, for purposes of Article 143, "exploitation" means using another person with the intent to

Engage them in forced labor, criminal or other antisocial activity, or prostitution;
Subject them to sexual exploitation or other work;
Put them under modern conditions of slavery; or
Use human organs, part of a human organ, or its cells for transplantation or other purposes.

Putting persons under modern conditions of slavery means to:

Take away their ID;
Limit their right for free transportation;

Prohibiting them to contact their families (by correspondence or telephone);

Putting them in cultural isolation;

Forcing them to work for free or give them inadequate compensation; or

Putting them in conditions that assault human dignity.

Article 143: Trafficking in Underage Persons

1. Selling or buying of underage persons, or subjecting them to other illegal deals, also recruiting, transporting, harboring, or taking them on for purposes of exploitation;
   —Is punishable by imprisonment from 8 to 15 years.
2. The same offense, committed:
   a. Repeatedly;
   b. With force, blackmail, or deception;
   c. Against two or more underage persons;
   d. By taking a victim abroad;
   e. With the use of life threatening or health threatening coercion, or threatening to use such force;
   f. With the abuse of official authority;
   g. Knowingly, against a vulnerable person, or against a person who is financially or otherwise dependent on the offender;
   —Is punishable by imprisonment from 12 to 17 years.
3. Offense, stipulated by first and second paragraphs of this article:
   a. Committed by an organized group;
   b. Which resulted in a death of an underage person or caused other serious consequences;
   —Is punishable by imprisonment from 15 to 20 years, or by life imprisonment.

The UN Protocol did not provide specific sanctions against offenders—that is left to the states' parties. For example, in the Republic of Georgia, in legislation from June 2003, after their ratification of the protocol, penalties were provided for first offenders and for repeat offenders. The lawmakers also provided severe penalties for traffickers who trafficked more than one person at a time and who trafficked a pregnant woman. In addition, the UN Protocol did not mention trafficking in human organs, but the Republic of Georgia statute includes that behavior.

Another state definition of trafficking in persons that is worthy of note is that of the Union of Myanmar (formerly known as Burma). The Anti-Trafficking in Persons Law of the Union of Myanmar, similar to that of Georgia, has some interesting features but included all of the UN 2000 Protocol. On

September 2005, the Union of Myanmar promulgated the Anti-Trafficking in Persons Law, and defined trafficking in persons, as follows:

1. Trafficking in Persons means recruitment, transportation, transfer, sale, purchase, lending, hiring, harbouring or receipt of persons after committing any of the following acts for the purpose of exploitation of a person with or without his consent:
   a. threat, use of force or other form of coercion;
   b. abduction;
   c. fraud;
   d. deception;
   e. abuse of power or of position taking advantage of the vulnerability of a person;
   f. giving or receiving of money or benefit to obtain the consent of the person having control over another person.
      i. Exploitation includes receipt or agreement for receipt of money or benefit for the prostitution of one person by another, other forms of sexual exploitation, forced labor, forced service, slavery, servitude, debt-bondage or the removal and sale of organs from the body.
      ii. Prostitution means any act, use, consummation, or scheme involving the use of person by another, for sexual intercourse or lascivious conduct in exchange for money, benefit or any other consideration.
      iii. Debt-bondage means the pledging by the debtor of his/her personal labor or services or those of a person under his/her control as payment or security for a debt, when the length and nature of service is not clearly defined or when the values of the services as reasonably assessed is not applied toward the liquidation of the debt.
      iv. Pornography means representation through exhibition, indecent show, publication, cinematography or by use of modern information technology of a sexual activity or of the sexual parts of a person for primarily sexual purpose.[5]

The Union of Myanmar Anti-Trafficking in Persons Law provides the scope of that nation's jurisdiction on the offense. The statute specified that the Union of Myanmar shall have jurisdiction on any person who commits "any offense cognizable under the law in the Union of Myanmar, or on board a vessel or aircraft registered under the existing law of the Union of Myanmar, or on a Myanmar citizen or foreigner residing permanently in the Union of Myanmar who commits the said offense outside the country."[6]

You can see some additions made by the Union of Myanmar in its definitions of exploitation, prostitution, debt-bondage, and pornography. Furthermore, the Union of Myanmar added that a citizen of Myanmar who commits the crime of trafficking in women and children while residing in another country will be prosecuted when he or she returns to Myanmar.

Following the increased waves of trafficking in women and children, on October 7, 2005, the Senate of the United States of America gave its advice and consent to ratification of the "United Nations Protocol to prevent, suppress, and punish trafficking in persons, especially women and children." The U.S. Senate sees this protocol as an important multicultural component of the worldwide effort to combat what has been described as modern-day slavery. [7]

The U.S. government definition of trafficking in persons encompasses "All acts involved in the transport, harboring, or sale of persons within national or across international borders through coercion, force, kidnapping, deception or fraud, for purposes of placing persons in situation of forced labor or services, such as forced prostitution, domestic servitude, debt bondage or other slavery-like practices." In the case of minors, there is a general agreement in the United States that the trafficking term applies whether a child was taken forcibly or voluntarily. Trafficking is distinguished from alien smuggling, which involves the provision of a service, albeit illegal, to people who knowingly buy the service in order to get into a foreign country. [8]

Now that we have given the working definition of the problem, the organization and order of presentation of the rest of the text follows.

This text has two parts: Part I has four chapters, which include this chapter; Chapter 2, "The Nature and Scope of Trafficking in Women and Children"; Chapter 3, "Causes of Trafficking in Women and Children"; and Chapter 4, "Control and Prevention of Trafficking in Women and Children."

Notes

1. http://www.captive.org?byandaboutCD/CDdocuments/cddefinitionoftrafficking.htm.
2. http://www.unode.org/unodc/en/trafficking_victim_consents.htm.
3. http://www.inet.co.th/org/gaatw/soliderity/action/HRSLetter.htm.
4. http://www.trafficinginpersons.com/about_trafficking.htm.
5. The Union of Myanmar: The State Peace and Development Council Law (The Anti-Trafficking in Persons Law) No. 5/2005.
6. Ibid.
7. http://www.humantrafficking.org/countries/eap/United_States/news/2005_10us_action_un_pro.
8. Trafficking in Women and Children: The U.S. and Int'l Response: http://www.usinfor.state.gov/topical/global/traffic/cs0510.htm.

References

A. Adepoju, Review of research and data on human trafficking in sub-Saharan Africa. In: *Data and Research on Human Trafficking: A Global Survey*, ed. Frank Laczko and Elzvieta Gozdziak, IOM, Geneva, 2005, pp. 75–90.

O. Agbu, Corruption and human trafficking: The Nigerian case, *West African Review*, 2003, 15: 18–29.

A.A. Aronowitz, Smuggling and trafficking in human beings: The phenomenon, the markets that drive it and the organizations that promote it, *European Journal on Criminal Policy and Research*, 2001, 9: 163–165.

A.A. Aronowitz, Illegal practices and criminal networks involved in smuggling of Filipinos to Italy. In: *United Nations Global Program Against Trafficking in Human Beings*. United Nations, Vienna, 2002.

Australian Crime Commission, Sex slavery in Australia, http://www.news.ninemsn.com.au/article.aspx?id=54134, 2005.

K. Bales, Expendable people: Slavery in the age of globalization, *Journal of International Affairs*, 2000, 53(2): 461–484.

K. Bales, The social psychology of modern slavery, *Scientific American*, 2002, 286(4): 80–88.

K. Bales and P.T. Robbins, No one shall be held in slavery or servitude: A critical analysis of international slavery agreements and concepts of slavery, *Journal of International Affairs*, 2001, 2(2): 18–37.

A.M. Bertone, Sexual trafficking in women: International political economy and the politics of sex, *Gender Issues*, 2000, 18(1): 4–18.

D. Brennan, Methodological challenges in research with trafficked persons: Tales from the field. In: *Data and Research on Human Trafficking: A Global Survey*, ed. Frank Laczko and Elzbieta Gozdziak, IOM, Geneva, 2005, pp. 17–34.

C. Campbell, *Social Problems*, Free Press, New York, 1981.

M. Clinard, *The Sociology of Deviant Behavior*, Holt, Rinehart, and Winston, New York, 1958.

J. Doezema, Loose women or lost women? The re-emergence of white slavery in contemporary discourses of trafficking in women, *Gender Issues*, 2000, 18(1): 23–55.

O.N.I. Ebbe, Political-criminal nexus in Nigeria, *Trends in Organized Crime*, 1997, 3(1): 3–10.

O.N.I. Ebbe, Political-criminal nexus. The Nigerian case: slicing Nigeria's "national cake," *Trends in Organized Crime*, 1999, 4(3): 29–59.

O.N.I. Ebbe, Slicing Nigeria's "national cake." In Roy Godson, ed. *Menace to Society: Political-Criminal Collaborations around the World*. New Brunswick: Transaction Publishers, 2003, 137–174.

L. Esadze, Trafficking in women and children: A case study of Georgia. Paper presented at the 2004 ISPAC of the United Nations Crime Prevention and Criminal Justice Programmes held in Courmeuyer, Mont Blanc, Italy, 2004.

R.J. Estes, *The Sexual Exploitation of Children: A Working Guide to the Empirical Literature*, Philadelphia, University of Pennsylvania, 2001, pg. 5.

Global Alliance Against Trafficking in Women, A proposal to replace the convention for the suppression of the traffic in persons and of the exploitation of the prostitution of others, Global Alliance Against Trafficking in Women, Utrecht, 1994.

Global Survival Network, *Crime and Servitude*, Washington, D.C., Global Survival Network, 1997.

B.D. Gushulak and D.W. MacPherson, Health issues associated with the smuggling and trafficking of migrants, *Journal of Immigrant Health,* 2000, 2(2): 67–78.

H. Heikkinen and R. Lohrmann, Involvement of Organized Crime in the Trafficking of Migrants, IOM, Geneva, 1998, http://migration.ucdavis.edu/mm21/Lohrmann.html.

N. Heyzer, *Combating Trafficking in Women and Children: A Gender and Human Rights Framework*, Vienna, UN Development Fund for Women, 2002.

W.F. Horn, U.S. Human Service Agency's Responding to Trafficking, *U.S. Department of Health and Human Services* (June), 2003.

D.M. Hughes, The Natasha trade—The transnational shadow market of trafficking in women, *Journal of International Affairs,* 2000, 25: 18–28.

Human Rights Watch, *Owed Justice: Thai Women Trafficked into Debt Bondage in Japan*, Human Rights Watch, New York, 2000.

Human Rights Watch, Hidden in the home: Abuse of domestic workers with special visas in the United States, http://www.hrw.org/reports/2001/usadom/.

Human Rights Watch, *Borderline Slavery: Child Trafficking in Togo*, United Nations, Human Rights Division, 2002a.

Human Rights Watch, *The Invisible Exodus: North Koreans in the People's Republic of China*, Human Rights Watch, New York, 2002b.

Human Rights Watch, *Hopes Betrayed: Trafficking of Women and Girls to Post-Conflict Bosnia and Herzegovina for Forced Prostitution*, Human Rights Watch, New York, 2002c.

Human Rights Watch, *Nepali Women Trafficked to India*, Human Rights Watch, New York, 2002d.

Human Rights Watch, *Trafficking of Women and Girls*, United Nations High Commission for Refugees, 2003.

K.F. Hyland, The impact of the protocol to prevent, suppress and punish trafficking in persons, especially women and children, Human Rights Briefs, http://www.wcl.american.edu/pub/humanright/brief/index.htm.

International Organization for Migration, *Paths of Exploitation: Studies on the Trafficking of Women and Children Between Cambodia, Thailand, and Vietnam*, IOM, Geneva.

International Organization for Migration, New IOM figures on the global scale of trafficking, *Trafficking in Migrant Quarterly Bulletin* (April), 2001.

International Organization for Migration, *Trafficking in Women to Italy for Sexual Exploitation*, IOM, Geneva, 2002.

S.L. Ivey and E.J. Kramer, Immigrant women and the emergency department: The juncture with welfare and immigration reform, *Journal of American Medicine Women's Association,* 1998, 53: 94–95.

F. Laczko and E. Gozdziak, eds., *Data and Research on Human Trafficking: A Global Survey*, IOM, Geneva, 2005.

North Atlantic Treaty Organisation, Resolution 323 on Trafficking in Human Beings, Parliamentary Assembly, Committee on Civil Dimension of Security, NATO, 2003.

G.O. Okereke, The international trade in human beings: A critical look at the causal factor, *Contemporary Criminal Justice Review,* 2005, 21(86): 4–17.

A. Popoola, Combating trafficking in human beings through legislation in Africa: Challenges, problems and prospects, presented at the First Pan-African Conference on Human Trafficking, held in Abuja, Nigeria, 2001.

L. Shelley, Trafficking and smuggling in human beings, presented at Corruption without Security Forces: A Threat to National Security Conference, Garmisch, May 14–18, 2001.

L. Shelley, Trafficking in women: The business model approach, *Brown Journal of World Affairs,* 2003a, 10(1): 119–131.

L. Shelley, Trade in people in and from the former Soviet Union, *Crime, Law and Social Change,* 2003b, 40(2–3): 231–249.

G. Tyldum and A. Brunovskis, Describing the unobserved: Methodological challenges in empirical studies on human trafficking. In: *Data and Research on Human Trafficking: A Global Survey,* ed. Frank Laczko and Elzbieta Gozdziak, IOM, Geneva, 2005.

United Nations, *Trafficking in Women and Girls,* Report of the Secretary General, United Nations, Geneva, 2000.

United Nations, Trafficking in Human Misery, http://www.unfpa.org/gender/trafficking.htm.

United Nations, *Significant Progress in the Fight against Trafficking in Human Beings in West African States,* United Nations, Geneva, 2001b.

U.S. Department of State, Victims of Trafficking and Violence Protection Act of 2000: Trafficking in Persons Report 2001, U.S. Department of State, Washington, DC, 2001.

U.S. Department of State, Victims of Trafficking and Violence Protection Act of 2000: Trafficking in Persons Report 2002, U.S. Department of State, Washington, DC, 2002.

U.S. Department of State, Victims of Trafficking and Violence Protection Act of 2000: Trafficking in Persons Report 2003, U.S. Department of State, Washington, DC, 2003.

U.S. Department of State, Victims of Trafficking and Violence Protection Act of 2000: Trafficking in Persons Report 2004, U.S. Department of State, Washington, DC, 2004.

S. Zhang and K.-L. Chin, Characteristics of Chinese Human Smugglers: A Cross-National Study, Final Report, U.S. Department of Justice Grant 99-IL-CX-0028, 2003.

The Nature and Scope of Trafficking in Women and Children

2

OBI N.I. EBBE

Contents

2.1 The International Scope of Trafficking in Women and Children

The origination countries of trafficking in women and children can be classified as coming from four regions of the world. These are East and Central Europe, East and Southeast Asia, South and Central America—including Mexico in the North, and Africa. The origination countries in East and Central Europe are Russia, Ukraine, Poland, Hungary, the Republic of Georgia, Slovakia, Bosnia-Herzegovina, the Czech Republic, Latvia, Estonia, Romania, Albania, and so on. In East and Southeast Asia the countries are India, China, Thailand, Cambodia, Sri Lanka, Pakistan, Vietnam, Indonesia, Taiwan, South Korea, Malaysia, Myanmar, and the Philippines. In South and Central (Latin) America they are Brazil, Argentina, El Salvador, Panama, Venezuela, Colombia, Guatemala, Nicaragua, and Honduras. Mexico is the only country of origin in North America. In Africa, the major source countries are Nigeria, South Africa, Ghana, Sierra Leone, Ivory Coast, Togo, Benin Republic, Rwanda, Burundi, Liberia, Uganda, Kenya, Ethiopia, Cameroon, Zimbabwe, Sudan, Chad, Zaire, Somalia, Tanzania, Mozambique, and Angola.

Destination countries for trafficked women and children include many Western European countries, especially Italy, the Netherlands, Germany, France, the United Kingdom, and Spain. Other destination countries are the Nordic states, Canada, the United States, Israel, Australia, Japan, and Middle East.

Nations that are both origination and destination countries are China, India, Nigeria, Russia, Hungary, Ukraine, South Africa, and Kenya.

According to the International Organization for Migration (IOM), more that 500,000 women and children are trafficked into Western European countries annually. Most of the women and girls came from the Newly Independent States (NIS) of the former Soviet Union. According to CIA and FBI reports (cited in Richard, 2000), over 45,000 persons are trafficked into the United States annually, and over 2000 Asians are trafficked into Canada annually. Studies on trafficking of women and children in African countries show that most of the African women trafficked were disposed of in Western European countries (Ebbe, 1999, 2003; Adepoju, 2005). The United States and Canada are destinations for women from Russia, NIS, Mexico, South and Central America, China, and Southeast Asia (see Figure 2.1).

Israel, Japan, and Australia are destinations for women from Russia, NIS, China, and Southeast Asia—especially Vietnam, Thailand, Indonesia, China, South Korea, and Malaysia.

Unmistakably, India, China, Nigeria, Russia, Hungary, the Ukraine, South Africa, and Kenya experience both intraregional and interregional trafficking. That is, although these countries are origination countries, some of them—such as India, Nigeria, Russia, Ukraine, South Africa, and Kenya—also have brothels that import women from within and outside of their countries and continents. Hungary is just a transit stop for the Eastern European women being trafficked to Western Europe (Bertone, 2000; Esadze, 2004). Brothels in India receive women from Indonesia, Thailand, and Vietnam. Brothels in South Africa and Kenya also have the Chinese triads and Japanese Yakuza supplying them with women from China, Indonesia, Taiwan, and Thailand.

The major organized crime groups involved in trafficking in women are Russian, East European, and Asian syndicates (Richard, 2000). The Russian, Ukrainian, Chinese, and Japanese criminal groups operate in small crime rings in the major cities of Western Europe, Nordic states, Canada, and the United States. They are loosely connected with each other. Unlike in traditional organized crime, they are not in competition with each other; instead, they complement each other. This means that a trafficked woman could be sold three times to different brothel owners, subjecting her to a life of perpetual sexual servitude. In the process of trafficking in women and children, these syndicates participate in extortion, racketeering, money laundering, bribery of government officials, drug use, document forgery, and gambling in their enterprises.

Throughout the major cities of the United States, Great Britain, France, Germany, Italy, Canada, and the Netherlands, studies have shown that Russian individuals and Russian organized crime groups are importing women from Russia, the Ukraine, the Baltic States, and Central Europe for the sex industry via the stripping, prostitution, peep and show club service, massage service, and escort service industries, among others (Foundation of Women Forum, 1998; Bertone, 2000; Richard, 2000; Esadze, 2004). In countries like the United States, where brothels are illegal (except in some counties in Nevada), Russian and Chinese organized crime groups establish massage parlors, spas, suntanning parlors, and beauty salons as fronts for the brothels (Richard, 2000).

The Chinese triads involved in smuggling and trafficking in women and children include the Sun-lee On Triad, 14K Triad, Wo Hop To Triad, United Bamboo Gang, and Fuk China Gang. They are reportedly known to operate in the United States, Canada, and various European countries. In addition, reports indicate that they supply women to brothels in South Africa and Kenya (FWF, 1998; Doezema, 2000; Gushulak and MacPherson, 2000; Richard, 2000).

Undeniably, based on the data on Nigeria and on the available literature, the women from the countries of origin did not find themselves in foreign countries by their own free will or on their own terms. In the Ukraine, Russia, and the Republic of Georgia, there are organized crime syndicates dealing with women trafficking, using fraudulent schemes.

According to a report on trafficking in Australia (Australian Crime Commission [ACC] Act, 2005), "at least 1,000 women are kept in debt-bonded prostitution in Australia, where they are raped, beaten and starved." The report also states that traffickers brought the women from Thailand and Burma (Myanmar) to work in legal brothels as prostitutes until they paid off their illegal transportation "debts"—up to $50,000 each.

According to an Australian-based nongovernmental organization (NGO), Project Reach, "Australia's sex slavery laws are failing and police are not doing enough to free enslaved women" (ACC, 2005). The ACC estimated that 300 women are trafficked into Australia each year, and about 1000 of them currently work as sex slaves.

There are small groups of traffickers of women and children from Southeast Asia who support the activities of both the Chinese Triads and the Japanese Yakuza. They transport women and children all over the world. Unlike with the traditional organized crime families, however, there is no evidence of division of territory among the various groups of women and children traffickers. In fact, according to Richard's (2000) study, they have a loose confederation.

The Mexican and South and Central American traffickers have ethnic and familial structures. Similar to some Nigerian traffickers, the women trafficked by Mexican and South and Central American groups are transported by their relatives, friends, and acquaintances. A Mexican brothel raided by the FBI in Florida showed that most of the women, who were held against their will in the brothel, had some consanguineous relationship with the brothel owner. However, from newspaper reports and arrest records in the

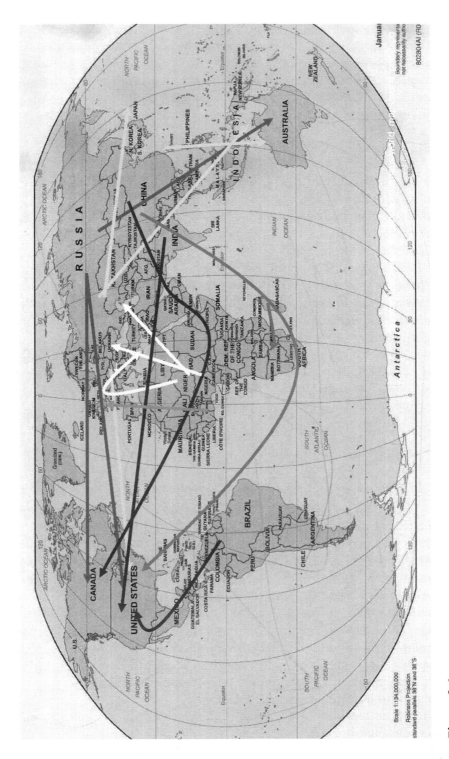

Figure 2.1

United States, it can be seen that the Latin American and Mexican smugglers and traffickers, similar to the Nigerian traffickers, are not as well organized as the crime groups of Russia, China, Japan, and the Ukraine. The Mexican, Nigerian, and Latin American traffickers operate as individuals, primary groups, and small *ad hoc* groups.

There are various factors involved in the trafficking and exploitation of women and children: child trafficking, child labor, forced prostitution, slave labor, sexual slavery, child pornography, exploitation of female migrants, and debt bondage. The trafficking and criminal exploitation of women and children can further be explained as the fraudulent transportation of women and children, domestically or internationally, for slave labor, child labor, forced prostitution, exploitation of migrant labor, sexual slavery, child pornography, and indentured servitude.

Trafficking in women and children is a crime in which victims are transported from poor nations to rich countries or from rural towns to the cities for the traffickers to amass huge profits. This trafficking of women and children grows fastest in Central and Eastern Europe and the former Soviet Union. In Asia, very young girls, ages 13–16 years, from rural towns in Nepal and Bangladesh are sold to brothels in India for $1000 each. In addition, young women and girls from Thailand, the Philippines, and elsewhere in Southeast Asia are trafficked to different parts of Europe, North Africa, Middle East, and Australia. Europol estimates that the sex industry is now worth several billion dollars annually.

However, the trafficking of women and children is not confined to the sex industry. Children are trafficked to work in sweatshops as bonded labor, and young men and boys work illegally in the "three-D" jobs (jobs that are dirty, difficult, and dangerous). The United Nations (UN) Children's Fund estimates that more than 200,000 children are enslaved by cross-border smuggling in West, East, North, and Central Africa alone. The children are often "sold" or trustingly given out by unsuspecting parents who believe that their children are going to be looked after, learn a trade, or be educated.

Very often, trafficking patterns are related to war zones, and even the presence of UN peacekeeping forces—as in Kosovo—and natural disasters create opportunities for traffickers. Some local law enforcement officers and peacekeepers even join in the illegal enterprise. Trafficking in women and children is a form of organized crime, and it threatens sustainable development and rule of law in the country of origin because illicit profits are used for corruption and to finance other criminal activities—including terrorism.

In some places, the women and children are picked up from their towns or countries under false pretenses of giving them a "better life," in terms of jobs, in another city or country. In reality, however, the traffickers sell the innocent women and children to the highest bidder in a foreign city or country. The financial aspect of the deal is completed before the transportation of the individuals even begins. The young woman, boy, or girl has no idea of what is really going to happen to him or her.

2.2   Modus Operandi of the Traffickers

The Nigeria data presented below and reports from Eastern and Central Europe, South and Central America, and Southeast Asia show that the traffickers target poor, helpless, single women in underdeveloped countries, countries at war or coming out of war, or countries that have recently suffered a natural disaster. The traffickers make fake promises to the women and paint them an unrealistically rosy picture of life in Western Europe, the United States, Canada, Israel, Australia, or Japan. To many of the women, the offer is like winning the lottery. Unfortunately, instead of going to the nirvana that has been described, they are heading into a tortuous and agonizing adventure.

In all studies of trafficking in women, the traffickers promised the women high wages and good working conditions in the foreign economies. They point out to their innocent victims the great cities of Tokyo, Sydney, London, Paris, Frankfurt, Munich, New York, Chicago, Los Angeles, Atlanta, Milan, Rome, Amsterdam, Geneva, and so on, as one of their possible destinations. For the unsuspecting women—and for young boys and girls, too—it sounds like a dream come true. These victims are women and juveniles who are looking for a way to escape their hopeless existence in their home countries.

The traffickers and their middlemen go to towns and villages, to small cities, and even to churches to recruit their victims. The types of employment that they promise for the women are jobs as waitresses, bartenders, nannies, models, housemaids, workers in salon shops, and so on. In Southeast Asia, Russia, and the Ukraine, the traffickers may prepare bogus contracts and sign them with the young women to give the deal a whiff of legitimacy (Richard, 2000; Esadze, 2004). In Russia, South and Central Europe, and East and Southeast Asia, the traffickers advertise for female service jobs purportedly available in various countries in Western Europe, the United States, Canada, Israel, Italy, and so on. In addition, some traffickers collaborate with travel agencies and matchmaking agencies to recruit their victims. The traffickers provide travel documents, some of which are even genuine but obtained through bribing corrupt embassy and immigration officials, and some of which forged with a superimposed photo of the person being illegally transported placed on the genuine passport and visa of someone else.

In all source or origination countries, some women and children are kidnapped and smuggled into the United States, Western Europe, Australia, or Japan. These kidnapped women are the women who are sold two or three times to different brothels. The voluntarily and fraudulently trafficked women are the ones who very often end up in debt bondage because the trafficker decided to exploit them by requiring them to pay $10,000–$50,000 U.S. dollars before they would be "free" to live on their own. Kidnapping, threatening, and intimidating are some of the methods of recruitment used in all origination countries. For instance, according to Richard's (2000) reports, in a 1997 trafficking case in California, a 22-year-old Chinese woman was kidnapped in China and smuggled to California on a Taiwanese fishing trawler without any travel documents. She was then forced to work as a prostitute in Los Angeles and continuously "confined, raped, and tortured."

In Nigeria, "Pat," a 21-year-old female—a high school graduate—was fraudulently recruited by her mother's close friend, "Grace," to work in her hair salon in Milan, Italy.[10] Below is part of Pat's paraphrased testimony before the U.S. Immigration Court in Manhattan, New York.

Between July and August 1999, Grace visited Pat's parents four times dressed in very gorgeous attire. Pat was never present when Grace spoke to her mother. After the final visit, Grace invited Pat to her house in Bini. Grace then asked Pat what she was doing for a living. Pat replied that she was experienced in hair dressing but that she had no job at that time. Grace offered to take Pat to Rome to work in the hair salon she ran there. She told Pat that she has spoken to her parents and that they agreed with this move. Grace further told Pat how great life was in Rome and how she could make a lot of money there and help her poor parents. Grace painted Pat a rosy picture of the life that she would have in Italy.

She told Pat that there were other Nigerians settled in Italy and that there was a much higher standard of living there, with a far more promising future, than in Nigeria. She also told her that there was a great demand for the type of salon she owns, catering to the needs of black customers. The way Grace looked and talked spelled confidence and success and of the positive things awaiting Pat.

Pat decided to go with Grace and told her mother so. In October, Grace and Pat left by bus from Benin City for Milan via the Republic of Benin and Paris. In Milan, they took a train to Padova. Pat said little throughout the entire trip, as she found the experience unsettling: "I felt like a fish out of water, taken out of my familiar pond and finding it hard to swim in the ocean" she testified.

When Grace and Pat arrived at a location, Grace approached a man who appeared to be waiting for her. Both talked out of earshot, and then both came to where Pat was waiting. Grace introduced the man to Pat as her husband, "Christopher." They loaded their luggage into Christopher's car and then drove for perhaps 20 minutes before reaching an apartment on the second floor of a four-story building.

The apartment had only one bedroom, which Grace and Christopher occupied. Pat slept on a thin foam mattress on the floor in the sitting room. Grace spoke to Pat in Bini but spoke English with Christopher (an Igbo).

The morning after Pat's arrival (a weekday), Grace and Christopher went out, leaving Pat in the apartment alone. When they returned, Grace told Pat that she needed to renew her salon license, which was why she was running around all the time. The next day, Grace disappeared again, leaving Christopher and Pat in the apartment. At night, Christopher raped Pat several times and told her that he paid 50,000,000 Lira (US$25,000) to bring her to Italy and that she had to work as a prostitute in the street until he recovered his money. He added that he would be with her in the street to protect her. When Pat asked him about Grace, he said that Grace had gone back to Nigeria to bring another woman and added that Grace was not actually his wife.

According to Pat, when she refused to be a prostitute, Christopher beat her so badly that, coupled with his starving her, she nearly died. At long last, Pat said that she agreed to prostitute for Christopher. Christopher started taking her to the street at night, where he collected money from some men and forced Pat to have sex with them in their car. Pat testified that after she had sex three times, on three different occasions, with one of her clients, she seized an opportunity when Christopher was out of earshot and told her client how she was brought to Italy and that she wanted to run away. She told him that Christopher was raping her every day and night, no matter how tired she was, and that Christopher had also seized her passport. The man told Pat that anywhere she ran to in Italy, Christopher would find her and possibly kill her. He then told Pat that he would find a Christian organization (NGO) that would help her leave Italy. According to Pat's testimony, the man did exactly as he promised. He collected Pat's full name, date of birth, nationality, and so on. Within a week, he told Pat the night the escape would take place and that the NGO had obtained a passport and arranged with an airline to take her to the United States.

On the night of Pat's planned escape, Christopher and Pat went to their usual location. Pat's "escape man" had arranged for another man to lure Christopher's attention away from him and Pat: When he and Pat entered his car to pretend to have sex, the decoy presented himself to Christopher as the next man wanting to have sex with Pat and led Christopher to a corner. Then the escape man drove away with Pat to the NGO's designed rendezvous. That night, Pat was led to the airport and flown to the United States. At JFK International Airport, she was detained and taken to New York's immigration detention camp, where the U.S. Citizenship and Immigration Services gave her a deportation order. Pat then contacted a cousin who lived in Boston, Massachusetts, who helped her apply for immigrant classification on the basis of asylum. However, a U.S. Immigration Court denied the application and ordered her deportation. Pat's lawyer could not find a solid ground for an appeal, but about a week later, Pat's lawyer, by happenstance, spoke about the case to a professor at American University. The professor told Pat's attorney that she should look for Professor Ebbe, who had published an article in

Trends in Organized Crime in 1999, titled "Political-Criminal Nexus: 'Slicing Nigeria's National Cake': The Nigerian Case," which asserted that if such a trafficked woman is deported to her country of origin, she would be killed by those who trafficked her out of that country within 2 weeks of her return. Thus, I was consulted to testify. I testified on Pat's behalf by an affidavit in 2001 before the U.S. Court of Immigration Appeals. After reading my affidavit and comparing it with the defendant's testimony, the appeals court sent the case back to the lower court, where the case had started (this court had not read my publication or testimony). At the lower court, after the court had read my testimony, Pat was granted asylum in the United States.

Pat's case is typical of the modus operandi of the traffickers in Southeast Asia, Russia, Latin America, and East and Central Europe. In Nigeria, the traffickers are in a category of organized crime called 419. The trafficking groups have from two to five members who specialize in fraudulent schemes.

In Southeast Asia, the trafficking of women and children is so endemic that it almost appears to be a legitimate way of life in a region where poverty and armed conflicts have led many women and children to flee their homeland. In Southeast Asia, organized crime groups smuggle women and girls to work in Malaysian brothels and bars from such places as Thailand, the Philippines, Indonesia, Cambodia, Sri Lanka, Pakistan, India, Taiwan, and Myanmar. In addition, women and girls from the Ukraine and Russia can also be seen in this region of the world.

In Australia, the nature and scope of trafficking in women and children presents a whole different picture. Australia has a sex industry and, like the Middle East, is a center of sex slavery.

The Australian Center for the Study of Sexual Assault published research that looked into developments in trafficking in women for sexual exploitation in the early 1990s. The findings, written by Lara Fergus, state that:[4]

In 1998–99, 237 women illegally in Australia were deported after being found in brothels. At that time, immigration officials were not required to question the women as to whether they had been trafficked. Sometimes the traffickers turn them in to DIMIA (the Department of Immigration) to be deported because they're no longer a fresh face. There are at least 1,000 adult women in Australia in any one year who have been brought here to work as prostitutes and most have their passports removed and are subjected to violence and rape. They are usually locked in the brothel or a house with other trafficked women. This is often the period where the women experience the most violence. The sexual violence teaches them that they are there simply to satisfy customers and cannot refuse any type of customers or any sexual act, including sex without condoms. Some victims report being shown pornographic images or videos and told that is what they will be required to do. Rape, physical violence, starvation, and threats of harm to the women's families are all used to instill fear and punish those who resist or try to escape. Legislation outlawing human trafficking passed federal parliament in June 2005, delivering a 12-year sentence for trading adults and 20 years for children. A joint parliamentary committee and Australian Crime Commission's response to trafficking in women for sexual servitude handed down a report into its year-long investigation in June last year. The federal government committed $20 million over four years to combat trafficking for sexual exploitation in 2003.

In addition, according to Project Reach, an Australia-based NGO, "Australia's sex slavery laws are failing and police are not doing enough to free enslaved women." Project Reach also reported that a sex industry insider confided to them that traffickers are, for example, turning to Korean women after police crack down on the importation of Thai sex slaves. There were also unsuccessful prosecutions for sexual servitude in Australia, according to the report, and more than 100 people had been summoned by the ACC because of alleged sex slavery.[5]

The ACC reported to a parliamentary committee that 107 people have been summoned and interviewed in Sydney, Melbourne, Adelaide, Perth, Brisbane, and Kalgoorie since 2003. About a third of the interviews were done with prostitutes, who mostly came from South Korea, Thailand, and China. Interviews were also conducted with the owners of premises, associates, financiers, and customers.[6] The ACC estimated that 300 women each year come to Australia for the purpose of prostitution, and about 1000 of them currently work as sex slaves. [7]

The traffickers target poor parents in underdeveloped countries who have many children to feed. The traffickers make fake promises to the parents of the children, telling the poor parents that they have found a good future for their children. These unfortunate parents then hand over their children to the fraudulent traffickers with trust and hope. The traffickers promise the parents that the innocent boys and girls will be employed as house servants and housemaids at a very good wage and that their children would start to send them money in a very short time.

Single, skilled women are promised jobs in restaurants, airlines, supermarkets, and so on in Europe, the United States, Canada, the Middle East, or Australia. The young women have no idea that the rosy promises made to them are all fake. For children, the traffickers are determined to deploy them in bonded labor, prostitution, and domestic slavery (Torstein, 1996; Ebbe, 1999, 2003:151).

According to a Nigerian human rights group and the Constitutional Rights Project Report, middlemen go out scouting for families with more children than they can care for. They convince such families of the juicy employment opportunities waiting for their wards in the cities inside and outside of Nigeria.

Ten-year-old Chukwudi Joseph was recruited and shipped to work in a logging company in Gabon. After three years, Gabonese authorities deported him to Nigeria. He had never been paid.

Thirteen-year old Tope came from neighboring Benin (Republic) on the promise of work, but when she arrived in Lagos (Nigeria) found that work was in a brothel. When she became pregnant she was abandoned on the street. (Torstein, 1996)

In war-torn regions of the world, such as Rwanda, former Yugoslavia, Bosnia, Kosovo, Congo, Sudan, Sierra Leone, Liberia, Afghanistan, and Iraq, the illegal traffickers promise young women, mothers, and their children that they will remove them from the war zones and settle them in safer countries. These helpless, frustrated refugees accept any offer made to take them to a safe zone. However, most of them are handed over to men who take them and deploy them in illegal ventures as slaves. In addition, the illegal traffickers go to refugee camps and entice young women and children out of the camps and transport them to towns and countries, where they are either sold into slavery or deployed in forced prostitution.

Unmistakably, some of the traffickers in women and children are actually those who should protect women and children—the police and UN peace-keepers. Some police officers in different countries and some UN peace-keeping soldiers have been arrested for their participation in trafficking in women for prostitution and sexual slavery. For instance, UN police officers and four foreigners were arrested for human trafficking in the UN-administered province of Kosovo. In addition, on October 5, 2005, the UN police (CIVPOL) and the local Kosovo Police Service (KPS) arrested an international policeman suspected of human trafficking; less than a week earlier, two local police officers were also arrested on human trafficking charges in Northern Kosovo (Krasmigi, 2005).

At present, about 3753 international police officers from 49 countries are serving in Kosovo, which has been under the administration of the UN Mission (UNMIK) since the end of the 1999 war. In addition, there are 6000 local postwar police officers in the region. There is also a specialized unit within UNMIK that is responsible for providing protection to the people and fighting human trafficking and other forms of organized crime. The UN spokesman in the region says that, "Kosovo, like other Western Balkan countries has a serious human trafficking problem" (Krasmigi, 2005).

Amnesty International stated that the presence of international peace-keepers in Kosovo has been fueling the sexual exploitation of women and encouraging trafficking. In addition, Amnesty International claims that the UN and North Atlantic Treaty Organisation troops in the region are using the trafficked women and girls for sex and that some of the soldiers have been involved in trafficking in women and girls. The Amnesty International report on combating trafficking in Kosovo claims that, "girls as young as 11 from Eastern European countries are being sold into sex slavery."

Amnesty International held interviews with women and girls who had been trafficked from Moldova, Bulgaria, and the Ukraine to service Kosovo's sex industry. They reported that sex victims are moved illegally across borders and sold in "trading houses," where they are sometimes drugged and "broken in" before being sold from one trafficker to another for prices ranging from 50 to 3500 euros. The report includes harrowing testimonies of the abduction, deprivation, and torture of the women, including beatings and rape.

The report also condemns the role of the international peacekeepers in furthering the problem, alleging that since the arrival of the peacekeepers in 1999, the number of places in Kosovo where trafficked women and girls may be exploited, such as nightclubs, bars, restaurants, hotels, and cafes, increased—from 18 in 1999 to more that 200 in 2003 (Krasmigi, 2005).

Undeniably, records show that the countries of Southeast Europe have not taken effective measures to curb human trafficking in the region. In fact, the U.S. State Department's report in 2004 showed that Western Balkan countries of Abania, Macedonia, Kosovo, Serbia, Montenegro, Bosnia Herzegovina, and Croatia are origination and transit countries for trafficking women and children to Western Europe and other destination countries for sexual exploitation and forced labor. A United Nations Children's Fund report also asserted that "the main targets of the traffickers are young women and girls between the ages of 15 and 17 who are often sold into sexual slavery, or children under the age of 13, who are trafficked for forced labor and begging (Krasmigi, 2005).

The degree of trafficking in women and children appears to be mind-boggling in every region of the world discussed, but the situation in the Middle East, particularly Lebanon, is more mind-boggling than most. Sexual slavery, child labor exploitation, child slavery, statutory rape, and violation of the human rights of migrants and trafficked women, girls, and boys in Lebanon have gone beyond epidemic proportions. The situation was so bad, as reported by Amnesty International, that it reached the point at which the UN had to send an expert on trafficking in persons to visit Lebanon and investigate. Sigma Huda, Special Rapporteur of the United Nations Commission on Human Rights on Trafficking in Persons, and especially women and children, informed the media of his finding in Beirut on September 15, 2005, when he ended the visit. It was a 9-day fact-finding mission, a small part of which, taken from Huda's presentation to the press in Beirut, is presented here, showing the degree of trafficking in persons and human rights violations in Lebanon:

In the course of my mission, I have found that a significant number of human beings, women in majority, are trafficked into and within Lebanon. Unfortunately, their plight seems to remain unknown to significant parts of Lebanese society, perhaps because the victims tend to be foreign nationals or are considered to be of low social status. Lebanon's victims of trafficking are often invisible victims because they suffer in places that remain hidden to the public eye such as private homes or hotel rooms. Many of my interlocutors, including senior government officials, also acknowledged that widely held attitudes of discrimination on the basis of race, colour, ethnicity, and gender contribute to the prevalence of human trafficking. Social and cultural taboos preventing public discussion of issues related to sexual exploitation are also a factor (Huda, 2005).

According to Huda, between 150,000 and 200,000 domestic migrant workers in Lebanon are victims of human trafficking. The 1946 Labor Code of Lebanon does not protect foreign domestic workers, and most of the women involved come from Asia and Africa. According to Huda, they have no access to the Lebanese Labour Courts. Huda reported that the migrants signed a contract with an overseas employment agency in their country of origin, but upon arrival in Lebanon they are deceived and forced to sign a second, "markedly more disadvantageous contract that is drafted in Arabic," which is a language they do not understand. These migrants are held liable for 16-hour working days, 7 days a week, and for withholding some of their wages. They did not know that this was what they agreed to by signing the new contract. Undeniably, this type of unilateral contract is fraudulent and malicious treatment. In addition, some of the migrants who tried to run away from their masters or from Lebanon were caught, abused, thrown into detention without trial, raped, and deported penniless (Huda, 2005). Huda also noted that some women find themselves in debt-bondage in Lebanon and will never find a way to go back to their countries of origin. In addition, while these women are in Lebanon, they are treated like outcastes or untouchables.

Women trafficked to Lebanon and other Islamic countries for forced prostitution suffer multiple hazards. Islamic Sharia Law prohibits prostitution. Therefore, any woman engaging in prostitution in an Islamic country, whether forced or voluntarily, can be prosecuted, imprisoned, and deported or executed. Unfortunately and contradictorily, the Islamic men who patronize the prostitutes go free. In 2003, a young Nigerian Moslem woman got pregnant without a husband, and the Northern Nigerian Islamic State government wanted to execute her according to Sharia Code. International outcry and the Nigerian Supreme Court saved the woman, but nothing was done to the Moslem man who impregnated her. Nigeria is not an Islamic country, but think of what could have happened to such a woman in one.

In many Islamic countries, they have "super night clubs" to which trafficked women are brought by their keepers for Islamic men to enjoy. In some of these clubs, one can see women not only from Africa and Asia but also from Eastern and Central Europe being paraded for the highest bidder (Huda, 2005).

Huda's findings in Lebanon are the epitome of what is happening in different parts of the world today, including in more advanced countries. Many trafficked women and children from Mexico, Asia, and Latin American countries are found in the countries of the Middle East, including Israel. Some of these women are willing international prostitutes, who can also be found in cities in Nigeria, Ghana, Kenya, and South Africa. Some of these women paid to be trafficked and became free and live on their own after their debt-bondage ended. Some of such women who succeed have become well to do and fly back to their countries of origin to ensnare other women. Some of these successful international prostitutes can be found not only in African cities but also in the United States, Germany, France, the United Kingdom, Israel, and Russia.

The professional traffickers belong to organized crime syndicates that have machines and the technology to produce many countries' passports. For more advanced countries, such as the United States, Germany, France, Italy, and the United Kingdom, these organized crime document forgers can superimpose a photo of an illegal immigrant on the passport of another person who has a legitimate visa to enter the United States, Canada, the United Kingdom, France, Italy, or Germany. This type of organized crime document fraud has been going on since the 1970s. With forged passports and visas, the traffickers can fly to any country. Sometimes, syndicated traffickers even collude with embassy or consulate officials to ease the difficulty of getting passports or visas.

2.3   Conclusion

Trafficking in women and children is a global phenomenon. It is an attack on the dignity of the human race. Human trafficking and the type of inhumane treatment meted out to trafficked women and children in various parts of the world portray an abject decay of morality and the absence of a cult of good manners. Many countries, particularly the developed nations, were too slow to respond to the challenges of trafficking in women and children. Many religious organizations and NGOs have been sounding alarms in various nations since the 1970s about the issues of trafficking. But their lamentations fell on deaf ears until the UN Palermo Protocol of 2000, which gave states' parties a ratification deadline of December 12, 2002. The protocol was open to all states for signature December 12–15, 2000, in Palermo, Italy. It had to be at the UN Headquarters in New York by December 12, 2002. However, the United States and Myanmar did not ratify the protocol until September and October 2005. That delay shows how reluctant some countries are about responding to the trouble of trafficking in women and children. It is very heartrending to observe that some men in authority positions tend to ignore the pains of women.

Notes

1. Fact sheet on human trafficking: http://www.unodc.org/unodc/en/trafficking_victim_consents.html.
2. About Human Trafficking: http://www.humantrafficking.org/about/trafficking.html.
3. Malaysia Annual Report: http://www/humantrafficking.org/countries/eap/malaysia/news/2005_07/hrc_seeks_crackdown.
4. Report on Trafficking in Australia: http://www.humantrafficking.org/countries/ eap/australia/news/2005_07/ACSSA_trafficking_rep....
5. Sex slavery in Australia: http://www.optusnet.com.au.13_August_2005.
6. Ibid.
7. "Australian Crime Commission Acts on Sex Slavery," AAP, August 11, 2005. http://www.minermsn.com.au/article.aspx?id=54134.

References

A. Adepoju, Review of research and data on human trafficking in sub-Saharan Africa. In: *Data and Research on Human Trafficking: A Global Survey*, ed. Frank Laczko and Elzvieta Gozdziak. IOM, Geneva, 2005, pp. 75–80.

Australian Crime Commission Act, Sex Slavery in Australia, 2005.

A.M. Bertone, Sexual trafficking in women: International political economy and the politics of sex, *Geneva Issues*, 2000, 18(1): 4–18.

J. Doezema, Loose women or lost women? The re-emergence of white slavery in contemporary discourse of trafficking in women. *Gender Issues*, 2000, 18(1): 23–55.

O.N.I. Ebbe, Political-criminal nexus "Slicing Nigeria's national cake: The Nigerian case," *Trends in Organized Crime*, 1999, 4(3): 29–59.

O.N.I. Ebbe, Slicing Nigeria's "national cake." In: Roy Godson, ed. *Menace to Society: Political–Criminal Collaborations around the World*. New Brunswick: Transaction Publishers, 2003, 137–174.

L. Esadze, Trafficking in Women and Children: A Case Study of Georgia, paper presented at the 2004 ISPAC of the United Nations Crime Prevention and Criminal Justice Programmes, held in Courmayeur, Mont Blanc, Italy, 2004.

Foundation of Women Forum, Trafficking in women for the purpose of sexual exploitation, The Swedish Ministry for Foreign Affairs, http://www.nmi.utc.edu/w?NH.DBI.EVKQE.RVnMYV.FDdEQ.CeQVPQW.K, 1998.

B.D. Gushulak and W.W. MacPherson, Health issues associated with the smuggling and trafficking of migrants, *Journal of Immigrant Health*, 2000, 2(2): 67–78.

S. Huda, Human trafficking: Expert on trafficking in persons end visit to Lebanon, http://www.humantrafficking.org/collaboration/regional/ame/news/2005_ 09/expert_statement.

E. Krasmigi, ISN Security Watch, http://www.humantrafficking.org/collaboration/ regional/seur/news/2005_09/combating.htm.

A.O. Richard, *International Trafficking in Women in the United States: A Contemporary Manifestation of Slavery and Organized Crime*, Center for the Study of Intelligence, Washington, D.C., 2000.

M. Torstein, *Child Slavery: Nigerian Human Rights Group Reporting*, Press Digest, Lagos, Nigeria, 1996.

Causes of Trafficking in Women and Children

3

OBI N.I. EBBE

Contents

3.1 Theoretical Explanations

There are various sociological theories that explain trafficking of women and children. In explaining the etiology of this fraudulent type of crime, we can look at the effect of criminality and economic conditions (Bonger, 1916), poverty (More, 1516), anomie (Merton, 1968; Durkheim, 1964), hedonism (Beccaria, 1819; Bentham, 1967), social control (Hirschi, 1969), class and crime (Chambliss and Mankoff, 1976; Quinney, 1977), greed (McCaghy, 1980), and globalization.

Starting with criminality and economic conditions, Bonger asserted that when a society is divided into haves and have-nots, the have-nots try to get even with the haves. In other words, the theory is that when the economy is bad, some individuals who are determined to survive will try alternative means of making it—however illegitimate. In many developing countries, the economy has been in a state of depression since the 1970s without an end in sight. As a consequence, trafficking in women and children from developing countries to more advanced countries for the purposes of prostitution, housekeeping, housemaid services, babysitting, child pornography, slave labor, and sexual slavery became an alternative, illegal moneymaking mechanism. In more advanced countries, greed (McCaghy) drives the rich and powerful to get richer by utilizing the cheap labor of illegal aliens and that of women and children, by housing girls twice or thrice their age as personal sex slaves, and by providing apartments hidden from their wives for these young girls.

Furthermore, domestic conflicts and wars taking place in some under-developed economies, emanating from postindependence tribal struggles for control of the government, wholesale corruption, crony capitalism, and crony democracy, have created social disorganization and anomie (Merton, 1968; Durkheim, 1964) in those countries. In effect, there is a breakdown in law enforcement as social control mechanisms are weakened to a point of lawlessness (Hirschi, 1969). In these former colonial regimes, intertribal or interethnic conflicts gave rise to dictatorships and predatory states. Such regimes have been recorded in Nigeria, Zaire, Uganda, Liberia, Bosnia-Herzegovina, former Yugoslavia, Haiti, Myanmar, Pakistan, Sudan, Sri Lanka, Zimbabwe, and so on. The police in this sort of state are used to protect the dictatorial and predatory state's political agenda at the expense of crime control and the safety of the nation's private citizens. The large mass population of unemployed and destitute individuals hang around hopelessly, living at the mercy of the fraudulent human traffickers. As a result, some young men and groups in such dictatorial regimes have found single women and children, struggling for survival, to be easy targets for trafficking exploitation.

Poverty is not a universal theory of crime. In other words, poverty cannot explain crime in all cultures. However, poverty explains a significant amount of crime in developed, industrialized nations and, to a small degree, in poor nations. As Thomas More (1516) put it before the British Parliament of his time, if a man has determined to be alive, but his basic needs are not provided, he must steal. In agreement with this line of thought, the economic conditions of some developed and underdeveloped nations produced waves of unemployment for both skilled and unskilled individuals in the 1980s, and as a consequence, many university and high school graduates engaged themselves in all types of transnational crimes, including transnational trafficking in women and children. Beccaria (1819) and Bentham (1967) of the Classical School of Criminology asserted that man is hedonistic: In effect, man will continue to seek pleasure wherever he can find it. Therefore, hedonism and greed combine to spur some middle- and upper-class individuals in Western, Eastern, and Central Europe; the United States; Canada; the Middle East; Africa; South America; Australia; and Japan to import innocent, illegally transported women and children to serve as housemaids, houseboys, sex slaves, or slave laborers.

3.2 Immediate Causes of Trafficking in Women and Children

Wars in Asia, Africa, Eastern Europe, the Middle East, and South America, as well as the many national disasters that took place in many regions of the world from the 1960s through the 1990s, created many orphans and orphan-ages in Indonesia, Cambodia, India, Africa, the Middle East, and so on. These orphans and orphanages brought about adoption hysteria, and consequently, some child predators found the orphanages and other orphan concentration areas to contain readily available populations for trafficking in children. In Southeast Asia, there are so many orphans that the orphanages could not handle them all, especially in Thailand (Bales, 2002). Some of these orphans roam the streets and are easy prey to the traffickers and sex tourists who flood Southeast Asia for the sole purpose of sexually abusing these minors. Illegally transporting these homeless children from Southeast Asia to loca-tions in Africa, the United States, Europe, and the Middle East has become an easy venture because the children have no parents or caring guardians to obstruct the trafficking.

The wars and national disasters mentioned here created new opportuni-ties for the emergence of transnational human smuggling and trafficking in addition to the opportunities already present in the parts of the world that are traditionally poor regions. In Southeast Asia, Cambodia is one of the least developed nations in the world, with a per capita income of $280 U.S. dollars per year. Most of the workers in Cambodian garment factories are single women between the ages of 18 and 25 years. Most of these women were born and raised in provinces in Northern Thailand, where there are no job opportunities at all. These women receive, on average, $40 a month, and they are forced to pay a 6-month procurement fee of $240 just to obtain the job. They also bear the stresses of having to send money home to their parents and loved ones and of getting out of debt.[1] In effect, these single women feel the pressure to prostitute themselves to meet their family obligations and to pay their own rent and transportation to work. With the addition of loneli-ness, long hours of work (sometimes 16 hours a day), poor living conditions, poor nutrition, and lack of meaningful guidance, many of these women fall prey to Western tourists and organized crime traffickers who make fake promises about great lives waiting for them in the United States, Germany, the United Kingdom, Canada, France, and so on. Many of these women are running from the frying pan into fire (Bales, 2002; Ehrenreich, 2002; Lan, 2002; Parrerias, 2002).

There exists a similar situation in the poverty-stricken regions of the heartland of Southeast Asia. In Northern Thailand, in the Hill Tribes, the people live in poverty and have a dire lack of education. Most parents are addicted to drugs such as heroin, and as a result, their children start working at a very early age. Some of these young kids are easily stolen or enticed to leave the poor area by traffickers and are then trafficked and sold into slavery (Bales, 2002).

In terms of the exploitation of women and children in the form of child and slave labor, Southeast Asia, and particularly Thailand and Cambodia, stands out. Some children under the age of 18 years are made to work 16 hours a day in village factories. In Phnom Penh, capital of Cambodia, the home of the country's garment industry, 90 percent of the workers are women. These women either get little money or have no money left after paying their bills. The exploitation of women and children is not found only in Cambodia, of course. One can find the same situation in Gabon and Equatorial Guinea in Southwest Africa, where boys are forced to work in plantations without pay and those who are paid are under bonded labor. This means that at the end of the month, they are already further in debt to their masters. Some of the boys who voluntarily entered these two countries but who want to go back to their home countries cannot because they do not even have the money for public transportation.

Another causal factor in the trafficking of women and children is globalization. The idea of shared political policies, culture, trade, and regional treaties that will eliminate the demand for visas at the borders of, for example, Economic Cooperation of West African States nations, European Union/North Atlantic Treaty Organisation nations, the North American States, and so on made the trafficking of women and children across international borders very easy, especially among the states that were parties to the treaty.

In fact, enacting legislation without stringent enforcement of the law is tantamount to the criminalizing of the masses. When laws are made to control a certain aberrant behavior but are not enforced, it causes some people in society to commit other crimes far and above those theoretically prohibited. This is because individuals in such a society form the belief that punishments for violations are not enforced. In addition, plea bargaining is not a stringent law enforcement system. Traffickers in women and children know that law enforcement officials are not keen on enforcing the law in many regions, both in developed and developing countries, especially when it is a matter of prosecuting the sexual abuse of women. In addition, some law enforcement officials are corrupt. In effect, then, trafficking in women and children is not scary to potential traffickers because they are aware of the existence of such weak social control systems. Individually, plea bargaining and a nonchalant attitude toward stringent law enforcement both weaken the anger of penal law.

3.3   Conclusion

Economic determinism is a pivotal factor in trafficking in women and children. Both the rich and the poor want the good things of life: The rich want to get richer, and the poor do not want to go to prison. Both are pursuing wealth through various means—but some want to get wealthy by all means. Therefore, controlling the excesses of some people in their pursuit of wealth is the only way out of this mess. The trafficking of women and children is a nerve-racking problem in some regions of the world, where resources for human survival are very scarce, such as Northern Thailand, rural Cambodia, disorganized Newly Independent States of Eastern Europe, arid regions of Africa, and countries whose populations grow faster than available resources, such as India, Mexico, and several Latin American nations. In these regions, abject poverty neutralizes any sense of guilt among the youth in kidnapping and fraudulent trafficking in women and children. Unmistakably, in these situations, abject poverty nullifies morality in an attempt to survive.

Notes

1. Restoration Center for Garment Factory workers: http://www.traffickingin-persons.com/restoration.htm

References

K. Bales, Because she looks like a child. In: *Global Woman: Nannies, Maids, and Sex Workers in the New Economy*, ed. Barbara Ehrenreich and Arlie Russell Hochschild, Henry Holt, New York, 2002.

C. Beccaria, *On Crimes and Punishment*, trans. Edward D. Ingraham, 2nd ed., Philip H. Nicklin, Philadelphia, 1819.

J. Bentham, *A Fragment on Government and an Introduction to the Principles of Morals and Legislation*, Basil Blackwell, Oxford, 1967.

W. Bonger, *Criminality and Economic Conditions*, trans. Henry P. Horton, Dryden Press, New York, 1916.

W. Chambliss and M. Mankoff, *Whose Law? What Order? A Conflict Approach to Criminology*, John Wiley and Sons, New York, 1976.

E. Durkheim, *Division of Labor in Society*, Free Press, New York, 1964.

B. Ehrenreich, Maid to Order. In: *Global Woman: Nannies, Maids, and Sex Workers in the New Economy*, ed. Barbara Ehrenreich and Arlie Russell Hochschild, Henry Holt, New York, 2002.

T. Hirschi, *The Causes of Delinquency*, University of California Press, Berkeley, 1969.

P. Lan, Among women: Migrant domestics and their Taiwanese employers across generations. In: *Global Woman: Nannies, Maids, and Sex Workers in the New Economy*, ed. Barbara Ehrenreich and Arlie Russell Hochschild, New York: Henry Holt, New York, 2002.

C. McCaghy, *Crime in America*, Free Press, New York, 1980.

R.K. Merton, *Social Theory and Social Structure*, Free Press, New York, 1968.

T. More, *Utopia*, trans. H.B.S. Ogden, Appletone-Century Crofts, New York, 1516 (1949).

R.S. Parrerias, The care crisis in the Philippines: Children and transnational families in the new global economy. In: *Global Woman: Nannies, Maids, and Sex Workers in the New Economy*, ed. Barbara Ehrenreich and Arlie Russell Hochschild, Henry Holt, New York, 2002.

R. Quinney, *Class, State and Crime: On the Theory and Practice of Criminal Justice*, David McKay, New York, 1977.

Control and Prevention of Trafficking in Women and Children

4

OBI N.I. EBBE

Contents

4.1   Control Strategies

The crime of trafficking in women and children is so horrendous that without some meaningful and speedy effort to control it, the sanctity and quality of humanity will be obliterated. Many women and children have been killed, some have committed suicide, and others are living in perpetual anguish during their existence as trafficked human beings. Those who survived the inhuman treatment of living in debt-bondage, sexual slavery, forced prostitution, and child labor live in the nightmares of their painful past. The United Nations (UN), governments, humanitarian nongovernmental organizations (NGOs), Amnesty International, and some religious organizations are determined to control and prevent this inhuman trade.

We discuss here the efforts made by the UN and the other organizations to save the lives of innocent women and children who found themselves in pitiful conditions that they never imagined. There are laws and methods already in place for control of trafficking in women and children. However, we suggest here additional methods to prevent the trafficking in women and children out of their countries of origin.

As far back as 1949, the UN Geneva Convention (IV) Relative to the Protection of Civilian Persons in Time of War prohibited the illegal transportation of women and children. Furthermore, the 1968 UN Convention on the Non-Applicability of Statutory Limitations to War Crimes and Crimes Against Humanity Art 1 (b); the 1969 Inter-American Convention of Human Rights, Art 4; and the 1973 UN Convention on the Prevention and

Punishment of Crimes Against Internationally Protected Persons Including Diplomatic Agents all implicitly prohibit trafficking in women and children. Furthermore, the 1993 Hague Convention on Protection of Children and Cooperation in Respect of Inter-Country Adoptions; the 2000 Optional Protocol II to the Convention on the Rights of the Child, Child Prostitution and Child Pornography, Art 2 (a); and the 2000 Palermo, Italy, Protocol to Prevent, Suppress and Punish Trafficking in Persons, Especially Women and Children, Art 3 (a) and Arts 4–6 are all international laws prohibiting trafficking in women and children for child labor, pornography, forced prostitution, slavery, debt-bondage, and sexual slavery.

The UN, through its office on Drugs and Crime (UNODC), has set up a program to deal with trafficking in human beings. The UN Global Programme Against Trafficking in Human Beings (GPAT) was designed by the UNODC in collaboration with the UN Interregional Crime and Justice Research Institute and was launched in March 1999 to assist member states in their efforts to combat trafficking in human beings. GPAT emphasizes the involvement of organized crime syndicates in human trafficking and promotes the development of effective methods to crack down on the perpetrators.

Whereas GPAT assists UN member states in cracking down on human trafficking, its key components in this effort are data collection, assessment, and technical cooperation. With the cooperation of UN Interregional Crime and Justice Research Institute, data are collected on various smuggling routes and on the methods being used by organized criminal syndicates for trafficking women and children. GPAT also keeps a database containing trafficking trends, routes, and information about victims and traffickers to assist policymakers, practitioners, researchers, and the NGO community.[1]

The countries selected by GPAT for study come from Asia, Europe, Africa, and Latin America and are assessed according to smuggling routes and forms of exploitation of trafficked persons; to cooperation among law enforcement agencies, prosecution, and the judiciary; and to government efforts to respond, including recent legislative reforms.

On the basis of GPAT assessments, seven countries are now involved in technical cooperation projects. Specific intervention measures have been introduced that are designed to strengthen the capacity of the nations to combat all forms of trafficking at the national and international levels. It is expected that these measures will help countries of origination, transit, and destination of the trafficked persons to develop joint strategies and practical actions.

Furthermore, the UNODC gives direct assistance to specific countries that are ravaged by poverty and disturbed by human trafficking hysteria. At present, UNODC is helping Vietnamese judicial system and law enforcement agencies to improve their ability to combat human trafficking in Vietnam. In fact, the second phase of the project captioned Strengthening the Legal and Law Enforcement Institutions in Preventing and Combating Trafficking in

Persons was signed by the Deputy Minister of Public Security, Senior Lieu-tenant General Le The Tiem, and the Chief of the UNODC's Vietnam Repre-sentative office, Narumi Yamada, in Hanoi on August 26, 2005. The project aims at consolidating current mechanisms that prevent and combat human trafficking by creating favorable conditions for judicial and law enforcement agencies and improving criminal investigations, prosecution procedures, and judges' skills, as well as training officers of related agencies.[2] The project was designed to help Vietnam ratify the UN 2000 Protocol.

Many national governments have promulgated laws making traffick-ing in human beings a serious felonious offense with a sentence of years of imprisonment if convicted. The United States, for example, has passed a law making trafficking in human beings, and particularly women and children, a felony. In addition to issuing an annual Trafficking in Persons Report, which has helped spur government action globally, the United States has given nearly $300 million to antitrafficking programs abroad in the past 4 years. In addition, it has spent millions of dollars more on antitrafficking efforts domestically, including stepping up prosecutions of trafficking and increasing assistance to victims of trafficking (Miller, 2005). Finally, on Sep-tember 21, 2005, the governor of California, Arnold Schwarzenegger, signed a human trafficking bill into law: The California Trafficking Victims Protec-tion Act makes human trafficking a felony in California.

Undeniably, the severest penalty for trafficking in human being is found in Myanmar (Burma). Almost 3 months after the United States named Myanmar, North Korea, and Cambodia the worst offenders for human traf-ficking in Asia, Myanmar, on September 13, 2005, banned the practice of trafficking in human beings and made it punishable by a maximum of life in prison and possibly also a fine. In Myanmar the minimum sentence for trafficking in women and children is 10 years in prison. The Union of Myan-mar statute also ordered that, "Whoever is guilty of trafficking in persons other than women, children, and youth shall on conviction be punished with imprisonment for a term which may extend from a minimum of 5 years to a maximum of 10 years and may also be liable to a fine."[3] The statute added, among other things, that anybody found "guilty of trafficking in persons with organized crime group … [will] be punished with imprisonment for a minimum of 20 years to a maximum of imprisonment for life and may also be liable to a fine."[4]

Given the horrendous and pitiful nature of the criminal transportation of women and children, many religious organizations have brought the prob-lem of human trafficking to the attention of many governments throughout the world. As a consequence, many governments on various continents have promulgated laws prohibiting the illegal transportation of women and chil-dren. In addition, many governments have also established task forces for the protection of women and children and are investigating allegations of illegal trafficking in women and children.

Some religious organizations have established orphanages in Cambodia, Indonesia, India, Congo, Sierra Leone, Rwanda, Bosnia-Herzegovina, and Kosovo as a way to protect the children from child traffickers. In addition, these religious organizations gather information on traffickers' *modus operandi* and inform the governments of the countries where they operate. In Southeast Asia, one can find orphanages like Church Orphan Home and Warm Blankets Homes, which pull some of the children from the streets of Cambodia and Indonesia. Below are testimonies of two orphans who found a better life at Warm Blankets Homes:[5]

> Once an orphan … I don't remember my father. He died when I was very young. My mother died of malaria when I was nine. No one wanted me. I felt so lonely and ashamed. I thought it was my fault. My uncle took me to a man who gave him money, but I was forced to do things I didn't want to do. I cried and he would beat me. It was very painful. I wanted to die. One night I ran away. I hid in the back of a house of a woman who sold soup near the hotel. She found me crying so she wrapped me in a blanket and took me to Warm Blankets orphan home. That was 4 years ago. Now, I have the Lord and know I am clean. I want to be a pastor and help those like me.
>
> Child soldier transformed to a man of God … I was born in a Khmer Rouge–ruled province. Some of us boys were taught that it was brave to be a soldier for the Khmer Rouge. My nickname is Crocodile. I was forced to kill at age 12 in the Killing Fields of Cambodia. I was fearless. I became chief body guard for the main Khmer Rouge general. I stood up to assassins and was spared. I had no peace in my life till a pastor told me about Jesus, then I felt my rage leave. At 16, I entered a Warm Blankets home. I received the Lord and now, 6 years later, I married a pastor's daughter and I am now pastor in a training church. Children should never have to be soldiers. Thank you for helping me become a man of God and not a man of hate.

The religious organizations involved in orphanage cases have saved many lives. Children who otherwise would have been dead or ended up in perpetual servitude and mental anguish are now saved by the orphanages.

There are NGOs like Amnesty International; the Coalition Against Trafficking in Women (CATW, founded in 1988); National Women Union and Can Tho City Women's Union (both in Cambodia); and Acting for Women in Distressing Circumstances, a French NGO; the Israeli Coalition Against Trafficking in Women; and so on, have launched many control, protection, and prevention methods against trafficking in women and children.

CATW promotes human rights by working internationally to combat sexual exploitation in all its forms. It is said that CATW was the first NGO to focus on human trafficking, especially sex trafficking of women and girls.

In fact, in 1989, CATW received Category II Consultative Status from the UN Economic and Social Council.[6] The Israel Coalition Against Trafficking in women is one of the NGOs that has waged tireless war against trafficking in women and girls for prostitution and sexual slavery. Reproduced here is a letter from the Israeli Coalition Against Trafficking in Women to the UNODC Headquarters in Vienna, Austria, requesting Global International Day Against Trafficking in Women:[7]

> We are writing this letter on behalf of the Israeli Coalition Against Trafficking in Women. The Coalition was established in 1997 and is comprised of a number of human-rights organizations and private individuals who are working together to eradicate the phenomenon of trafficking in women and to care for the women who have been trafficked into the sex industry in Israel. The Coalition believes it is the responsibility of the State of Israel to take care of the victims of such trafficking and see to their initial rehabilitation and recuperation after their terrible experience in the country.
>
> This letter is to formally request that the United Nations declare August 16th "International Day Against Trafficking in Women." August 16th is a symbolic and tragic day in the story of trafficked women. Five years ago, on this day, an Israeli brothel was set on fire and four women who were locked in it were burned alive. We believe the memory of these women should serve as a reminder of the tragedy that befalls all women who are forced into the life of prostitution. If their memory can be used as an impetus for change, then perhaps their senseless deaths and tragic lives will not have been in vain.
>
> The trafficking in women has been a plague on Israeli society and unfortunately much of the world. Most of the women sold into Israel's modern day slavery are from the former Soviet states. Some are aware that they will be working as prostitutes when they come here; many are not. They are forced to work in brothels for almost no wages in order to one day buy back their freedom. Their fate when they return to their homeland may be as bad as their ordeal in Israel, especially if they choose to cooperate with authorities against their captors, who are often connected with organized crime and retain strong ties to the former USSR.
>
> Our principal goal is to influence the state to do all in her power to act against trafficking in women and help the victims of trafficking. With the help of the United Nations, we hope August 16th can become a day of hope and increased awareness of the plight of too many of the world's women. The trafficking of women is an international problem and it can only be eradicated with international support and cooperation. It is our hope that this International Day will bring an end to this crime against women.

The NGOs are all watchdogs against trafficking in women and children. Furthermore, there are concerted efforts being made by NGOs and government agencies to identify the illegal traffickers in women and children. In addition, some NGOs and designated government agencies have taken the responsibility of rescuing women and children who are in bondage in many parts of the world. Finally, governments have been warned through the UN not to deport illegally transported women and children to their countries of origin after they have been rescued to avoid the traffickers' taking reprisal on those they had victimized.

Efforts are being made by many governments to protect the victims of trafficking in women and children. The UN 2000 Protocol Article 6, "Assistance to and protection of victims of trafficking in persons," stipulated the roles of states' parties in reintegrating victims of trafficking. Both origination and destination countries are advised not to treat victims of trafficking in persons as criminals but, rather, give them all the medical, psychological, economic, and educational assistance that they need. In addition, destination countries are advised not to deport trafficked women and children without ascertaining the safety of the victim on his or her return to his or her country of origin.

Some governments like those of Sri Lanka, India, and the Philippines have established programs in their embassies for helping their citizens who were trafficked to other countries to settle wherever they choose.

4.2   Conclusion and Recommendation

There are tremendous efforts being made all over the world by governments to eliminate trafficking in women and children. These efforts are spearheaded by the UN, NGOs, and some governments, but a great deal of damage had already been done against women and children before the UN and the governments were alerted to the problem.

Undeniably, it is a mistake for anybody to think that trafficking in women and girls will be entirely eliminated—there is just too much money involved in the trafficking. Trying to eliminate trafficking in women and girls is like trying to eliminate smuggling narcotics drugs when the market is available. Trafficking in women and children involves billions of dollars annually. Cooperative efforts are needed among governments to bring the occurrence of this crime to the lowest minimum, but in a situation where some government leaders run with the hare and hunt with the hounds, controlling trafficking in women and children becomes a wild goose chase.

Trafficking in women and children is a form of cancer ravaging the human race. It is, in the main, sex trafficking. Trafficking in women and children is also a national and international crime in which both the rich and the poor cooperate. Globalization has made it so that no country in the world is immune from trafficking in women and children. Although trafficking can serve as an escape or safe haven for some women, for most of them, the exploitation and the inhuman treatment meted out is not worth the risk.

Although tremendous efforts are being made by some governments all over the world to eliminate trafficking in women and children, for some governments, trafficking in women is a source of economic survival. In effect, in such situations, these governments do not want to do anything to stop the crime; this is particularly the case with governments in Southeast Asia, which often encourage sex tourism as a means of obtaining Western currency. It is also necessary to realize that prostitution network associations are opposed to antitrafficking laws in countries with brothels. Finally, law enforcement agencies of all nations must be made morally responsible for enforcing the laws against trafficking.

In addition, nations of the world should tackle the problem of poverty. The UN and more advanced countries should help to reduce poverty to a minimum if trafficking in women and children may be eliminated, given that some poor parents sell some of their children to survive while others encourage their daughters to engage in prostitution as a way to survive poverty. Absolute poverty, especially, can lead to depraved crimes and acts of mind-boggling complexity.

The proverb that prevention is better than a cure, is very important in the case of the criminal exploitation of women and children. We suggest that governments, religious organizations, and local communities should be alerted to the problem so that they can encourage local women and girls not to be carried away by the traffickers' rosy promises of good jobs in their national cities and other countries. Parents and single women should be warned to look before they leap into what may turn out to be false promises and disastrous situations. We recommend mass education on the existence of illegal traffickers in women and children and how to avoid them, and religious organizations should create a program of global spiritual revival to curb irrational pursuit of wealth and hysterical sexual deviancy. For this inhuman enterprise to come to an end, governments of both origination and destination countries of innocent women and children must wage a tireless war against the traffickers.

Notes

1. UN global programme against trafficking in human beings: http://www.unodc.org/unodc/en/trafficking_human_beings.html.
2. Human trafficking in Vietnam: http://www.humantrafficking.org/countries/eap/Vietnam/news/2005_08/ht_capactiy_building.htm.
3. The Union of Myanmar: The State Peace and Development Council Law (The Anti-Trafficking in Person Law) Nov. 5/2005.
4. Ibid.
5. Trafficking in Persons: http://www.traffickinginpersons.com/voices.htm.

References

J.R. Miller, *United States Senate Consent to Ratification of UN Protocol on Trafficking*, Office to Monitor and Combat Trafficking in Persons, U.S. Department of State, Washington, DC, 2005.

Part II

**Case Studies
in Trafficking
in Women and
Children**

Trafficking in Women and Children in Japan

5

HARUHIKO HIGUCHI

Contents

5.1 Introduction

Japan is one of the richest countries in the world. In 2002, the per capita income was US$22,550,[1] and the gross domestic product amounted to US$4 trillion. However, the Japanese still have various problems related to trafficking in women and children in ways different from developing countries. This study is based on ethnographic observation. There are very few official data available on trafficking in women and children in Japan.

5.2 Child Prostitution and Child Pornography

Child prostitution and child pornography are matters of growing concern, and the Law for Punishing Acts Related to Child Prostitution and Child Pornography was enacted in 1999. In 2003 alone, 7304 juveniles were victimized, of which 1731 were cleared cases of child prostitution, about 12.2% of which involved the use of telephone clubs,[2] and 45.7% were related to online services.[3] Also, there are 214 cleared cases of child pornography, and 47.7% of them involved the use of the Internet. The number of victimized girls taken from online dating services is on the increase: A survey in December 2002 conducted by the Society for the Research of Internet Contents Harmful to Juveniles indicated the following:

- 40.2% of junior high school students and 88.9% of high school students have a cellular phone.
- Among high school students, 17.6% of the girls and 32.9% of the boys have used online dating services.
- Among the high school students having used online dating services, 47.1% of the girls and 41.5% of the boys really met a partner whom they got to know through the Internet services.

5.3   Juvenile Delinquency

In Japan recently, juvenile delinquency has emerged as a major social problem. In 2003, the percentage of juveniles recorded as penal code offenders came up to 38.0%, and 66.0% of the street crimes, such as purse snatching and street robbery, were committed by juveniles. Prostitution by high school and junior high school girls has become one of the most characteristic delinquencies. Also in 2003, 4412 juveniles were placed under guidance or taken into protective custody for sexual misconduct. Of course, this number is just the tip of the iceberg.

These delinquent girls are really exploited by shameless adults, but to make matters worse, many of them are not forced to sell their bodies. That is, they engaged in prostitution spontaneously, as a business. In fact, the telephone clubs and online dating services mentioned above are known to be the easier methods for girls to use to look for their customers.

Most of them are from middle-class families and have never experienced hardships in life. Though they receive a good amount of pocket money[4] from their parents, they just want extra money for fashionable cosmetics, brand-new bags and clothes, tickets for discos and concerts, updating their cellular phones, and so on. They often describe their misconducts as *Enjo-Kosai*, or simply *En-Ko*, which means "supportive intercourse" in English. According to a survey performed in 2002, 41.2% of the delinquent juveniles protected by the authorities had committed sexual misconduct to get money for going to the cinema.[5] This loss of morality may be attributed to recent failures within the educational system. After World War II, the occupying forces revised all the Japanese governmental systems drastically. In modern Japanese educational structure, the teaching of "morality" and "discipline" has been neglected as a result of the false charge that they comprised the core of Japan's former militarism. The delinquent girls now say, "We are free to do anything we want," and modern Japanese society, having lost its traditional values, has nothing to offer them as counterargument.

5.4 The Lolita Complex

There are a growing number of men with a Lolita complex, generally called *Lolicon*, who are perverts who have sexual desires for girls under 12 years of age. In Japan, as a result of the nation's rapid Westernization after the Second World War, women are getting stronger both physically and mentally. As a result, some men who are disenchanted by assertive adult females are interested in young girls, who are still obedient. The growth of *Lolicon* is also attributed to the development of sophisticated animation programs and computer games showing idealized young heroines.

Lolicon men collect miniature figures, pictures, and comics of young girls. The comic market, abbreviated to *Comike*, is held annually in Tokyo and sells comics with cartoons of sexually abused children to more than 400,000 buyers. Some *Lolicon* men have participated in Enjo-Kosai with young girls, but they are worried about investigation by the Japanese police, so now they are going to Southeast Asian countries, where they can easily find prostitution houses full of young girls.

5.5 Japanese Law

The Japanese Law for Punishing Acts related to Child Prostitution and Child Pornography can punish a Japanese citizen who has committed sexual crimes abroad, but practically, the investigation of such crimes is quite difficult, because the victims are watched by their masters and are afraid to report the violations to the authorities. *Lolicon* men's indecent behavior is extremely humiliating to the Japanese as a nation, but the Japanese police need international cooperation to help them enforce the country's laws against sex trafficking.

5.6 Prostitution and Human Trafficking

5.6.1 Prostitution Business

In Japan, you can see "soapland" shops deep in the back streets of amusement quarters. As prostitution is banned by the Anti-Prostitution Law and other regulations, these shops are officially there to provide bathing services in a private room, but actually most of the bathing attendants are said to offer prostitution services as well. There were 1310 "soapland" shops nationwide in 2003. Massage shops called "fashion health" stores are also providing sexual services like oral sex; there were around 18,000 "fashion health" enterprises in Japan in 2003. Recently, non–shop type "fashion health" enterprises intended to dispatch masseuses to customers have been growing rapidly.

According to Takashi Kadokura (2002), the chief economist of the Dai-Ichi Life Research Institute, the scale of prostitution business in Japan was estimated at around 1.2 trillion yen (0.2% of the gross domestic product) in 1999. Among them, "soapland" shops represented 57.6% and "fashion health" 23.2% of all prostitution earnings. Enjo-Kosai prostitution amounted to 4.9% of the total, which was more than double the amount earned by foreign prostitutes, who constitute 2.3% of the total.

In Japan today, because of the strong economy and a well-established social welfare system, there are almost no people living below the poverty line. However, there are prostitutes who willingly entered the business just to get more money. In the emerging "fashion health" business, for example, there is a large number of young ladies who just want to afford a better life—buying a new sports car, going abroad for sightseeing, collecting high-grade goods, and so on. There are also many part-time prostitutes who are also housewives or office ladies.

In 2003, the Japanese police cleared 2411 offenses (in which the perpetrators were identified) of the Anti-Prostitution Law and arrested 1244 persons. As many as 85.8% of the offenses are related to *Hotetoru* businesses dispatching a prostitute to a customer's hotel room or his residence. (*Hotetoru* is the business of taking a prostitute to a male customer, who has paid for the services, at his hotel or home. Just like delivering a pizza.) These businesses lure customers with advertisement cards, sexual photos, and a cellular phone number. Anywhere in amusement quarters, you can see telephone booths whose walls are fully covered with sex cards.

Among 235 foreign prostitutes arrested in Japan in 2003, Chinese foreign nationals accounted for 33.2%, followed by Thais (23.8%), Koreans (14.5%), Colombians (12.3%), and Taiwanese (11.1%). *Boryokudan*, commonly referred to as *Yakuza*, are organized crime groups indigenous to Japan[6]; the prostitution business is one of their major sources of income. According to available information, 22.7% of arrested offenders of the Anti-Prostitution Law in 2003 were Yakuza members.

5.6.2 Human Trafficking

Japan is regarded as a destination country for trafficked women, who are mostly used for sexual exploitation. The typical case is as follows: Brokers reel in victims with promises of work in Japan as dancers, maids, or hostesses with good pay, but after their arrival, they are forced to do prostitution or strip dancing to pay off a "loan" of several million yen (several thousand U.S. dollars) charged for their travel expenses. Frequently, they are brought under the control of Boryokudan members.

In 2003, 20 women trafficking cases were cleared in Japan, involving 88 women. Among the 88 victims, Colombians accounted for 51.8%, followed by Thais (25.3%), and Taiwanese (14.5%). The rest were from China, Indonesia, and Cambodia. In investigating trafficking cases, the police sometimes have difficulty in getting witnesses for victimized foreigners.

If the foreign women were desperate to escape, they could go to one of 15,000 police boxes on the street for protection, but they do not. That is because they fear being deported by the Japanese immigration authorities, and they really want to stay in Japan to get money for their families at home. That situation makes it easier for trafficking organizations to exploit them. Still, the women hate the dirty business they are in.

In the Trafficking in Persons Report 2003 by the U.S. Department of State, Japan is categorized in Tier 2, which consists of countries whose governments do not fully comply with the Trafficking Victims Protection Act's minimum standards, but that are making significant efforts to bring themselves into compliance with those standards. There is no advanced nation other than Japan in Tier 2. The report pointed out the problems with the antitrafficking measures used in Japan, such as the low number of prosecuted traffickers and the weak penalties used against offenders. In the existing migration laws in Japan, as mentioned before, victims are treated as illegal migrants and are susceptible to deportation, which is considered one of the major obstacles hindering victims from seeking legal remedies from Japanese authorities.

To ratify the Protocol to Prevent, Suppress and Punish Trafficking Persons, Especially Women and Children, and in response to the disgraceful evaluation in the U.S. report, the Japanese government has already launched various projects to tackle the trafficking issues and is now planning the revision of the migration laws. The National Police Agency has also been instructing local police forces to pay more attention to careful handling of trafficked victims as well as distributing educational pamphlets and videos to police officers on the front line.

5.7   Conclusion

To fight against the crime of abducting and trafficking in women and children is not an easy task. Each country or region must consider its own economic and cultural background when adopting methods to control this type of crime. In China, for example, the prevention of the crime of abducting and trafficking in women and children is believed to be a comprehensive project.

The elimination of a single cause of trafficking cannot get rid of this type of crime completely. Thus, various authorities should be called to work together to fight against this type of crime. However, international cooperation and experience sharing definitely enhance the effectiveness of preventing this kind of activity.

Excessive desire for sex is a global problem, but the problem is exacerbated in Japan by the presence of fabulous wealth in the country. Some men, when they have a lot of money in their pockets, look for young women, and some women easily sell themselves to men with money. The Japanese government and people need to go back to their traditional values and engage in stringent enforcement of its immigration laws.

Notes

1. http://www.worldbank.org/ (April 5, 2004).
2. Telephone clubs have their shops in amusement quarters. Men are invited into a cell with a telephone, at a rate of a few thousand yen per hour, and receive phone calls from women outside. To urge women to make these calls, telephone clubs distribute small gifts with their phone number to women on the street. Many girls making calls to telephone clubs out of curiosity have subsequently become victims of sexual offenses.
3. "Most of on-line dating services are fee-charging websites of cellular phones. Men and women exchange their own profile through the sites and search for a partner who suits their taste. Many victims have suffered in the same way as telephone clubs."
4. The average monthly pocket money of high school students in Japan was 6324 yen (about US$60) in 2003. (http://www.saveinfo.or.jp/kinyu/yoron/per03.html#04, July 16, 2004).
5. Cabinet Office. *White Paper on Youth in Japan* (2003).
6. As of the end of 2002, Boryokudan membership stands at about 85,300, with 43,600 full members and 41,700 associates.

Trafficking in Women and Children in China

6

GU MINKANG

Contents

6.1 Nature and Extent of Trafficking in Women and Children in China

In China, the most serious criminal exploitation is the crime of abducting and trafficking of women and children. In fact, through stringent government enforcement and severe punishment, this kind of crime was almost nonexistent after the People's Republic of China was established in 1949. However, it emerged again in China in the 1970s, and since the 1980s, this offense has become more and more frequent.

Chinese law enforcement records show that many women are abducted and trafficked to jurisdictions outside China, especially to Taiwan, Hong Kong, and Macao. Most of these women are forced to engage in prostitution.[1] There are various reasons for this kind of crime, but it often can be attributed to the unique social factors in China.

6.2   Causes of the Crime

There are ideological factors in China that contribute to the trafficking and exploitation of women and children. China has a social system that makes both domestic and international trafficking in women and children both inevitable and easy to accomplish. The fundamental factors involved are the feudal ideology and the poor economic situation in the remote countryside, such as in villages in Anhui or Jiangsu provinces. It has been reported that most traffickers are from underdeveloped areas such as these, where the people have a deep-rooted feudal ideology. Thus, it is reasonable to say that the crime of abducting and trafficking women and children is connected with feudalism, ignorance, underdevelopment, and poverty. Thus, a boy who is purchased is expected to support the buyer when he gets older (*yang er fang lao*), and a wife is purchased because the buyer is usually in a poor situation, and no woman will willingly marry him. However, a man's getting a wife is mainly aimed at meeting his desire to get subsequent generations (*chuan zhong jie dai*)—to prolong his own genealogy. In China, local cadres are assumed to know the laws and to be model citizens in the enforcement of government policies. In these poor, rural areas, however, the buyers are often cadres of the villages, buying because they want to get either a son or a wife. Some cadres go to buyers' families to drink the happy wine (*xi jiu*). This cooperation between the buyers and the cadres creates a false impression that to buy an abducted woman to be one's wife is approved or recognized by the state. Even the local police will close their eyes to such illegal activities, because buyers are usually their relatives or good friends. In the extreme cases, the local police may hinder rescue efforts by releasing important information to buyers, or simply by paying little attention to the situation. As for local authorities who are in charge of the birth policy,[2] they do not interfere with the birth situation solely because these trafficked wives are from other areas throughout China, and thus their registered permanent residences are not in the local areas and their birth situation does not affect the local birth control policy.[3]

6.3   Economic Background

Another important factor in trafficking in China is that there are markets for selling swindled or abducted women or children. It is known in China that men in poor, remote countryside are sometimes unable to get wives either because women are trying to escape from their poverty by seeking a better life elsewhere or because women from other rich areas do not want to go to those poor areas. In this situation, abducted women become the best source for those men to get their wives, because these trafficked women will be isolated and helpless. It is also known that the Chinese one-child policy may affect those who want to have their own son. Thus, male children are more welcomed than girls.

The buyer's market is active mainly because buyers care only about the price paid—not where those women and children come from. In their estimation, it is reasonable to buy the women or child because they have paid a price—a quid pro quo. Because of their ignorance of the relevant laws and regulations, the buyers believe that they are also victims if their purchased wives or sons are rescued and taken away from them. In one case, the "husband" was arrested for raping his 15-year-old "wife," who was purchased from a criminal. In the detention house, the man insisted that police should return his RMB 7000 to him in spite of his being told that his conduct had violated China's criminal law. In his eyes, the police snatched his wife away.[4] In worse situations, buyers use illegal force against law enforcement personnel. In one case, a policeman was beaten to death by a buyer and his relatives.[5]

6.4   Lenient Punishment to Buyers

The criminal law provides punishment for those who purchase women and children, but it is rare to hear that the buyers have been seriously punished, partly because of an understanding that the buyers are also victims in certain aspects. As the result of this lenient treatment, potential buyers have few or no fears about trafficking in women and children.

6.5   Ignorance of the Law

Poverty and ignorance usually go together. In one case, criminals used written contracts to sell more than 10 women. These contracts contain formal languages. In accordance with Chinese Civil Law Principles and the Contract Law, the gift giver (seller in fact) and gift receiver (buyer in fact) both agree to formulate this contract, and nobody can modify or cancel this contract unless it has been done in accordance with the relevant provisions of these laws. Under this disguised contract, each woman was sold for a price between RMB 150,000 and RMB 180,000 yuan.[6]

6.6   Economic Incentive

The abducting of and trafficking in women and children is very, very profitable in China. In accordance with Karl Marx's theory, the more profit the business generates, the more likely the actor will ignore or break the existing law. This is similar to the idea of criminal economy. In other words, the high profit return will stimulate high desire to commit this kind of crime and a willingness to possibly face severe punishment. It has been reported that the price for selling one child ranges from a few thousand yuan to more than 10,000 yuan. In one case, a baby girl who was less than 1 year old was sold for RMB 1500 yuan ($12,000 US) to be the buyer's "child wife." Though she was rescued by the police, her life was in danger because of the lack of care.[7] In another case, abducting and trafficking in women and children can generate takings equivalent to 1 year's income in some poor areas.[8] In addition, because there is a high demand from the buyers, criminals have a strong motivation to commit this kind of crime again and again.

6.7   The Prosperity of Yellow Industry in China

In China, the phrase "yellow industry" refers to the prostitution business. Prostitution is strictly prohibited in China, but the government does not have sufficient force to eliminate this phenomenon as it did in the 1950s. It has been reported that, to date, there are more than 6 million prostitutes in China.[9] Recently, in Zhuhai, Guangdong Province, there was a sensational prostitution case. On September 16, 2003, a Japanese company held a party in Zhuhai International Convention Hotel to reward the good performance of its employees. That night, more than 300 prostitutes were called to serve the employees. It was reported that on that one night, 185 prostitutes completed their business, and the money paid amounted to more than 300,000 yuan (US$2,400,000). Many Chinese people were shocked by this news. On December 17, 2003, 14 principal criminals were convicted for organizing prostitution. The same day, the International Police at China National Center issued red orders to search for three Japanese criminals.[10] In this case, one fact is very certain: 300 prostitutes could be organized efficiently on short notice. In other words, people can buy sex easily in China despite governmental efforts to crack down on yellow industry. In fact, as a result of the high demand for women and children in China, these individuals are abducted with impunity for the yellow industry.

The crime of abducting, trafficking, kidnapping, and selling 50 young girls took place in Jiangsu Province. This crime shocked many people in the province, and on January 18, 2001, three of the criminals, Zhang Hongdeng, Shi Deping, and Shi Yanli, were given the death penalty, and a few other criminals received severe prison terms. This was the severest penalty given to criminals in China since the establishment of the People's Republic of China.

6.7.1 Elder Sister Entrapped Younger Sister

In this case, there were five principal criminals. Zhang Hongdent and Shi Yanli were husband and wife, and Shi Yanli, Shi Deping, Shi Deyong, and Shi Yanhong were brothers and sisters of the same blood. The Shi family was located in a poor village in the Jiangsu Province. Shi Deping was the eldest son (aged 35 years), and Shi Yanli was the second child (aged 31 years). Shi Yongde was the third child (aged 29 years), and Shi Yanhong was the youngest (aged 25 years). Among those four brothers and sisters, only Shi Deping had a high school education; the other three had only primary school educations. In the view of their neighbors, these siblings were fond of food but averse to work. They had never taken any serious jobs.

In 1994, the Chinese Spring Festival had just ended when several creditors asked Shi Yanli to repay her debts. Shi Yanli discussed this matter with her husband, Zhang Hongdeng, who mentioned that his aunt, Zhang Meiling, was engaging in the prostitution business in Hainan Province and earned a remarkable amount of money that way. Shi Yanli thought that this might be the best way to make quick money. She asked her husband to take care of their child and went to the Hainan Island.

After 1 year as a working girl, Shi Yanli had earned a lot of money through her prostitution business. On the second day of the Chinese New Year in 1995, Shi Yanli went back to her village to see her mother. Her mother was impressed by her daughter's expensive attire and asked Shi Yanli to take the youngest daughter, Shi Yanhong, with her to make more money.

Shi Yanli took Shi Yanhong to the Hainan Island. On the first day of her arrival, it was arranged for Shi Yanhong to work as a prostitute. After performing her "work," Shi Yanhong cried and showed Shi Yanli her underwear, which contained blood. Shi Yanhong told Shi Yanli that she was going to report this rape case to the local police. Shi Yanli, however, was not surprised by the blood and tried her best to convince Shi Yanhong that prostitution was the only way to make more money. After Shi Yanhong's "education," she started to believe that nothing could be lost again, since she was no longer a virgin.

Based on this understanding, Shi Yanhong engaged in prostitution actively. She requested RMB 5000 yuan (US$40,000) from her second client for his "sleeping with a virgin." She then pretended to be a virgin again and asked for RMB 5000 yuan from her third client for the same privilege.

Shi Yanhong saw that a virgin could easily make a lot of money—more than an experienced prostitute—and proposed that Shi Yanli get more young girls from their hometown. Shi Yanli thought this was a great idea and instructed her husband, Zhang Hongdeng, and her brothers, Shi Deping and Shi Deyong, to recruit young girls. Thus, a plan was made and implemented.

6.7.2   Kidnapping Young Girls for Prostitution

The gang of five decided that their targets would be young girls who were aged from 14 to 18 years old. The girls were from poor families, were unable to continue school, and had no idea of what the outside world was like. Zhang Hongdeng had rich experience in dealing with people and knew some Chinese Gongfu. He took on the role as agent of a company and recruited young girls on behalf of nonexistent factories. All the families of those young girls were promised that they would earn good salaries. To cheat the parents, Shi Yanli forced those girls to phone home within a fixed time period and to tell their parents everything was fine. Furthermore, Shi Yanli sent 400–500 yuan ($3200–4000) to each girl's parents per month as the victim's salary. One parent was grateful for the daughter's good treatment and introduced another 11 young girls to Zhang Hongdeng. To build the recruits' zeal, Zhang Hongdeng pretended to interview those girls and accepted only eight girls for the nonexistent factory jobs. The other three, "unqualified," girls were sad and managed to go "back door" (that is, the girls tried to bribe Zhang to hire them for the company), but Zhang Hongdeng refused. This story spread and became an advertisement for Zhang Hondeng's business.

From 1997 to 1999, this criminal organization swindled and abducted 50 young girls, moving them to Hainan Island. Once they arrived, hoping to work in a factory, they were forced to be prostitutes. Among those 50 young girls, two were below 14 years old, nine were just 14 years old, 27 were between 15 and 18 years old, and 12 were above 18 years old. Shi and other criminals used force to take those girls' naked pictures and threatened to distributing them if the girls did not work. To control the young girls, Shi Yanli and Shi Yanhong asked their brothers, Shi Deping and Shi Deyong, to go to the Hainan Island. The job of the two brothers was to organize the young girls, especially when working at the haircut shops opened by the Shi sisters. Because Shi's haircut shops had an adequate supply of girls, and those girls were "fresh," Shi's haircut shops became very famous on Hainan Island, and many clients came to request sex service. Within 2 years, a profit of about RMB 500,000 yuan (US$4,000,000) was made by the criminals.

6.7.3   Miserable Life of the Young Girls

The criminals were enjoying their life, spending money made by the girls on the good things in life. The young girls were in utter misery. Two girls took an opportunity to use the bathroom and escaped with RMB 50 yuan. When they arrived at Haikou, the biggest city on Hainan Island, they had only RMB 10 yuan left. They needed money to buy tickets and decided to sell their blood. Unfortunately, they were not allowed to do so because they did not have their identification cards. They had to call Shi Deyong, whom they naively thought might help them to go back home, because they were all from the same hometown. As the result, the two girls were caught by the criminals and taken back to the haircut shop. Shi Yanli ordered them to write to their parents to tell them that they had been found, and then 10 men who had consumed sexual medications tortured them under the guise of "reeducation." The whole process was videotaped for the purpose of "educating" or threatening the other girls. These two girls were severely injured by the abuse and could not move for several days.

On Hainan Island, many gamblers and businessmen believed that to have sex with a virgin and to see the blood from the hymen after sex would bring them good luck. Thus, virgins were in high demand, but high prices had to be paid. To make more money, the Shi sisters forced the young girls under their control to pretend to be virgins; that is, during sex, those girls had to damage their sex organs so that the clients could see blood and believe that the girls were virgins. As reported, each girl had to pretend to be a virgin three times and would thus generate an additional RMB 8000 for the Shi sisters.

Furthermore, more than 10 of the girls were forced to have sex with Zhang Hongdeng, Shi Deping, and Shi Deyong. Among them, Zuo Ruolan, Dai Chunyan, and Liu Li were convinced and eventually turned from victims into accomplices.

6.7.4   Justice at Last

On August 31, 1999, the police received a report that several girls were betrayed and abducted to Hainan Island, where they were forced to be prostitutes. The police started an investigation and successfully arrested Zhang Hongdeng, Shi Deping, Shi Yanli, Shi Deyong, Shi Yanhong, Dai Chunyan, and Zuo Ruolan. All of the young girls were rescued and sent back to their hometowns. On January 18, 2001, the judgment was announced publicly as follows: Zhang Hongdeng, Shi Deping, and Shi Yanli were given the death penalty and executed immediately. Their political rights were deprived, and they forfeited their personal properties. All other criminals were given severe punishments, including prison terms.

6.7.5   Lower Educational Background

Most of the victims were not highly educated. As a result, they were easily deceived and persuaded to go with strangers. Because of their lower educational backgrounds, it was difficult for them to find an ideal job, and once they see a chance to work for an attractive salary, they follow the traffickers without any hesitation.

6.8   Government Control of Trafficking in Women and Children

The Central Committee of the Chinese Communist Party and the National Government have paid serious attention to the abduction of women and children. In 1987, both offices of the Central Committee of the Chinese Communist Party and the State Council offered a warning against the crime of kidnapping and selling of women and children. Furthermore, in 1991, the National People's Congress adopted the Decision on Severe Punishment for Criminals Committing the Crime of Kidnapping and Selling Women and Children. In 1997, the Amendment of the Criminal Law was adopted by the Eighth National People's Congress at its Fifth Conference. This kind of crime was made subject to severe punishment under the Criminal Law:

Article 240 specified that[11] those abducting and trafficking women and children are to be sentenced to from 5 to 10 years in prison and fined. Those committing especially serious crimes are to be sentenced to death in addition to having their property confiscated. Those falling into one or more of the following groups are to be sentenced to 10 years or more in prison or given life sentences, in addition to being fined and having their property confiscated:

1. Primary elements of rings engaging in abducting and trafficking women or children;
2. Abducting and trafficking more than three women or children;
3. Raping abducted women;
4. Seducing, tricking, or forcing abducted women into prostitution, or those selling abducted women to others who in turn force them into prostitution;
5. Kidnapping women or children using force, coercion, or narcotics, for the purpose of selling them;
6. Stealing or robbing infants or babies for the purpose of selling them;
7. Causing abducted women or children, or their family members, serious injuries or death, or causing other grave consequences; and
8. Selling abducted women or children outside the country.

"Abducting and trafficking women or children" refers to abducting, kidnapping, buying, selling, transporting, or transshipping women or children.

Article 241 states that those buying women or children are to be sentenced to 3 years or less in prison or put under criminal detention or surveillance. Those individuals buying abducted women and forcing them to have sex with them are to be punished according to stipulations of article 236. Those buying abducted women or children and illegally depriving them of or restricting their physical freedom, or injuring or insulting them, are to be punished according to relevant stipulations of this statute.

Article 242 provides that those using force or coercion to obstruct workers from state organs from rescuing sold women or children are to be punished according to article 277 of this law.

Ringleaders who lead other people to obstruct the workers from state organizations from rescuing bought women or children are to be sentenced to 5 years or less in prison or put under criminal detention. Other individuals who use force or coercion are to be punished according to paragraph one of this article.

In addition to these laws and regulations, several national campaigns have been organized to fight against this type of crime, and many criminals have been subject to severe punishment, including the death penalty. [12]

Severe punishments can deter individuals from pursuing the crime of abducting and trafficking women and children once, but they may not eliminate the crime altogether. It has been suggested that the way to stop the criminals is to crack down on the buyers' markets. If the buyers' markets have been successfully closed, it could effectively stop the growth tendency to transport women and children. In addition, there is a need to change the poor life and feudal ideology of the citizens in the countries of origin, because this sort of societal change will effectively eliminate the phenomenon of swindling and selling women and children.

In addition, fighting this kind of crime is not a task just for the police departments. Rather, these crimes are a social problem and need the entire society to cooperate with the police to solve the problem. The best approach is a comprehensive one involving the police, civil departments, and so on. For example, after women are rescued, it is important to help them regain their self-respect, to cure their weakened spirit, and most important, to resolve their living problems. Otherwise, they might be swindled and sold again. Furthermore, to fight against this type of crime, our efforts must be constant, for if they are not, criminals will engage in this type of crime again.

One of the recommended methods of reducing these types of crime is to make good use of the networks. Thanks to the high development of the computer networks, it is now possible to share information among many law enforcement authorities. In addition, it is now possible to share information internationally, so that the abduction and trafficking of women across the borders could be effectively controlled.

It is also advised that a wide range of propaganda programs should be conducted to teach potential victims to be aware of the crime of abduction and trafficking of women and children. The following tips for potential victims could effectively prevent this type of crime: do not look for a job blindly, do not trust strangers easily, and do not eat or drink foods offered by strangers.[13]

6.9   Conclusion

The population of China is very large, and so is its land mass. As a result, controlling the movement of the people becomes cumbersome. The Chinese policy of one child per family and the Chinese cultural preference for male children have created a scarcity of women. As a consequence, basic economic principles take their course: When demand is more than supply, price rises. That means that the fewer women who live in a country, the more the cost of getting a wife goes up, as does the price of getting sex partners.

To the many men chasing very few women, China has created a very good market for organized crime. Despite the fact that many efforts have been made by various local governments to crack down on prostitution, the phenomenon is still seen everywhere in China. The reasons noted earlier helped contribute to this kind of problem. In addition, the actions against prostitution that are being taken are unevenly applied throughout the regions of China, and prostitutes move from one place to another, making prostitution very hard to control. Finally, prostitutes are controlled by criminal organizations, and there are many illegal organizations, brokers, and hotels that share in the profit of making young girls available for sex or forced marriage.

Notes

1. On August 26, 2003, 26 women were being smuggled by boat to Taiwan. Before the boat arrived in Taiwan, the Taiwanese Security Police stopped the ship to check it. To cover the illegal activity, the captain of the boat ordered that all the women be thrown overboard into the sea. As a result, six of the women died and one was seriously injured. http://www.big5.hauxia.com/ca/mtcz/00116887.html (February 14, 2004).
2. One-child policy is enforced throughout China.
3. http://www.gazx.gov.en/text_view.asp?newsID=807 (February 1, 2004).
4. http://www.law.westen.com/ztbd/daguai/31.htm (February 13, 2004).
5. http://www.bjyouth.com.cn/Bq6/20000527/GB/4261%5ED0527B0214.htm (February 13, 2004).
6. http://www.dailynews.sina.com.cn/society/2000-09-01/122773.htm (February 1, 2004).
7. http://www.legaldaily.com.en/gb/content/2002-08/09content_41296.htm (February 1, 2004).
8. http://www.gazx.gov.cn/text_view.asp?newsID=807 (February 1, 2004).
9. http://www.news.bbc.co.uk/li/chinese/talking_point/newsid_30830801.stm (February 1, 2004).
10. http://www.en.news.yahoo.com/031217/55/1xr3g.html (February 14, 2004).
11. The English version can be seen at http://www.gis.net/Chinalaw/lawtranl.htm (February 13, 2004).

12. In Yunnan Province, for example, the police at various levels cooperated with each other and adopted the methods of cracking down, prevention, and rescue concurrently. As the result of this method, many cases have been uncovered. From 1995 to May 2000, Yunnan Province uncovered 3230 cases of abducting and trafficking women and children, 7752 criminals were arrested and 923 criminal organizations were destroyed, and about 6543 women and children had been rescued successfully. All criminals involved in this type of crime were given death penalty, life imprisonment, and fixed-term imprisonment. See http://www.legaldaily.com.cn/gb/content/2000-10/12/content_6518.htm (February 14, 2004).

13. It should be noted that in some cases, the victims refuse to be rescued, because they have given birth to some babies, and as they are from poor areas, they worry that their lives will be miserable if they go back to their hometowns. They prefer to take the status quo and live with the "husbands" who purchased them. Another reason is that in some cases, people blame the victims and look down on them when they go back to their hometowns.

Child Labor and the Trafficking Industry in India

7

CHANDRIKA M. KELSO

Contents

7.1   Introduction

India, with an estimated 155 million child workers aged 5–14 years, has the third largest labor force of child workers. It has a higher proportion of girls than boys engaged in labor, with the girls working under far worse conditions than those faced by boys. Many of the working children in India are engaged in hazardous occupations (Fatima, 2003). The cottonseed fields in India that are owned, operated, or subsidized by international and multinational companies employ an estimated hundreds of thousands of children in the 6–14-year age group. These children account for 88% of the total labor force, 78% of whom are girls (Businessline, 2004).

Children in underdeveloped countries are put to work at a very young age, which impedes their physical, psychological, and intellectual development. Many parents in Western countries encourage their children to do chores in and around the house or at outside agencies and stores and then pay them for the services. This is done to improve the children's individual and independent values and development, but such is not the case in poor countries. In underdeveloped countries, children are used as primary and secondary sources of family income. Some adults simply exploit the children in pursuit of financial gains. These children are paid as children but treated as adults, work long hours, and engage in physical labor. They are denied educational and growth opportunities, and without education or vocational training, they are unable to compete in the work force as adults, and are thus confined to being victims and to endless life of poverty. On average, these children work 12 hours a day, earning 18 rupees a day (38 cents) (Thapa et al., 1996; Mathews et al., 2003).

Children are employed in various sectors such as making hand-knotted wool carpets, explosive fireworks, footwear, hand-blown glass bangles, hand-made locks, hand-dipped matches, hand-broken quarried stones, hand-spun silk thread, hand-loomed silk cloth, hand-made bricks and bindis (hand-rolled cigarettes), brasswares, seed production, chemicals, pesticides, garments, pharmaceuticals, housewares, glass, and limestone and working in the electrical and steel industries. They are also employed as bonded laborers, domestic servants, agricultural and horticultural laborers, rag pickers, trash and garbage collectors, lunch delivery and errand boys, paper deliverers, vegetable and flower vendors, restaurant service employees, house cleaners, petrol station service employees, and workers in cottage industries. A number of children also work out of their homes making clothes, food products, incense sticks, and tobacco products; designing/printing; cutting gems; and packaging goods for export.

7.2   Nature and Extent of the Problem

The first generation of child employment is attributed to the Factory Act of 1881, followed by the Child Labor Act of 1933, which prohibited the employment of children under the age of 14 years. The 1986 enactment of the Child Labor Act regulated the employment of children in certain types of fields and areas that are hazardous in nature. The ultimate overhaul was seen following the enactment and implementation of the Juvenile Justice Act (1986 and 1987), which created extensive measures to curtail, prevent, and prohibit the trafficking, abuse, and exploitation of India's children (Ahuja, 2001). However, the deplorable state of child labor continues unabated all over India. Despite international and Indian laws prohibiting the trafficking and exploitation of children, some of these child laborers are still being sold into debt-bondage at home and in far distant countries in Southeast Asia and the Middle East, working excruciatingly long hours to pay off their parental or ancestral debts (Venkateswarlu et al., 2003).

The Indian agricultural sector, including plantations, commercial farms, and subsistence farms, employs 80% of the country's child workers and accounts for 70% of working children globally. These children are exposed to hazardous work and living conditions without protective gear or basic amenities such as fresh water, education, proper nutrition, and recreation. The problem of child labor is further exacerbated by the spread of diseases such as HIV/AIDS, which increases discrimination against these children and reduces their opportunities or access to alternative careers. In addition, some female child laborers are sexually molested by their masters or supervisors. The rural parts of the country do not recognize mother-to-child risk of disease transmission, with the affluent classes thinking that HIV is a poor man's disease and the poor classes suffering from high rates of infection resulting from a lack of awareness. The children of infected parents pay heavily for this convoluted understanding of the disease. These children are ostracized and forced into isolation by Indian society. Some seek employment in hazardous factories just for survival, and some seek solace in homes that cater for infected persons, where they are shackled to their cots, confined to small spaces, and denied medicine and food if they protest.

The selling of children and women into bonded labor, domestic servitude (as happens to an estimated 15 million children in India), brothels, and the commercial sex industry is rampant in India (Chakrabarthi, 2002; Dutt, 2003; Majumdar, 2003; Mathews et al., 2003; Venkateswarlu et al., 2003). Because of the presence of broken glass, dangling electrical wires, and lack of protective equipment and ventilation, combined with the intense heat of the furnaces, the International Labor Rights Education and Research Fund described the glass factories in India as resembling Dante's Inferno. Child labor is a profitable venture in India. India's exports to the United States alone in 1993 were worth the following: carpets totaled $170 million; there were $1 billion worth of gem stones; more than $2 million worth of glass and glassware products; and more than $107 million worth of footwear. In 1995, silk exports from India to the United States alone totaled $260 million, and they were worth another $300 million in 1996 (FOIL, 1996; Tucker & Ganesan, 1997). Most of these exports are products of child labor.

7.3 Poverty, Education and Gender Issues in Child Labor

Lower levels of educational attainment are tied to a higher incidence of poverty, and poverty in turn leads to denial or prevention of educational opportunities. In India, 28.6% of the population lived below the national poverty line in 2000. Child labor, poverty, and adult unemployment are strongly connected. When a family's income from non-child-labor sources decreases significantly, children are forced by their parents to enter the labor market. Adult unemployment in many developing countries is also influenced by child labor, as employers can pay children lower wages than adults (Ray, 2000).

One of the strong indicators of development is adult literacy rate. The literacy rate in India is 76% for males and 54% for females. The long-term benefits of investing in the education of children in the 6–14-year age group, especially that of girls, are already known to society. Approximately, half of India's 220 million children, aged 6–14 years, are out of school, and 60% of them are girls. Indian illiteracy rates for women and children are higher than those of men and boys (Joshi and Smith, 2002; Fatima, 2003). Women's high illiteracy rates further add to the problems of child labor and poverty: Lack of education predicts a future life of poverty. Indian children are also environmental victims and suffer from malnutrition, resulting in diarrhea and respiratory infections (Ramaswamy, 2002).

There are gender-based differences in the labor market. Multinational and national companies that own and operate the hybrid cottonseed farms contribute to the gender-based child worker discrimination, where female workers are employed for emasculation and pollination work on long-term contracts based on advances and loans to their parents by the local seed producers. Although girls as young as 7 years old are employed by the seed and agriculture-based companies, the most preferable children are those in the age bracket of 9–13 years; those above 13 years of age are generally not even considered by the companies. These girls are paid less than the boys, work longer hours, and are often more compliant than boys. Because these companies prefer girl (female) employees, citing reasons such as better physical dexterity, the males and boys in the respective households withdraw from the family and financial responsibilities, leaving them to the female children. The same preferences are seen in the match and fireworks industries, where the girl-to-boy ratio is 3:1 (Businessline, 2004).

Debt servitude and bonded labor, though illegal since 1933, are still flourishing in India. At the same time, India provides a large market for bonded labor in the Middle East, North Africa, Australia, and Southeast Asia. Families, unable to pay their debts, submit a child as bonded labor to the employer. As a result, the child works for the employer for free, and the family, having lost an earning worker, borrows more to sustain itself, adding more years of bonded labor service to the child. The penalties, if the employer is caught, are minor, so the practice continues. In addition, these bonded children are mistreated. They are abused physically, sexually, and emotionally and are expected to be on call all day. They rarely receive any breaks from their hard work.

7.4   International Exploitation

Multinational and national companies have children employed in their workforce: Novartis, Advanta (3000 child workers), Emergent Genetics, Bayer offshoot Proagro (2000 child workers), Syngenta (6500 child workers), Mahyco-Monsanto (17,000 child workers), and Unilever subsidiary

Hindustan Lever Limited (25,000 child workers). They produce and market hybrid cottonseed, exacerbating the child labor problems in India. These companies are aware of their employment of child laborers, who earn wages ranging from 18 to 20 rupees per day and are exposed to poisonous pesticides like Endosulphan during their work, yet claim that they are unaware of the related health problems of these child workers. They thus fail to address the children's health problems (Venkateswarlu et al., 2003). The working children in fireworks and match factories earn an average of 20–30 rupees per working day, which begins at 7 a.m. and ends at 6:30 p.m. These children are housed in small and cramped places, work in unsafe conditions, and are subjected to severe punishments if they do not adhere to the rules and procedures established by the contractor or the employer.

For each acre of cotton crop meant for hybrid seed production, about 10 children are employed in cultivation. In 2000–2001, five transnational companies accounted for nearly 21.6% (5350 of 24,783 acres) of the total area under hybrid cottonseed production in the state of Andhra Pradesh. The children's parents are paid an advance loan amount of about 1500 rupees per child, who are made to work an average of 13 hours a day from 5 a.m. until 7 p.m. and make 30% less wages than an adult female and 55% less than the adult wage market rate. In addition, after the children are done with field work for the day, some are also expected to do chores around the employer's house (Businessline, 2004).

7.5   Health and Behavioral Implications

The total expenditure on health as a percentage of gross domestic product in India totaled 4.9% in 2000. India's poor do not have easy access to health care subsidies, and India is among the top five worst countries in terms of what they offer as poor health subsidies in the public sector. Each year, thousands of new formulations are seen in the pesticide and fertilizer sectors, with over a million synthetic chemicals being used in these products, leading to illnesses in children such as acute respiratory infections, chronic obstructive lung diseases such as asthma and chronic bronchitis, lung cancer, and adverse pregnancy outcomes (Bahuguna, 2003; Businessline, 2004). The United States–based companies such as Monsanto, which produces genetically engineered products and is prohibited from selling their products in the United States and Europe, have created themselves a profitable niche in countries such as India, Nigeria, Kenya, and other Third World countries. The genetically engineered soybeans they sell contain antibiotic-resistant genes, adding to the complications of treating related illnesses (Shiva, 2002).

India has an agrarian economy, with the majority of the Indian population and 26% of its gross domestic product reliant on agriculture. With the introduction of new methods to increase food grain production in India, and the fact that these varieties are more labor-demanding, the intensive use of these new methods increases the need for inputs such as irrigation, pesticides, and fertilizers. These substances contribute heavily to the contamination and pollution of the environment and also have a negative effect on the health of the agricultural workers (Shetty, 2002; Krishna et al., 2003). The World Health Organization classifies pesticides into class I (a, extremely, and b, highly hazardous) and class II (moderately hazardous). However, the farmers in India do not pay heed to any of the instructions on the pesticide containers and continue to mix dosages that are dangerous, use pesticides without any protective gear, and not follow the recommended intervals and schedules for spraying. Children who work in the fields are forced to handle these pesticides without any precautions, and thus contract the associated illnesses and diseases. The class I and II pesticides are known to cause reactions ranging from weakness, fatigue, headache, nausea, to serious problems such as diarrhea, vomiting, nasal discharge, eye problem, itching, burning, and so on (Shetty, 2002).

About 30% of the pesticides that are sold in developing countries fall short of the internationally accepted standards. They are also known to pose serious threats to the environment and human health. However since the market value of this pesticides use is around $900 million, most corporations are reluctant to lose the profit. "The notorious 'dirty dozen' of pesticides—Aldicard (Temik), Camphechlor (Toxaphene), Chlordane, Heptachlor, Chlordimeform, DBCP, DDT, Aldrin, Dieldrin, Endrin, EDB, HCH/BHC, Lindane, Paraquat, Parathion, Methyl Parathion and Pentachlorophenol—have been widely used in India, despite warnings by environmental and health groups. The size of the Indian pesticide market is about Rs 4,000 crore per year and no player would ever risk forgoing this hugely attractive market" (Businessline, 2004).

Cancer, nerve damage, birth defects, headaches, respiratory ailments, convulsions, fainting spells, skin and eye irritations, dizziness, and pesticide poisoning are some of the health problems exhibited by the children employed in the seed and agricultural industries. These issues are attributed to both direct and indirect exposure to pesticides and chemicals. The children involved are not provided with any information on how to protect themselves and do not have access to clean supplies, further increasing their risk of health problems (Mathews et al., 2003; Businessline, 2004).

Pesticide residues are seen in 20% (tolerance level is 2%) of Indian food products—only 49% of Indian food products are residue free. Most of the rural Indian mothers already suffer from anemia and malnutrition, and the growth of children and fetuses is also impaired by exposure to chemicals, pesticides, and environmental contaminants. Forty-five percent of all child mortality in India is attributed to environmental causes, and 55% is to prenatal causes. Pediatric cancers, neurological impairments, mental retardation, low birth weight, chronic anemia, and stillbirths are also evident.

The lack of awareness of the farmers involved also adds to the prevalence of diseases associated with pesticide and chemical usage. For instance, the farmers employ unusual agronomic practices and an uncommon combination of pesticides to overcome the problem of insect pests, with defective spraying equipment leading to an inadvertently increased dosage of the pesticides. The farmers also exceed the recommended number of pesticide sprays, spraying 15–20 time per season instead of the required eight (Shetty, 2002).

In the silk industry, the child workers are frequently scalded, burned, or blistered from having to dip silk threads into boiling water, they cut their hands and fingers on the threads, they are exposed to the risk of infection from handling the dead silk worms, and they also breathe in machine-generated toxic fumes and smoke that cause lung and other infectious diseases. The silk industry has a two-phase production processes: the first involves silk reeling and twisting, followed by weaving and working on handlooms. Children are employed in both sectors almost 100% of the time. The state of Karnataka, which has received large sums of money from the World Bank to support its sericulture, has approximately 100,000 bonded children in the silk industry (Tucker and Ganesan, 1997; Suri, 2003).

The boys who work as reelers palpate the cocoons, kept in scalding water, to check whether the silk threads are unwound. The use of spoons or other instruments is prohibited because of the belief that only touch can determine whether the threads are ready to reel. The silk looms are kept in poorly ventilated rooms, and children weave the silk under these conditions. They work an average of 10 hours a day, and some at night and suffer from various skin diseases and infections, such as tuberculosis, eye infections, asthma, bronchitis, backaches, and physical injuries. Interestingly, digestive disorders and tuberculosis are considered to be occupational diseases of the weaving community, and as such, first aid or medical attention offered by the employer is a rare occurrence, and those who fall sick lose their wages when they do not work (Tucker and Ganesan, 1997; Suri, 2003).

Children in the diamond industry suffer from malaria, discoloration of their hair, rotten teeth, dysentery, eyestrain, headaches, and leg and shoulder pain. The children who work in the glassware factories suffer from tuberculosis, mental retardation, asthma, bronchitis, liver ailments, chronic anemia, severe burns (which are not treated), and even fundamental damage to their genetic matter (FOIL, 1996).

Those who are employed in the match and fireworks industries are exposed to hazardous substances such as phosphorous, paint thinners, and sulphur and perform tasks ranging from dyeing, printing, spinning, weaving, varnishing, laminating, scoring, welding work, and quarrying units to making cracker fuses and paper pipes (Krishnakumar, 2000). Lead poisoning from multiple sources, such as the ingestion and consumption of medications and food products, and exposure to automobile fuel, food can soldering, lead-based paints and pigments, leaded cooking utensils, and drinking water systems are other problems faced by child workers in India. The flour mills, mining and smelting, the textile industries, battery repair and recycling, and the cosmetics and cottage industries have child workers who work with lead-based products, resulting in experiencing lead poisoning and long-term health effects. Lead poisoning can lead to permanent brain damage, particularly among young children (Blood Weekly, 1999; Falk, 2003).

The emotional and psychological toll on these children is equally distressing. They are separated from their families, and the normal process of childhood development is truncated. They work such long hours that they have no time for any other recreational activities such as are enjoyed by their counterparts in other sections of the world. They suffer from depression and other forms of mental distress. In addition, those employed in the sand plants and glass industry are exposed to silica. They suffer from silicosis, though the symptoms of chronic chest pain, coughing, breathlessness are often misdiagnosed as tuberculosis, resulting in unnecessary medical expenses that they cannot afford (Johnson, 2003). All these practices contribute significantly to the socioeconomic, health, and environmental profile of the country.

7.6   Occupational Safety and Health Law

The founding member of the International Labor Organization was the nation of India, but it has ratified only a few occupational safety and health laws. The year 1983 saw the inclusion of the Occupational Safety and Health Law (OHS) in National Health Policy, intended to address and strengthen public health and elements of disease prevention, health promotion, and rehabilitation. The Factories Act of 1948, the main legal instrument of OHS in India, has oversight over the health and safety in factories having power (i.e., electrical energy or any other form of energy that is mechanically transmitted and is not generated by humans or animals) and 10 or more workers. This act is enforced by the state governments through the inspectorate, assisted by other inspectors; physicians and surgeons are also appointed to certify the adolescent workers. Because of the severe manpower and funding deficits, the enforcements are not always a priority, and in some cases they are rarely considered (Sloan, 1983; Joshi and Smith, 2002).

The nonunionized and unorganized working sector in India, though it represents the bulk of the country's workforce (90.6%), suffers from lack of health and safety regulations because OHS is not seen as a priority. Examples are seen in the agricultural sector, with home-based workers and cottage industries, and in the chemical and pharmaceutical industries, where regulation, supervision, and enforcement of the law is difficult (Joshi and Smith, 2002).

7.7   Policy Implications

Though the 1986 Child Labor (Prohibition and Regulation) Act forbids child labor, this act does not have jurisdiction over the employment practices of the cottage industries. Therefore, these employers often circumvent the law and continue to exploit children all over India. Horrifying examples are seen in the fireworks and match industries in the state of Tamil Nadu alone, where an average of 33,000 children in the 6–14-year age bracket are employed.

The Explosives Act and the Arms Act were aimed at prosecuting fireworks manufacturers who employ children. However, in 1998, 26 of the 55 cases that went to trial were acquitted, and 34 of 125 cases that went to trial in 1999 were also acquitted simply on minor legal loopholes. Another 49 cases in 1988–1990 were quashed because the presiding judge decided that the Deputy Chief Inspector of factories was not a competent authority to certify a worker's age, as legally, anyone over the age of 14 years can be employed and would require a medical certificate as proof of age, with no additional requirement being needed to send questionable cases to the medical board for review. The manufacturers have carefully crafted methods to avoid prosecution under this law by subcontracting their work to contractors who hire children for paper pipe making and for fixing fuses on crackers and fireworks. Children are also used to roll, cut, and dye the paper pipes; fill them; and make fuses with poisonous chemicals including sulphur. The parents of these children are afraid of losing their only source of income and are reluctant to come forward and register complaints (Krishnakumar, 2000).

Between 1980 and 1995, the World Bank provided approximately $380 million to various silk industries in India to support and modernize the sericulture, production, and quality of the silk products. The rationale was that this step would create employment opportunities and help with the eradication of poverty, but this was not the result. The money from the World Bank actually indirectly supported the child labor and exploitation of children in the silk industries (Tucker and Ganesan, 1997).

The main determinants of national policy should be focused on the creation of a project-based plan, legal actions for general welfare, and development programs for the child workers and their families (Ahuja, 2001). Policies that address the two-pronged combined intervention models—using increased income and increased literacy—would be more effective in reducing child labor for both genders. The Indian government's Poverty Alleviation Project reserves 40% of its budget for women's projects. The Universal Elementary Education programs from the 1986 National Policy on Education have abolished tuition fees in the government-run school system, thereby making education accessible and affordable to all. Furthermore, families who remove their children from hazardous work environments and enroll them in school receive about 20,000 rupees as remuneration for the child's lost wages. The children are then taught on a fast track, where they complete the usual 5-year elementary school curriculum in 3 years (Thapa et al., 1996; Krishnakumar, 2000; Businessline, 2004; Dutt, 2003).

The World Bank's International Development Association has also loaned $2 billion to India for the establishment of 10,700 primary schools and 62,000 non–formal education projects countrywide, but the bank has been criticized by the National Alliance for the Fundamental Right to Education regarding the disbursement of the funds. On the alliance's agenda is equity in education and curriculum in all schools because of the current preferences among the Indians, where the affluent Indian families send their children to private schools with better facilities, qualified teachers, and a rigorous curriculum. The government schools suffer on all levels, with poorly run schools, lack of rigor and quality, and less-qualified teachers (Fatima, 2003).

7.8   Conclusion

"Children who receive adequate care, and creative opportunities for growth and development during early childhood are more likely to benefit from later education and other social services than those who did not. They are likely to be more productive and healthy citizens. Early years of age (0-8) are critical in the formation of intelligence, personality and social behavior."

Globalization's effect on India has been directly related to poverty, with destitution claiming children and women as a vast majority of its victims. Indian women and children are transported all over the world for prostitution and for paid or unpaid labor. Although the discovery and usage of new chemicals have aided the acceleration and acquisition of modern development, many of these new chemicals have neurotoxic effects, jeopardizing the workers' development of intelligence, language skills, attention span, and behavioral and social adjustments, along with increasing their risk of coma, respiratory paralysis, and death. India has been described as being trapped in environmental and human upheaval (Bahuguna, 2003). The backbone of the carpet industry is child labor that is condoned by the Indian government, with assistance from the International Monetary Fund. The footwear, seed, diamond, glassware, and other industries' needs, demands, and profits are also built on the toils of young children (FOIL, 1996). Laws, rules, and regulations exist on paper, but they do not seem to be implemented or enforced to the same degree of severity as seen in Western nations.

The amount of money that is raked in by the various industries that use and exploit children contradicts the traditional notion that poverty is at the root cause of major societal problems. To attribute the evils of society to poverty alone does not serve any useful purpose. Poverty should be seen not as a primary cause but as one of the many contributory factors to society's problems. The deplorable lack of health care services and medications and the financial weakness of the nation have increased health problems in India. Typically, the infrastructure in India and the cost of living are relatively affordable. However, the corruption that is embedded in the government circles eviscerates and excoriates any progress made by the country.

External funding received is not used wisely, and the majority of it sadly lines the deep pockets of the politicians. To address the problem of HIV alone, there are approximately 1800 nongovernmental organizations that receive funds. However, as many as 80% of these nongovernmental organizations are fraudulent enterprises, backed by the politicians and government employees. The Gates Foundation provided Rs480 crore for AIDS research in 2002, but how much of that money really reached the infected and affected children or adults remains to be seen. In addition, we need a thorough examination of our own religious and cultural beliefs that allow us to both indirectly and directly support trafficking in women and children by consuming products that may illuminate the human self and the house but in essence reek of blood. Perhaps an infusion and expression of collective consciousness among the Indians in control may be the most effective tools for the eradication and abrogation of child labor and exploitation.

References

R. Ahuja, *Social Problems in India*, Rawat, New Delhi, 2001.

N.J. Bahuguna, Toxic war on children. New Delhi: Women's feature service, retrieved March 11, 2003, from http://gateway.proquest.com/openurl?ver=z39.88_.

Blood Weekly, Environment: Lead poisoning threatens kids in India, retrieved March 2, 2004, from http://proquest.umi.com/pqdweb?index=75&did=0000 00234331271&SrchMode=1&sid=10&Fmt=3&VInst=PROD&VType=PQD&R QT=309&VName=PQD&TS=1079305641&clientId=29440.

Businessline, Rich reap more than poor from healthcare sops, retrieved March 12, 2004, from http://proquest.umi.com/pqdweb?index=0&did=00000052325270 1&SrchMode=1&sid=2&Fmt=3&VInst=PROD&VType=PQD&RQT=309&V Name=PQD&TS=1079298761&clientId=29440.

S. Chakrabarthi, The AIDS mess: Unaided victims, *India Today* 2002, 27(49). New Delhi, India.

E. Dutt, State Department reports faults India on human trafficking, *News India Times,* 2003, 34(25).

H. Falk, International environmental health for the pediatrician: Case study of lead poisoning, *Pediatrics*, 2003, 112(1).

A. Fatima, Development-India: Hub works on education for its children, Global Information Network, retrieved March 12, 2004, from http://gateway.proquest.com/openurl?url_ver=Z39.88-2004&res_dat=xri:pqd&rft_val_fmt=info:ofi/fmt:kev:mtx:journal&genre=article&rft_dat=xri:pqd:did=000000292207141.

FOIL, Those that are in bondage: Child labor and IMF strategy in India, retrieved March 10, 2004, from http://www.foil.org/economy/labor/chldlbr.html.

K. Johnson, Sweating it out for nothing, Women's Feature Service, New Delhi, 2003.

T.K. Joshi and K.R. Smith, Occupational health in India, *Occupational Medicine,* 2002, 17(3).

V.V. Krishna, N.G. Byju, and S. Amizheniyan, Integrated past management in Indian agriculture: A developing economy perspective, retrieved March 10, 2004, from http://ipmworld.umn.edu/chapters/Krishna.htm.

A. Krishnakumar, Children still at work, Frontline, Chennai, 2000.

S. Majumdar, Undone by HIV-AIDS, Women's Feature Service, New Delhi, 2003.

R. Mathews, C. Reis, and V. Iacopino, Child labor: A matter of health and human rights, *Journal of Ambulatory Care Management,* 2003, 26(2).

A. Ramaswamy, Decade of major gains, dispiriting failures: Crucial issues are stagnating infant mortality rate, quality of basic education, declining sex ratio, *News-India Times,* retrieved March 12, 2004, from http://proquest.umi.com/pqdweb?index=32&did=000000468012231&SrchMode=1&sid=2&Fmt=3&VInst=PROD&VType=PQD&RQT=309&VName=PQD&TS=1079300016&clientId=29440.

R. Ray, Child labor, child schooling, and their interaction with adult labor: Empirical evidence for Peru and Pakistan, *World Bank Economic Review,* 2000, 14(2).

P.K. Shetty, *Ecological Implications of Pesticide Use in Agro-Ecosystems in India,* National Institute of Advance Studies, Bangalore, 2002.

V. Shiva, Monsanto and the mustard seed, *Earth Island Journal,* 2002, 16(4).

I. Sloan, *Child Abuse: Governing Law and Legislation,* Oceana Publications, New York, 1983, 20(1).

S. Suri, Rights-India: Horror stories behind those veils of silk, Global Information Network, retrieved March 12, 2004, from http://gateway.proquest.com/openurl?url_ver=Z39.88-2004&res_dat=xri:pqd&rft_val_fmt=info:ofi/fmt:kev:mtx:journal&genre=article&rft_dat=xri:pqd:did=000000279887801.

S. Thapa, D. Chhetry, and R.H. Aryal, Poverty, literacy and child labor in Nepal: A district-level analysis: intervention programs aimed at reducing child labor need to focus on both alleviating poverty and increasing literacy, *Asia-Pacific Population Journal,* 1996, 11(3).

L. Tucker and A. Ganesan, The small hands of slavery: India's bonded child laborers and the World Bank, *Multinational Monitor,* retrieved from http://www.thirdworldtraveler.com/IMF_WB/SmallHands_MNM.html.

D. Venkateswarlu, J. Kasper, R. Mathews, and C. Reis, Child labor in India: A health and human rights perspective, *The Lancet,* 2003, 362.

Trafficking Children for Child Labor and Prostitution in Nigeria

8

OLAKUNLE MICHAEL FOLAMI

Contents

8.1 Introduction

Child labor involving youngsters between the ages of 7 and 16 years, rather than abating, continues to assume wider and more frightening dimensions. Highly vulnerable children, mostly elementary school–age students, continue to be lured away from their unsuspecting parents and guardians and deployed in slave labor.

In Nigeria, this problem has also experienced unprecedented growth compared to what was possible within the traditional social structure, in which parents used children as economic tools for further production of wealth in their farms. Domestic slavery predominated traditional society, and children were sometimes sold to honor social economic and religious obligations or pledged for money to pay for a dowry of an elder brother's would-be bride.

This traditional form of slavery still exists in sub-Saharan Africa, West Africa, and some other parts of Asia and Latin America. However, the associated crimes that take place during the trafficking of women and children in Nigeria, apart from child labor, are sexual slavery, women trafficking, child soldiering, and drug trafficking, among others. But the most prevalent crime in this criminal exploitation of children in Nigeria is child labor.

8.2   Statement of the Problem

The phenomenon of child labor has reached an unimaginable magnitude in Nigeria. Child labor is a major problem facing developing countries, where the most use of child labor takes place. About 800 million children are currently engaged in one form of child labor or another in Asia, Africa, and South and Central America. Child labor in Nigeria ranges between 20% and 30% of the population under 18 years of age, which makes up a part of the 41% of African children between 5 and 16 years old who are laborers.

The International Labor Organization (ILO), in a report released in 1999, noted that the majority of workers aged 10–14 years are found in Asia, which has 44.6 million—or 13% of the total number—of child workers in the world, but the highest percentages are found in Africa, where 23.6 million children—or 26.3% of the total—are working. Latin America is in third place, with 5.1 million (9.8%). Because of urban expansion, child labor is increasing inexorably in the Third World. However, despite urbanization, 9 of every 10 working children are still employed in rural areas.

In Nigeria, the localization of child labor has created its largest concentration in the major cities of Lagos, Ibadan, Port Harcourt, Kano, Abuja, Zaire, Calabar, Benin City, Solcoto, Maidugri, Kdduna, Jos, and Akure. Official statistics show that 4.1 million boys aged 10–14 years are at work in Nigeria, compared to 3.5 million girls. However, such figures often underestimate girls' work, because they do not take housework into account. Unmistakably, girls are more isolated from the public in Nigeria than in India.

Child labor has wide spectrum of exploitation. It can be seen in the form of "aggressive hawking," bus conducting, touting, or the most recent phenomenon, importing children from neighboring countries to serve as house servants when getting Nigerian boys or girls as servants is difficult. These children are captured like slaves and kept in a slavery camp until their services are required by those who need them. The traffickers are then paid a fee by whoever wants the services of the boys or girls, according to the duration of the service.

These children are either kidnapped for sale into slavery or prostitution or given away by parents who are fooled into believing that a better life awaits their wards. There are agents who collect all the earnings of the children who are hired out to affluent families to serve as house slaves, and there are agents who have some children on bonded labor. They give the children only a fraction of the earnings when their terms are over and they are ready to go back home. The females among the children are hired out to beer parlor operators, who also use them as prostitutes. These girls do double service for their masters, working as prostitutes and as waitresses, and some of them are simply kept as waitresses and sex slaves for their master. Some older women also hire some girls to serve as prostitutes in their whorehouses or beer parlors.

The trickle of emigrants from Nigeria in the 1970s turned into an exodus between 1980 and 1995. At the end of the route, what awaits the children are pain and penury. The story does not end better for the females among them who are trafficked out of the country and end up in prostitution houses. Almost all parts of Nigeria are involved in the trading of children for prostitution, and over 70% of domestic servants are constantly not paid their wages, live like condemned persons—exploited, out of school, abused, and deprived of the necessities of life. Starved and left alone under harsh and deplorable conditions, these individuals hawk wares, baby-sit, and work long hours taking on heavy responsibilities that, in most cases, are also hazardous to their health.

The areas in which child labor mostly occurs include construction sites in the semiformal sector, where children are employed to carry bricks. In public places, they are street vendors, shoe shiners, car washers, and feet washers. They also work in semipublic settings in cottage industries, such as vulcanizing, iron and metal works, hair dressing, and tailoring. Child labor also occurs in private homes, where thousands of children, especially girls aged 10 years and older, work as domestic servants and are often emotionally and sexually abused by adults.

The ILO (1996a) further stressed that child slaves were to be found in large numbers in agriculture, domestic service, the sex trade, the carpet and textile industries, quarries, and brick-making factories. It is said elsewhere that children have been exchanged like merchandise in employment contracts for adult services or for money.

The many wars that Nigeria has seen have also contributed to spreading the practice of trafficking in women and children. In fact, the Nigerian Civil War (1967–1970) played a significant role in the upsurge of women and children being trafficked in Nigeria.

Some girls are given out as domestic servants to families in exchange for their education or for their learning a trade. The experiences reported by some of them include deprivation and maltreatment. Some of these girls are sent out to hawk goods in the streets, and by so doing they become exposed to prostitution and sexual abuse. Some men offering to buy the girls' merchandise may agree to purchase the girls' goods in exchange for sex. Nnorom (2003) asserted that children are found in all parts of Lagos metropolis, hawking and running after moving vehicles ("aggressive hawkers"), trying to sell goods believed to belong to either their biological or their foster parents.

The ILO (1996b, 1998) stressed further that the acute need of many households to keep all family members fed and clothed forces many children to work full time for their own and their families' survival.

This ILO study also critically examines the sociopolitical and economic factors that encourage child labor in Nigeria as well as looking at the socioeconomic characteristics of children involved in child labor. This is an attempt to specifically address the trafficking and exploitation of children for child labor. It incidentally examines the economic motives behind the trafficking of these children into slavery and bonded labor by the traffickers.

8.3   Socioeconomic Factors in Child Labor

Economic conditions theory (Bonger, 1916) explains child labor beyond a culture of poverty theory. In a society in which there are "haves" and "have-nots," the "have-nots" will try to get even with the "haves." The culture of poverty theory sees the behavior of the poor as a response to the established and internalized cultural patterns. No individual wishes to remain pauperized and to transmit such pauperization generationally, but some extraneous social factors put in place an impediment to impoverished persons who are willing to scale above poverty line (Haralambos, 2004).

Most of the children who become child laborers are from indigent families. The existence of child labor throws into sharp relief the widening divide between the "haves" and the "have-nots." Children begging or hawking wares can usually be traced to the doorsteps of the poor in society—you are not likely to see the children of the well-to-do in society engaged in such an act. The rich make sure that their children receive all the good things of life and thus cannot be tempted to go into the streets as hawkers. Some daughters of the rich may engage in prostitution, as happens Japan, but not in aggressive hawking.

Chukwu (1996) posited that parents need to make choices about the kind of life they want their children to live, but many family heads fail to make this decision, and hence some of them, when they give birth, just throw their children away. Chukwu also pointed out that although some parents, at least to some extent, strive to care for their children, they still send them on very difficult errands, such as hawking in busy traffic and trading on the streets, to augment the family income.

The theory of situational constraints portrays the poor as being constrained by some social factors, social structure, low income, unemployment, and the like and that they respond to their situation using all means available instead of being subjugated by a culture of poverty.

Situational constraints theory also asserts that the poor would readily change their behaviors in response to a new set of circumstances once the constraints of poverty are removed (Haralambos, 2004). Haralambos also went on to say that the poor share the values of society as a whole but differ in their inability to translate many of those values into reality. So once the etiologies of poverty are removed, the poor have no difficulty adopting mainstream behavior patterns and seizing available opportunities.

This theory explains the upsurge in child labor in Nigeria. Socioeconomic and political circumstances beyond the control of the children and their families make them vulnerable to child labor. The Nigerian economy is so bad that even the child knows more about the economics of the home now. Foluke Sonubi, a businesswoman in Lagos, revealed to the researcher that when she was growing up, she never knew how food got to the table because her parents were up and working and because the economy was not that bad. Today, the social reality is that parents work very hard to bring in very little for the family. Sonubi added that today children have come to see themselves as partners in providing for the home.

David Omozuafoh, the Group Development Officer of Amnesty International (Nigeria), believes that the reasons advanced by parents who sell their children include the bad economy. Because of the economy, a child will be sold to meet the needs of the family or to pay the school fees of the other children in the family. More often than not, however, the father spends the money on beer or takes another wife.

According to Nnorom (2003), the dangers to which these children are exposed cannot be quantified in monetary terms. If a moving vehicle does not knock them down first, chances abound that they may become victims of rapists (in the case of a female child) or, in extreme cases, become targets of ritualists, who may entice the unsuspecting child with promises of buying all their goods but kill the child for her or his body parts for the practice of voodoo or other ritual sacrifices.

Arewa (1996) says that government has to be blamed because if there were normal economic growth in the country, even people from the poor families would still be able to get by very well. According to Arewa, in Nigeria it is only the upper echelons of society that live well, and there is nothing like the middle class anymore. She adds that government has failed to provide needed assistance, often in the form of subsidies, to parents desiring to educate their children.

8.4   Public Intervention in Child Labor

In the 1970s, especially during the General Yakubu Gowon administration, it was a serious offense for anyone to engage a child in any form of labor, particularly during the school hours. Any child caught working during school hours was apprehended and held until his or her parents or guardian came forth to plea for his or her release. Upon the release of the child, the parents or guardian paid a fine to the government worth about 100 Naira (US$1.85). However, the ouster of Gowon in 1975 led to the abrogation of the law.

In 2002, a bill was sponsored by the Center for Women's Affairs to again outlaw any form of child labor. Another bill was also sponsored by the WOMEN Trafficking and Child Labor Eradication Foundation (a nongovernmental organization owned and controlled by the wife of the vice-president of Nigeria, Mrs. Titi Abubakar) at the National Assembly to implement a law that would put an end to the problem of women trafficking and child labor in Nigeria. According to Mrs. Abubakar, the old laws did not even mention giving assistance to the victims, but this oversight has been eliminated by the new law. The Child Rights Bill, which was signed into law in 2001 by President Obasanjo, was initially rejected by the National Assembly—some legislators rejecting it for religious reasons, others for cultural reasons—when it was presented. However, after criticisms by civil rights groups, the legislators were forced to reintroduce the bill and pass it into law.

The bill seeks, among other things, to check the abuses to which Nigerian children have been exposed over the years. These include hawking, child trafficking, child labor, early marriage, and child prostitution. The United Nations Children's Fund Representative in Nigeria, Exio Giani Muzi, applauded the government for signing the bill into law. "We join Nigeria's children and other partners in applauding this proof of commitment to fulfilling the rights of Nigerian Children," said Muzi. The fund called for harsher punishments for parents who abuse their children. Some provisions of the new Child Rights Act prescribed a fine of about 2000 Naira (US$20), but the parliament wanted jail terms ranging from 10 years to life imprisonment for violators. It also demanded life imprisonment for perpetrators of child marriage, which under the new act carries a fine of 2000 Naira (US$20). This law will go a long way to putting an end to the barbaric attitudes expressed—more than the earlier law did, which handed out a jail term of just 2 years to violators. There is now pressure from the civil populace on the Nigerian federal government to implement the law.

8.4.1   Method

This study was carried out in Ifako/Ijaye, Lagos State, Nigeria. Ifako/Ijaye is a metropolitan town in Lagos state. Lagos state is the commercial nerve center of Nigeria. Most residents of Ifako/Ijaye engage in both formal and semiformal economic activities. Motor garage and open market structures are jointly operative in this locality.

The snowball research technique was employed to reach out to the respondents in this area. The primary source of data collection was designed to elicit information on the issue of child labor in Ifako/Ijaye. Unstructured interviews were conducted among children between the ages of 8 and 17 years, and the suppliers and receivers of child labor also were interviewed.

Another method employed to reach out to the suppliers and receivers of child labor was the purposive sampling technique. An unstructured interview method was adopted because of cost and time constraints. In addition, most of the interviewees are uneducated except for some of the employers of child labor.

Interviews were conducted among 116 respondents: 100 child laborers (including 14 itinerant hawkers, 13 house helpers, 13 bus conductors) and 12 and 14 suppliers and employers of child laborers, respectively.

8.4.2   Findings

8.4.2.1   Suppliers of Child Laborers

The interviews were conducted with women from Owo in Ondo State, Nigeria, where suppliers of child labor have been in the business for more than 13 years.

Other women interviewed came from Akwa Ibom. These women have combined child trafficking with petty trading, and some have been suppliers of child labor for almost 18 years. According to some of these women, child labor is nothing but the result of a patriotic call for the children to assist in growing the economy of their homes.

One respondent explained that child labor is a way of helping children whose parents cannot provide for their economic needs. The children between ages of 5 and 12 years are too young to detach from their parents, but both the economic and psychological needs of the families necessitate parents offering their wards for labor.

8.4.2.2   Sources of Child Labor Supply

One source of child labor is concentration camps, where the children are kept until their services are needed. Some respondents believed that these children were either kidnapped or voluntarily offered themselves for labor, or that their parents made them available for labor basically for economic gain.

Imeko, a border town in neighboring Ogun State, was mentioned as containing one of the camps. In addition, other sources of child labor are Ondo, Ogun, Osun, Abia, and Imo states, and Afikpo and Okigwe in Abia State. These areas are said to account for over 50% of the goods sold in Nigeria. The agents from the areas are also said to have spread beyond the Nigerian frontiers into Benin Republic, Togo, Ghana, and Mali Republic.

8.4.2.3   Economic Benefits

Some residents revealed that the child trade is a booming business. Some traders realize N560,000 (US$3810) annually. The receivers of child laborers pay N2,000 (4\$14) monthly for each child, but they make returns of N1500 (US$10) on the child, the N500 (US$4) surplus remains their gain. The "masters" also deduct N500 (US$4) for each child, and the remaining balance is sent to the individual child's parents or guardian. These children are considered bonded laborers and can be reacquired by their parents with prior agreement.

8.4.2.4   Receivers of Child Laborers

The end receivers of child laborers are housewives (who use them as housegirls or houseboys), restaurant operators, traders, shop owners, those in informal sectors of the economy, and so on.

One respondent said that she had steady receivers in the cities, particularly Ibadan and Lagos. She distributes child laborers to those in need of them in the cities, especially the households, traders, and the informal sectors of the economy. She revealed that children with low productivity face eventual repatriation to their camps and eventual replacement with new arrivals.

At times, according to her, she also arranged to provide children to those who smuggle them to foreign countries (international trafficking). The literature corroborates that children are trickling out of Nigeria. These trafficked children are ultimately transported to camps in the coastal towns, filtering in to neighboring Nigerian countries via buses and taxis to avoid detection. These children are promised paradise in foreign countries like Gabon, Equatorial Gunea, Saotome and Principle, Italy, Spain, Belgium, and so on, but they end up losing everything. Some never see their parents again.

8.4.2.5   Various Cases of Child Laborers' Exploitation

The Nigerian child community faces many sources of exploitation from pregnancy through birth into babyhood, infancy, and adolescence. Some are made into hawkers and roadside traders. Some are turned into prostitutes or beggars, and some are forced into child marriages. We provide six cases here as examples.

Case 1

Osuji Benedict, who ought to be in junior secondary school, is on the streets selling groundnuts. This is not because he does not want to continue his education, but because he has come to realize that his father cannot care for all six of his children due to the poor salary he receives as a night watchman. Osuji went further, saying that his mother devised another economic means to supplement the family income. He added that he makes up to N600 per day from the sales of groundnuts, of which the entire amount goes to his parents, who provide for the family.

Case 2

Aniamaka Nkem, a junior secondary school pupil, said that it is the excitement of being with her mates that brought her to the street to sell packaged water ("pure water") to augment the income of her family. She makes an average of N1000 per day. Her income goes to her mother, who uses it to meet the needs of the family. When told the advantages of being in school, Aniamaka said that she could not sit at home doing nothing when everybody else has gone out to do something lucrative. "The days I didn't go out, it would seem as if I am sick." She said that she is a girl and that someone out there would marry her someday, and that the little experience she has gained in pure water sales would assist her in setting up her own factory in the future.

Case 3

Oladayo Ojo looked younger than his 10 years. He was seen in the company of his little sister, Sayo, begging for alms with their wares beside them. Asked why he took to child labor, he revealed that his family could barely manage on the little earnings made by his mother. Oladayo does not know who his father is, as his mother is said to have separated from his father. His mother currently lives with her children in a one-room apartment somewhere in Lagos. He said that the proceeds from the wares belong to his mother, but the alms are for his upkeep.

Case 4

Dorcas, a Togolese, is 12 years old. Her parents offered her for labor because they could not provide for the 21 children in her family. She said that apart from helping her master in chores, she hawks household utensils. She revealed that her master pays her N1500 monthly, but this money is usually sent to her parents in Togo, a foreign country. She lamented that, for her, education is a forgone conclusion. She has never been to school.

Case 5

Ibrahim Adewumi, a little, 8-year-old boy, is a "bus conductor." He said that his father, who happens to be his master, the bus driver, refuses to send him to school. There are 13 members of his family, including two stepmothers. At the close of business every day, his father gives him N100, although other bus conductors are paid well, up to N1000 per day. He said that he would like to go back to school if he could get support from any source. When asked about his other siblings, he said that they also are involved in various child labor activities and generating money for the family.

Case 6

Sherifat, a 16-year-old girl, who had returned from Italy, said that she was in senior secondary school when her mother's friend approached her mother and introduced her to an agent who arranged for her being trafficked to Italy. The agent promised her mother that Sherifat would be given a decent job and a life full of promise in Italy, so her mother allowed her to be trafficked. When Sherifat got to Italy, however, she was confronted with the reality of her new situation. She worked to pay for money expended on her visa and airfares. When asked what kind of work she did in Italy, she replied "sex work"—"Ashawo" (prostitution), and that her master arranged for men to make love with her. The men paid her master directly. Sherifat said that she was forced into prostitution and was both ignorant of the dangers and lacking any information about its inherent exploitation.

8.5   Conclusion

This study set out to examine the upsurge of trafficking children for prostitution and child labor in contemporary Nigeria. In-depth interviews were undertaken to draw inferences and conclusions about the socioeconomic factors that tend to place children on the threshold of child labor and prostitution. In addition, we also undertook case studies of some child laborers in the Ifako/Ijaye area of Lagos State.

This study shows that apart from poverty, there are other social and economic reasons, such as social structure, low income, and unemployment, leading to child labor. A breakdown in the institution of the family has downplayed the societal value attached to children. The *modus operandi* of this modern slave trade (child labor) is similar to what was seen in the traditional slave trade, in which the slaves were put into camps before their departure for different destinations in America and Europe. The demand for child labor is supplied through kidnapping, false promises, and voluntary offering.

As in the Republic of India, in Nigeria, child labor yields enormous benefits to the operators, but the economic gains yielded cannot be quantified against the exploitation and danger facing child laborers. The suppliers of child laborers are parents and agents, and the receivers are households, restaurant operators, traders, shop owners, whorehouse operators, and others in the informal sectors of the economy. However, child prostitution appears to be the linchpin of child labor and exploitation, and the indications are that child prostitution will continue to grow. With AIDS on the prowl, it is said that the patrons are casting their gaze on fresh-blooded children, whom they believe do not have the dreaded disease. That is the attraction and the reason children are being recruited into this condemnable practice (Ikeano, 1998).

The Nigerian government should pass a bill prohibiting children of school age from being in the streets during school hours. Any child found wandering should be apprehended and transferred to the appropriate welfare home. Though the juvenile homes and juvenile courts have been eradicated in Nigeria, the present circumstances demand the resurrection of juvenile homes and juvenile courts as a panacea for child labor and prostitution in Nigeria. In addition, the health and education sectors should provide free and compulsory "medicare" for all children up to senior secondary level, and sound programs for eliminating poverty should be formed by the federal and state governments in Nigeria.

References

T. Arewa, Trauma of abuse, *Daily Times Newspaper*, May 14, 1996.

W.A. Bonger, *Criminality and Economic Conditions*, trans. Henry P. Horton, Dryden Press, New York, 1916.

H. Chukwu, Trauma of abuse, *Daily Times Newspaper*, May 14, 1996.

M. Haralambos, *Sociology: Theme and Perspectives*, 6th ed., Harper Collins, New York, 2004.

N. Ikeano, Child prostitution: A new social malaise, *Daily Times Newspaper*, March 20, 1998.

ILO, Children working in Asia, Africa, *New Nigeria*, November, 14, 1996a.

ILO, Poverty eradication programme, *New Nigeria*, July 11, 1996b.

ILO, Poverty main cause of child labor, *Punch Newspaper*, January 5, 1998.

C.C.P. Nnorom, Socio-economic characteristics of child hawkers in Lagos, Nigeria, paper presented at Tunisia, December 8–12, 2003.

Plight of Trafficked Women in Nepal

9

GOVIND PRASAD THAPA

Contents

9.1   Introduction

Women are generally subject to discrimination throughout the world in the social, economic, legal, and political spheres. Gender discrimination exists in varying degrees in the rural and urban areas of Nepal and seriously affects the nutrition, health, education, social status, and economic position of women in those areas. Women in Nepal are more subject to criminal victimization than males both inside and outside their homes. This victimization can include harassment, torture, abuse, and sometimes murder. Dowry (bride-price) atrocities, child abuse, and trafficking in women for sexual exploitation are—and have been—a disgrace to Nepalese society.

9.2   Features of Trafficking

An abundance of opportunities for trafficking in women in Nepal acts as a prime incentive to the traffickers. The vulnerability and haplessness of the potential victims, as well as a lack of proper legal safeguards, provide many opportunities for trafficking in women. The profile of a trafficked woman is nearly the same in all countries: She is poor, rustic, and semiliterate or illiterate. Many mail-order brides come from lower-middle-class backgrounds. Most trafficked women are single. Although poverty and lack of alternative opportunities are the main reasons, a woman who has gone through an unsuccessful marriage or a love affair also may be regarded as a potential victim. By and large, poverty, unemployment, displacement, social exclusion, and powerlessness can turn any woman into a potential victim. Research conducted by the writer revealed that 49% of the victims' families were broken in one way or other. Some had no fathers, some were without mothers, and still others were orphans (Thapa, 2002).

9.3   The Traffickers, Victims, and the Law

Trafficking is a slow, continuous, creeping, organized, lucrative, and silent activity. International crime syndicates are involved because of the high profit potential, difficulty of detection, and comparatively low penalties from the law. Even when trafficking rings are busted and exposed, it is very difficult to persuade victims to testify against the offenders. The victims are often frightened about retribution taken against their family members and ashamed to go home, and they lack an effective witness protection system (there is a law in place, but it is rarely enforced). In many cases, the traffickers are also heavily organized.

An organized crime syndicate is understood to be a group of two or more persons who, acting singly or collectively as a syndicate or gang, indulge in clandestine crime operations. Organized criminals are motivated by the large profits that can be earned in trafficking. They are generally involved in drug trafficking, financial fraud, gold smuggling, cyber pornography, arms and explosive hauling, human trafficking, terrorism, kidnapping, extortion, hijacking, counterfeiting, contract killings, and so on.

Cross-border trafficking has formed a set pattern that is followed across the entire Asian continent. Nepalese women are trafficked to India through the Indo–Nepal border. Thai pimps smuggle women across neighboring Myanmar. Groups of Bangladeshis trying to reach Pakistan through India to find employment often fall victims to traffickers or dalals (pimps), who are more often than not the guides on whom they have relied on and even paid to lead them through the subcontinent. The betrayed travelers can only look on mutely when armed local henchmen kidnap the women and girls in their group—the travelers' illegal immigration status prevents them from turning to the police for help.

In general, traffickers use two methods—deception and coercion. Any state of lawlessness or tacit impunity accorded to criminals is a factor that enhances the vulnerability of women and children and increases the opportunities for traffickers. The women involved are in desperate situations and are frantic to get help. As a result, they are easily made vulnerable to fraudulent promises. Trafficking in human beings is a violation of human rights and a deprivation of rights to sexual liberty and physical and emotional integrity.

The act of trafficking is inversely proportional with the amount of risk in carrying out the crime. The higher the risk, a trafficker had to take, the less the chances of trafficking. Therefore, effective law enforcement can definitely decrease the intensity of trafficking and other related crimes.

Notwithstanding elaborate plans, programs, debates, parliamentary deliberations, legal provisions and procedures, and the activities of a surfeit of nongovernmental organizations concerned about the fate of trafficked women and girls, the flesh trade continues to thrive globally. The daily newspapers carry headlines that scream the agonies and atrocities suffered by hapless women and children, yet the culprits always manage to get themselves acquitted by the very courts expected to condemn them for their debauchery. Such a state of affairs greatly encourages potential perpetrators to devise more innovative means and methods to carry out their criminal deals, and cases in which the offenders were punished and justice rendered to the victims are very few (Malla, 1998). In most cases, it is innocent people who have to face arrest, incarceration, and police brutality (Sangraula, 1999).

9.4   Thai Women Trafficked in Bangladesh

Today, it appears that criminals who are involved in the trafficking of women and children are changing their patterns and territorial locations. On January 10, 1999, 14 Thai women who were forced to engage in prostitution by a Korean hotel owner were rescued. The hotel owner was arrested, and the women were handed over to the Embassy of Thailand.

9.5   Deception

The trafficking of women and girls is a well-organized crime. In most cases, the families of the victims are deeply involved in the trafficking process as a result of their extreme poverty, avarice, and lack of awareness. Preventing trafficking or breaking the crime nexus are leviathan tasks because of widespread illiteracy among the poor and the failure of the government to provide viable alternative sources of income.

Prosecution of the criminals is quite often complicated by the victims having given their initial consent to be trafficked, either on their own initiative or under threat or parental pressure. The victims are ignorant and innocent, and the traffickers cash in on this innocence and ignorance—and quite often, the victims' silence is taken as their consent. For many victims, consent is willingly given to the traffickers by themselves or their parents, but many of the victims also are not aware of the nature and consequences of their agreement. The victims invariably give their consent either because of their ignorance about the consequences or under coercion, and they may give their consent without understanding what is being proposed and without knowledge of the alternatives. For example, 38 children who were rescued from the Apollo Circus of Delphi have told stories of their horrible experiences of exploitation and sexual abuse by the Apollo Circus staff. The victims have not filed any complaints against Apollo Circus, however, at least in part because their parents gave their consent for these children to go into the circus.[1]

Deception involves luring a potential victim by sheer treachery into a vulnerable situation. The lure could range from the promise of a good education, marriage, or a well-paid job to anything else under the sun. The victims eventually succumb to the overtures of the trafficker and end up in bonded labor or forced marriage. Some women thus deceived and trafficked are forced to work in sex industry.

Because of the lures offered and promises made, many girls fall victim to the traffickers' deception. Nepalese and Bangladeshi women and girls, lured by promises of a glamorous life in the city or career prospects in show business, or simply the promise of jobs in factories and households, find themselves locked up in brothels in India or Pakistan. The same false employment hopes have also victimized Indonesian women and children. Thai women bound for Canada, expecting to have work as hostesses, salespersons, and waitresses, are prostituted instead. Filipinos who go abroad as housemaids and entertainers are then sucked into the sex industry. Vietnamese women travel as tourists to foreign lands to look for work, and then the agencies that arrange these tours force them into prostitution in those countries. Sri Lankan women have fallen victim to offers of work in Japan and Korea, where they are brought ostensibly to undergo job training and then disappear.

9.6   Matrimonial Lure

Many women are tricked into sexual exploitation through spurious marriages. Quite often, two such bogus transactions—those of the matrimonial lure and the counterfeit marriage—are the most effective *modus operandi* of traffickers fishing out their catch. Examples from some Web sites include the following advertisements:

> Beautiful Russian Brides Seeking UK Men. Over 10,000 ladies from Russia and the former USSR seeking to meet men from UK for marriage. www.blue-sapphires.net
>
> Find an Asian Bride. Meet Asian and Oriental women for romance and marriage in the UK or internationally. Search member profiles and post your profile for free. www.asianeuro.com
>
> Beautiful Russian Women. UK-based agency introducing over 9,000 women from Russia who want to meet men from the US and Europe. A wealth of information is available, from trip reports, scams to avoid visa advice. www. eastmeetwest.com
>
> Mail order Bride! Free dating service! Single Russian women! Mail order Russian Bride! You can find pretty single women here! www.geocities.com/olik1975/mail_order_bride.html
>
> Zandy's Bride (1974 Zandy's Bride (1974)—Cast, Crew, reviews, Plot Summary, Comments, Discussion, Taglines, trailers, Posters, Photos, Show times, Link to official sites http://us.imdb.com/Title?0072435
>
> Mail order Bride (2003): Danny Aiello, Robert Capelli, Ivana Milicevic, Robert Capelli Reviews of the movie Mail order Bride (2003) the nation's top critics and audiences. Also includes movie info, trailer, interviews, articles, and box office figures....R for language and some sexual content Mail order Bride (2003) http://ofcs.rottentomatoes.com/movies-10003473/reviews.php
>
> Russian brides—Beautiful Russian Women—Single Russian girls—Russian dating service feature Russian women personals Beautiful Russian brides dating service. We present single Russian women and pretty Russian girls seeking marriage. Browse catalogue of pretty Russian women, beautiful Russian girls and sexy brides. Our Russian dating agency list free Russian...Russian

Another example is that of Minara, a Bangladesh girl, who was sold to Araf in Lahore. She stayed with him for 1 month and was married to him. He brought her to Karachi. Araf was about to have her married to another person in Karachi when she ran away. She was then caught by the police and was sent to Edhi Home (Ahmad, 1999).

The so-called mail-order bride business has made big profits by exploiting the adverse circumstances and economic hardships of women from various origination countries. Agencies in the United States, Canada, Australia, Japan, Great Britain, and Germany offer extensive matrimonial services. The prospective grooms come from Australia, Germany, Japan, and the Middle East. In many cases, the results of these marriages have been disastrous, with women experiencing violence at the hands of their husbands and even being pimped by some. The following news story is a testament to the existence of such incidents:

BBC News—A man who was sentenced to almost 29 years in prison for killing his mail order bride. Gifford King, Jr., strangled his wife, a woman half his age from the former Soviet Republic of Kyrgyzstan, to avoid the expensive second divorce. Anastasia's body was found in a shallow grave in 2000. King, 40, was convicted last month of first-degree murder and witness tampering. He was imprisoned for 28 years and 11 months.[2]

There are also immoral systems involving men having temporary wives. Arabs stationed for a short period in Pakistan take a wife who can cook, wash clothes, and provide sex. At the time of the husband's departure from the country, his wife is usually abandoned there. The women are then forced to take up the responsibility of bringing up their illegitimate children. The Philippines has been facing the brunt of this problem for many years, some Bangladeshi women became the "additional" wives of middle-aged Pakistani men from the semiurban lower middle class.

These women are brought into the sponsoring countries through deceit. The sponsors may not reveal their real age, real economic situation, or criminal records, if any. Although women generally view migration to a developed country from the standpoint of prospective economic relief, the sponsoring men are free to harm and inflict violence on the women because grooms are immune from investigations and legal actions.

9.7 Counterfeit Marriage

Women are increasingly being deceived and forced into counterfeit marriage alliances. For instance, Nepali girls are lured into false marriages and then trafficked. Vietnamese women are reportedly brought to China to become the wives or concubines of Chinese men who are often interned in remote places from where the women cannot escape. Web sites are becoming the easiest and effective means to attract many innocents into the net of trafficking. Some advertisements on the Web appear as follows:

Mail order Bride (1964)—Cast, Crew, reviews, Plot Summary, Comments, Discussion, Taglines, Trailers, Posters, Photos, Show times, Link to official site, Fan Sites http://us.umdb.com/Title?0058318

Singles list – Single Latin Women and Single Russian Women, Asian Women & Mail order Brides dating sites for single men and women. Contains links and profiles of Latin women and Russian women and other mail order brides. www.singleslist.net

Topsitedirectory.net—<Refueled> Comprehensive Directory guiding you to the Highest Quality Sites on the Net!...Get fast, reliable connections, a free e-Mail account, access to thousands of nationwide dial-up numbers, and great... www.topsitedirectory.net/links/dating/mailorderbrides.shtml

> Mail Order Russian Foreign Brides Mail order foreign Russian brides and
> pen-pals Profiles and photos on-line....A Mail order Brides.com Supreme
> Affiliate...site with free personal ads, marriage agency, dating service and a
> matchmaker. Foreign Bride Directory. Features Site...www.tigerlillies.com

In Nepal and Bangladesh, prospective grooms, accompanied by men posing as their brothers, cousins, fathers, or uncles, travel across the country, going from one impoverished village to another, seeking out families that are unable to feed themselves or marry their daughters. The travelers then offer to marry the girls and thus relieve the family of her burden. A large number of brides are collected in this manner.

Marriage matches voluntarily entered into by Nepali women frequently have had tragic ends for the enticed and tricked women. On their arrival, they are sold and resold by their supposed husbands and placed into brothels. In India, the business of exchanging Bangladeshi and Nepalese wives among prospective men for profit is clandestinely carried out—often, the prostituted women's clients are friends of their "husband."

9.8   Threat and Coercion

Forced labor, servitude, and slavery are crimes prohibited by international law. The core element of trafficking involves coercive and abusive conditions in which victims are forced to stay. People are trafficked into many types of jobs and situations, such as domestic, menial, or industrial work, and rape, kidnapping and abduction, physical torture, and drugging are some of the common methods used to get some women trafficked from one location to another. Some agents may also use force to abduct a victim and other violent means to blackmail and keep a trafficked person under control. In addition, traffickers often drug victims and then transfer them to their trafficking point under the pretense of taking the victims to emergency hospitals.

Trafficked persons have to depend on the traffickers for food, clothing, and housing and must submit to the demands of their captors. Traffickers usually restrict a victim's freedom of movement, such as by prohibiting victims from leaving the premises without an escort. Rape and physical torture are some of the common practices adopted to "straighten" the victims, as are threatening to kidnap their family members or throwing them into jail.

According to a study conducted by the Bangladesh National Women Lawyer Association, children aged between 5 and 10 years are being used inhumanly for camel jockeying—which sometimes causes the death of the children—in the United Arab Emirates. Other effects on the children of being trafficked include mental and physical disability, kidney failure, trauma, and serious injuries. The Bangladesh National Women Lawyer Association study estimates some 7000–10,000 children are being trafficked from Bangladesh to different Gulf States by air via India and Nepal every year. Their findings also show that the United Arab Emirates is the main destination for Bangladeshi children trafficked for camel jockeying. When the children are being trafficked, several of them are made to share a small room and sleep on the floor. They are often denied adequate food and are subjected to beatings if they perform badly (Kamal, 2004).

9.9   Detection, Reporting, and Registration

Women are subject to criminal victimization both inside and outside their homes. This victimization can include harassment, torture, abuse, and sometimes murder. Dowry atrocities, child prostitution, and trafficking in women for sexual exploitation are a disgrace to society, as is having a very large number of children being used for commercial sexual purposes every year—often ending up with their health being destroyed. Child sexual abuses are often unheard of and unspoken about in Nepalese society. These abuses are so hidden under layers of guilt, shame, and societal pressure that they go undetected and unpunished, but their victims live with this torment the rest of their lives. Prostituted children are raped, beaten, sodomized, emotionally abused, tortured, and even killed by pimps, brothel owners, and customers.

Unfortunately, the detection of such crimes is difficult. The reasons for this include the victims' fear of societal stigma, fear of perpetrators, threats, bribery, and personal guilt. Sometimes the lack of confidence in the ability of the law enforcement system to provide efficient and prompt delivery of a judgment discourages the reporting of crimes. In addition, in court the victims have to revive the memories of their exploitation when narrating the sordid account. They are then cross-examined and grilled by the defense counsel to prove that they were not raped and that they had willingly consented to the affair. This part of their ordeal is adding insult to injury. It is often argued that almost all law enforcement practices, in relation to prostitution, are aimed at the control of the prostitutes rather than at the men who exploit them. Sadly, under the current system, the victims are treated as criminals.

Quick delivery of justice is what every society craves. Unfortunately, this is easy to dream about but difficult to attain and more difficult to enforce. The reasons behind this could be individual or institutional. The legal investigation might take years, and the current justice system is so leaky that even after the case has been in the legal system for 15 years or more, there are still scores of ways for the perpetrator to get off scot-free. Normally, this is the result of corruption and inefficiency on the part of investigating officials, but the use of traditional investigation techniques without adding the know-how of modern scientific methodologies is also responsible for the current, inefficient justice system.

The nonreporting of cases is further exacerbated by the fact that 124 women and children were rescued by the Indian Police in 1996 from a Mumbai brothel and put in various rehabilitation centers (Ghimire, 1998). According to Durga Ghirmire, president of ABC Nepal, none of the 28 rescued victims rehabilitated in her center filed cases against the perpetrators.

In another study, of 180 rehabilitated victims in Maiti, Nepal, only 26 (14.44%) lodged complaints. When such a large number of victims in Kathmandu do not complain, the victims in remote areas cannot be expected to do so.

The mere existence of legal acts will not infuse the victims with the required courage and determination to report their cases to the police and thereby help in apprehending the culprit. However, easy access to justice and a proper support system to protect both victims and witnesses could result in an increase in the reporting of such crimes. In many places, people have successfully experimented with rewards and incentives and with taking a community approach to encourage victims to voice their indignation and protest their plight.

Nepal police have established 17 Women and Children Service Centers to help victims report and investigate such crimes. These centers have also been found very useful for women police officers. Apart from the Women and Children Service Centers, there have been more than 80 community centers established in conjunction with the police to prevent and investigate crimes. These centers have been very efficient in bringing such cases to light.

9.10 False Charges

Reports of the incident must be fully verified by the concerned agencies. Many cases have ended up being the result of false allegations. The following case is a testimony to that possiblity:[3]

Sita filed a complaint against Pushpa Adhikari alleging that he, together with Padam Bahadar Katuwal and Devi Katuwal, had trafficked and sold her in India. Sita claimed that the trio showed her a fake letter written by her husband from Kathmandu, asking her to travel there. She agreed to do so but instead of taking her to Kathmandu, the men took her to Saharanpus, India, and sold her. Later, however, Sita withdrew her allegations. She admitted that she had gone to Saharanpur on her own free will, and all of the accused were set free.[4]

The case of Tara is yet another example of a case withdrawn because of false evidence:[5]

Tara, a young Badi girl of 16 year of age, was married to a person from her own community. Because her husband worked in India, she stayed in her brother-in-law's house. One day, her uncle, aunt, and brother-in-law falsely informed her that her husband was in Delhi and wanted Tara to visit him. All of them took Tara to Delhi, but on reaching Delhi they sold Tara to a brothel. However, the Indian police raided the brothel the day following the incident, and Tara was rescued along with other sex workers in the brothel. Tara lodged a complaint against her uncle, aunt, brother-in-law, grandmother, and brother for trafficking her. In her complaint, she clearly stated the names of the persons who took her or who helped in taking her to Delhi and who sold her. The case was filed against the accused in the Banke District Court, and all were remanded to judicial custody.

However, on the day of the final hearing, the case took an unexpected turn. The court received a letter from Tara in which she asserted that she was not trafficked by anyone and was not rescued from the brothel. Instead, she said that the Indian police arrested her when she was walking the streets of Delhi. She blamed Maiti Nepal and the Nepal police for pressuring her to lodge a false complaint against her relatives. Therefore, she requested the court to release her uncle, aunt, brother-in-law, grandmother, and brother because they were innocent.

9.11   Evidence and Witnesses

Evidence constitutes a key factor in the investigation, prosecution, and subsequent conviction of an offender. It is mandatory to prove the *Corpus Delicti–Mens Rea* and *Actus Reus*, meaning the total guilt of the offender. The source of evidence can be the crime scene, the victim, the witnesses, and the offenders. Many cases having to do with trafficking get nowhere in court because of the absence of such evidence. A request letter sent to the Inspector General of Police of Nepal police by Maiti Nepal (Mumbai) may be quoted here:

Since we regularly repatriate rescued victims to Nepal, we could not produce them in court for evidence and statement in the course of trial, when required for prosecution of the criminals. Therefore trafficking agents and brothel keepers are acquitted by the court. And with this illusion, they are free to resume trafficking of Nepalese girls and women.[6]

Cases are also lost because of a lack of substantial evidence. This situation is best reflected in the Tulasa case:

Tulasa was kidnapped in 1980 from Nepal, when she was 12 years old, and was thrice sold to different brothels. The prosecutor's case was weak, as all the witnesses could not be produced. The judge expressed anguish over the handling of the case because original records were missing from the police files, including records from the JJ Hospital, where Tulasa was treated for 20 months (1982–1984) for a sexually transmitted disease and brain tuberculosis. Tulasa died some time in 1998. Recently, the city session's court acquitted the alleged perpetrator of the crime, Abdul Hameed Abdul Kareem, for want of substantial evidence. The Additional Sessions Judge, Judge K.U. Chandiwal, ordered Kareem's acquittal because the prosecution was not able to produce any direct evidence against him.

It is also difficult to collect physical evidence, especially in situations in which the victims are ignorant and cannot even recollect the names of their traffickers, the places to which they were trafficked, or *gharwali* (brothel owners). The offenders exploit this ignorance and innocence. In the case of *State vs. Salem Miya*, the court gave its verdict, saying that "the allegations against the accused could not be established."[7] In yet another case, the confession made by the offender was annulled in the absence of supporting witnesses or other evidence.[8]

In situations in which the police cannot produce required evidence in court, the victims of sexual abuse and trafficking often show frustration over the demand for evidence.[9] Parvati (name changed) was trafficked to Mumbai, India, where she was sold to a brothel. *Goondas* (henchmen) gang-raped her when she denied prostituting. She filed a complaint upon her return to Nepal. The courts asked to produce evidence to prove the guilt of the offenders, but Parvati did not have any: "What other big evidence can I produce than myself as the victim? What [evidence] can I give to the government?" was her question to the court during the investigation.[10] Unfortunately, such impassioned appeals made by the victims of sexual exploitation usually fall on deaf ears.

In another, similar, case, Sita was lured, trafficked, and then sold in India by Bir Bahadur, Lahure, and Kanchha. Although all three men were involved, Sita only knew Lahure. During the court investigation, Sita could not identify anyone except Lahure. She said, "I can identify only one of the accused and do not know the others," which gave the court a good reason to declare that, "The victim did not recognize Bir Bahadur." As a result, Bir Bahadur was acquitted.[11] Innocence, ignorance, and the incapacity of victims to explain and prove a crime often result in the acquittal of the traffickers.

In addition, some traffickers who will admit to the police that they committed a crime turn hostile in court. Bir Bahadur contended, "The police tortured me and while I was unconscious, they got my signature in the statement papers. That statement is false. I have not sold her. I do not know the victim and the other accused. The complaint is fictitious, concocted by her for revenge."[12]

In yet another decision, the district court of Sarlahi acquitted Panchamaya BK but punished Padam Bahadur Pathak, even though both of them had confessed their crime to the police. In the course of their interrogation, Panchamaya had even confessed to selling four other girls in India, but the district court maintained that "although Tulsi had accused Panchamaya and endorsed her document in court, she did not appear in court during the investigation. Panchamaya denied the accusations in the court. Padam Gahadur, despite his denial of the accusation, could not produce evidence to support his denial." Thus, Panchamaya got the benefit of doubt because Tulsi did not appear in court during the investigations.

In the case of *State vs. Norsang Lama*,[13] 15 girls were intercepted with their traffickers on their way to India. These girls were supposed to be taken to Saudi Arabia. All of them wore the apparel of Buddhist nuns, or *Bhikchhuni*, and their passports were later found to be fake. However, the court released all of the suspects on bail for want of evidence.[14]

9.12   Victims' Rights and Treatment

Victims have various experiences with the national criminal justice system. For many, the criminal justice system does not exist at all. Many helpless women and children do not have access to justice because they simply do not have the courage and confidence needed to approach the police. Even when they do, unfortunately, they are further insulted by society. When there are laws in place, there is often weak law enforcement, and as a consequence, the offenders might enjoy immunity. In addition, victimized women and children may be treated as perpetrators of crimes in certain circumstances, which can lead to victims' apathy, distrust and avoidance of the system. The most glaring issue is that these types of crimes are underreported.

It is quite often found that the duties and responsibilities of many law enforcement officials make them less concerned with human rights issues. Their duties sometimes make them rude and insensitive to human value, and they do not attend to the humanitarian aspects of policing: They neglect the human factor. The authority and power they wield make them feel great, and they end up turning a blind eye to the psychological state of many victims of sex crimes. It is extremely necessary that the Nepalese government harmonize the duties, authority, and power of the police force with the needs of humanity: Nepal needs to humanize the law enforcement system.

The special nature of this type of crime indicates a need for a special unit to investigate trafficking in women and children. This unit must have officers, especially women officers, who are particularly trained in the art of investigating such crimes. A combined investigation can also be an alternative to the implementation of this unit—police officers should be encouraged to seek the cooperation of other agencies' experts when dealing with such crimes.

On many occasions, the victim of rape or other forms of abuse is a loner without any kith or kin. She could be an orphan or have been disowned by her family for fear of them being censored by the society. Therefore, in the absence of government-run transit or rehabilitation houses, the law enforcers have to face the problem of providing transit or accommodating the victim until the end of their investigation.

The victims are normally innocent, young, and ignorant about the names and whereabouts of the perpetrators. They cannot even fathom the gravity of their own precarious situation. In fact, those who are just on the threshold of puberty cannot even correctly interpret the acts and relationships in which they are involved as being abusive. In addition, the offenders give their victims fake names and addresses, so if by chance the victims do manage to escape from one brothel, they can be caught and interned in another, which aggravates their suffering and humiliation. Finally, the more links the relay chains of illegitimate custody have, the more difficult it is to investigate and arrest the culprits.

Victims should be treated with compassion and with respect for their dignity. They are entitled to justice and to prompt redress, as provided for by national legislation, for the harm they have suffered. Judicial and administrative mechanisms should be established and strengthened where necessary to enable victims to obtain redress through both formal and informal procedures that are expeditious, fair, inexpensive, and accessible. Victims also should be informed of their rights when seeking redress through such mechanisms.[15]

The human rights of the victims should be protected during the delivery of justice. It is important to be aware that victims are already traumatized enough and are in need of comfort and solace. The investigating officer must be aware of the physical and mental state of a victim before interviewing her. The officer must also be aware of the victim's needs and should take care not to revictimize the victim in the course of the interview or investigation. Proper interviewing techniques and the use of modern science can help protect the victim from a continuous reliving of the tragedy. To assist in caring for the victims, it would help if female doctors and police officers perform any examinations and interviews.

Proper assistance to victims must be rendered throughout the legal process. Actions taken to minimize inconvenience to victims, to protect their privacy, and to ensure their safety, as well as that of their families and witnesses, from intimidation and retaliation must be well thought out. Unnecessary delays in the processing of cases and the execution of orders or decrees granting awards to victims must be avoided.

Offenders or third parties responsible for their behavior should, where appropriate, make fair restitution to victims and their families or dependants. Such restitution should include the return of property and payment for the harm or loss suffered, reimbursement of expenses incurred as a result of the victimization, provision of services, and restoration of rights.

In Nepal, there are no laws that address the problem of foreigners falling victim to trafficking. Therefore, it is normal practice for traffickers to deport such migrant women (or even men) without giving them a substantial amount of time to explain and justify their presence in the country. They are sent home before they can claim child support or outstanding wages or follow up on criminal charges made by them against their offenders. In such circumstances, migrant female workers are vulnerable not only to traffickers but also to police control and state punishment.

9.13   Trial and Prosecution

Evidence and witnesses both play important roles in facilitating the efficient and accurate delivery of justice. The collection and presentation of evidence, whether of *Mens Rea* or *Actus Reus*, and witnesses, including victims, are important. In Nepal, one of the studies revealed that the public prosecutor did not produce the witnesses in 56% of the past cases in the court. There could be many reasons for this, but it is certain that cooperation among police, public prosecutors, and the general public is highly warranted and valuable.

All law enforcement officers must be trained in various intervention skills. They should be adequately sensitized about the nature of these types of crimes, and instruction in the appropriate techniques used when dealing with various agencies must be sought. A well-planned program must be established to boost the morale and esteem of the law officers and imbue in them a much-needed sense of sincerity and commitment, in addition to making them efficient. Efficiency only is not enough—the Nepalese government must make its officers sensitive to human rights and feelings.

Often, the judges doubt the veracity of the opinions and evidence presented by experts, ostentatiously posing as if they know better than the experts. Such a myopic and parochial outlook hinders delivery of the right verdict (Tripathi, 1997). Because of the prolonged and cumbersome court procedures involved in the prosecution of these crimes, the witnesses tend to lose interest in the cases. In 43% of past cases, the witnesses were summoned within 91 to 270 days, and 41% within 90 days.[16] The study revealed that 31% of the cases took 361–720 days to dispose of; only 17% of the cases were dealt with within 90 days.

There are also indications that evidence, such as witnesses and material findings from the crime scene, is not considered important when delivering justice. The ruling of the Supreme Court is simply accepted as the final verdict, and whether the verdict is just or unjust becomes a secondary issue. Admission of guilt by the accused in police custody is accepted as the main impetus for criminal justice, and even private prosecutors treat such confessions as the prime evidence for conviction.

The prosecution's case must be based on more evidence than only confession or admission. A continuous hearing system should be introduced into the court proceedings, and the suspects should be cross-examined by the attorneys. The correct identification and address of the offender must be recorded at the time of investigation. The court proceedings should be made less prolonged and precise. The areas of administration and management must be further developed and updated. Separate courts for civil and criminal hearings must be established. Finally, the laws pertaining to criminal justice and administration must be reviewed and updated.

9.14   Conclusion

The need to protect women and children against all forms of exploitation has been agreed on and endorsed through various conventions such as the Convention on the Elimination of All Forms of Discrimination against Women. Yet women and children are battered, brutalized, traded, and subjected to innumerable criminal and ignominious injustices throughout the world. The investigations of these crimes and of violence against women and girls have required special skills and attitudes. The law enforcement officials must nurture positive attitudes toward the victims, as the children or women undergo untold trauma and anguish when they are victimized. Most of the victims complain of indifferent and callous behavior on the part of law enforcement officials, ranging from police to the courts, who often abuse them.

The various agencies responsible for execution of the criminal justice system have been kept distant from other sectors of development. As such, coordination and cooperation among the police, prosecutors, judges, physicians, forensic specialists, social activists, and jail administrators must be revitalized. Creating an enabling environment for a universally equitable and harmonious social life and existence and reducing the opportunities for such criminal activities are the only ways to contain this social malady.

Notes

1. (Kothima benchieto bhanda chhaina circus ma pugeka chelika pida). The plight of the circus girls are not less than those sold to brothels, *Nepal Samachar Patra*, July 23, 2003, year 9, no. 194, p. 2.

2. http://www.news.bbc.co.uk/hi/English/World/Americas/newid_1815000/ 1815537.stm.
3. Based on the interviews conducted by the writer of 145 individuals who were convicted criminals or who were detained inside three jails of Kathmandu Valley-Nakklu, Dillibazar, and Central Jail, Tripurewor, in 2001.
4. *State vs. Pushpa Adhikari*, 1995, one of the case studies selected for the research purpose by the writer.
5. Based on the report of the court observations of the Banke District Court, conducted by *Forum for Women Law and Development*, June 19, 2001.
6. Letter dated September 30, 2000, with an appeal to send the rescued girls to Mumbai when summoned by the courts.
7. Nepal Kamoon Patrika, 1990, section 31 no. 10, verdict no. 3938, p. 1019.
8. *State vs. Raju Tamang*, Nepal Kamoon Patrika 1990, no. 4, verdict no. 3788, p. 390.
9. (Afai uriera betha pokhda abud magne nyaya) The justice asking for evidence even when the victims relate the episode by herself. *Kanipur*, September 21, 2000, year 8, no. 216, p. 1.
10. "What evidence of trafficking can I give to the government?" *Alimalaya Times*, September 28, 2000, year 5, no. 271, p. 8.
11. *State vs. Bir Bahadur Biswokarma*, Nepal Kanoon Patrika, vol. 3, no. 10, verdict no. 4385, p. 618, 1991.
12. *State vs. Panchamaya* BK, case no. 103, April 25, 1992. It was found that the incident occurred on 13 April 1985. This case also proves the fact that many cases are registered several years after the occurrence of the crime. Sarlahi District Office, Nepal.
13. *State vs. NorSang Lama*, case no. 532, 1995, District Police Office, Kathmandu.
14. District Police Office, Kathmandu.
15. UN General Assembly, November 29, 1985 (Resolution 40/34).
16. Analysis and reform of the criminal justice systems in Nepal. Center for Legal Research and Resource Development, Kathmandu, 1999, p. 118.

References

N. Ahmad, Bangladesh in Karachi: Trafficking and/or migrated for work? Trafficking in women and children from Bangladesh to India and Pakistan, 1999, *Nepal News*, p. 30.
D. Ghimire, Life in hell: The true stories of girls rescued from Indian brothels, 1998, ABC Nepal, p. 3.
K. Kamal, Bangladesh Manobadhikar Sangbadik Forum, e-mail communication, 2004.
S. Malla, Cheliko Betha, 1998, year 2, no. 2, *Nepal Edit*. Srawan-Asanj 2055, p. 9.
G. Sangraula, Cheliko Betha, 1999, year 3, no. 1, *Nepal Edit*. Bansakh-Asa 2056, p. 17.
G.P. Thapa, Counteractive management of human trafficking in Nepal: The law and its enforcement, 2002, unpublished thesis.

H. Tripathi, Existing modality of criminal trial system in Nepal: The Lacunal, challenges and perspective refers, paper presented at the National Workshop on
Criminal Justice in Nepal: Existing reality and prospects for reformation, June
10–12, 1997.

The Emergence of Trafficking in Women and Children in Bosnia and Herzegovina: A Case Study

10

VELIBOR LALIĆ

Contents

10.1 Introduction

Trafficking in human beings for the purpose of forced prostitution has been the most typical form of criminal exploitation of women and children in Bosnia and Herzegovina in the postwar period and continues to be an important issue in Bosnia and Herzegovina. Bosnia and Herzegovina has unfortunately become a safe route for the trafficking in human beings and other forms of smuggling into Western European countries. According to Europol's analysis, Bosnia and Herzegovina is considered to be the primary Balkan route for trafficking in human beings to the European Union (Europol, 2001). Trafficking in women is an issue that will have a long-term effect on the regional stability and development of Southeast Europe.

The geopolitical map of Eastern and Southeastern Europe has changed dramatically in the past decade. The fall of the iron curtain created a flow of migration from east to west. Additional factors that have certainly helped cause the problem of trafficking in women and children have been globalization of the economic sector, followed by globalization of crime, as well as the outbreak of conflicts in the region.

The breakdown of the social, economic, and political structure resulting from the civil war in Bosnia and Herzegovina caused the expansion of various forms of organized crime, including trafficking in human beings. Disintegration of society and creation of an institutional vacuum offered maneuvering space to the criminal groups taking advantage of institutional weaknesses and the legal vacuum for realization of their criminal objectives. Trafficking in human beings for the purpose of forced prostitution is a complex phenomenon that includes issues of criminology, criminal law, human rights, migrations, labor, and gender equality. In a wider context, the trafficking in human beings produces an effect on local and regional stability and also affects the international position of the country.

Trafficking in women and children with the purpose of forced prostitution is a form of slavery that is growing to meet the needs of the expanding sex industry.

10.2   The Scope of Trafficking in Human Beings

The increase in trafficking in women and children has been motivated by the globalization of transportation, market economy, labor needs, poverty, women's socioeconomic insecurity, economic transition, and conflict (Kelly, 2002).

Economic liberalization has unintentionally helped create a fertile environment for transnational crimes, such as drug trafficking, migrant smuggling, and money laundering (Andreas, 2003). Organized crime is currently thriving. In fact, this is an era of globalization of crime, corresponding to increases in global trade, personal mobility, and high-tech communications. Traditional forms of transborder crime such as drug, weapon, and motor vehicle smuggling and money laundering continue to exist. At the same time, many organizations involved in these activities have expanded their portfolios to include the trafficking of migrants. The reasons are clear: Given the demand, there are profits to be made (International Organization for Migration, 1996).

In the late 1990s, the profits from trafficking in women exceeded the profits derived from drugs and arms smuggling. According to the U.S. Congressional Research Service in 2002, trafficking in women and children represents the third largest source of profit for organized crime, after drugs and arms (Kelly, 2002). Poverty is the root cause of the migration of individuals from their countries of origin to more economically developed regions of the world. In that way, poverty presents a fertile ground for the criminal exploitation of women and children. For example, more than 120 million people in Eastern Europe earn less than US$4 per day (Hughes, 2000). The privatization of state assets (property), which has accompanied the transition from a socialist state to capitalism, has disproportionately affected women because women are deprived of the social safety net of the socialist system and fail to gain their share in the redistribution of state property, which has been dominated by former party officials and crime groups (Shelley, 2002).

In the Ukraine, over 60% of the unemployed are women, and of those who have lost their jobs just since 1991, more than 80% are women. The average salary in Ukraine is about US$30 a month, but in small towns, it is only half of that (Hughes, 2000). Furthermore, conflict in the region has brought economic and social dislocation. The replacement of superpower conflicts with an increasing number of regional conflicts has compounded the problem and has made many women in war-torn areas not only destitute but also vulnerable to trafficking networks (Shelley, 2002). In addition to the social, economic, and political causes of trafficking, the crime can be seen as being rooted in the inability of people to migrate for political, financial, geographic, or other reasons. The gap between the increasing desire of people to migrate and their increasing inability to do so is most often filled by organized smuggling, and from these smuggling rackets come the trafficking syndicates.

There are no precise statistics kept on trafficking in human beings at the global or regional levels, but governmental and nongovernmental experts in the field estimate that between about 700,000 and 2,000,000 women and children are trafficked globally each year. This number is a preliminary estimate and represents both cross-border and international trafficking. It does not, however, include internal trafficking within countries such as Thailand, Nigeria, Ghana, China, Indonesia, South Africa, Mexico, and India (Richard, 2000; Ebbe, 2006). The International Organization for Migration (1996) estimates that 300,000 women a year (in 1998) are trafficked into Europe. The European Commission estimates the figure to be 120,000 (Hughes, 2000). For example, the Ukrainian Ministry of the Interior estimates that 400,000 women have been trafficked out of the country in the past decade alone (Hughes, 2000). Data point out that trafficking in women and children is a serious global problem, although the figures are not precise and are based on estimations.

10.3   An Analysis of Trafficking in Human Beings in Southeastern Europe

Conflicts in Southeastern Europe have marked the last decade of the 20th century and have reshaped the geopolitical map of the region. The area has been militarily, politically, and economically divided; new states have been created, and new borders established. The countries of Southeastern Europe have been seriously affected by the problems of organized crime and corruption, which have been the main obstructions to further development and regional stability.

Because of the limited economic resources available, governments in the region have not been able to establish an effective control over economic fraud and other forms of organized crime, including trafficking in women. The region of Southeast Europe has been an area of destination and transit, as well as an origination point, of trafficking in women and children for the last 15 years (Limanowska, 2003). Organized criminal groups in the region have successfully exploited insufficiently controlled borders, corruption, a legislative vacuum, and the lack of regional cooperation in the fight against organized crime. In addition, the geographical proximity of the Eastern and Central European countries has had an effect on the trafficking of human beings in Southeastern Europe, because the former East Block countries have been adversely affected by the aftermath of the collapse of the Soviet Union.

The International Organization for Migration calls the rise in demand for Slavic women a "fourth wave of victims involving women and children from Central Eastern Europe, including Russia and Ukraine that began in the early 1990s and continues at present time." The fourth wave of human trafficking from East Europe to Central Europe has included the Southeastern European countries as well, primarily because of their geographical proximity, similar history, and collection of problems that currently face these post-Soviet societies. The most prevalent form of crime in Southeastern Europe remains smuggling of drugs, arms, and cigarettes, which was the most lucrative form of transnational crime throughout the 1990s, although smuggling and trafficking in persons become more prolific toward the end of that decade.

As a transnational crime, trafficking in human beings should be tackled through an integrated approach at national, regional, and international levels. By signing the Stability Pact Trafficking Task Force Ministerial Declaration for South Eastern Europe in Palermo, Italy, the governments of the

Southeastern European countries acknowledged that they should play a leading role in antitrafficking activities. A system of regional cooperation, coordinated by the Stability Pact Trafficking Task Force, has been developed, and each country has set out to produce a unified, structured system to combat trafficking in the form of National Plans of Action (NPAs). The NPAs involve governmental, nongovernmental, and international agencies and have thus far proven to be very useful and effective as a theoretical framework (Limanowska, 2003).

10.4   Conflict in Bosnia and Herzegovina

Bosnia and Herzegovina was part of the Socialist Federal Republic of Yugoslavia until 1991. Civil war broke out in Bosnia and Herzegovina in April 1992 and ended with the signing of the Dayton Peace Agreement in Ohio in November 1995. With the Dayton Peace Agreement, Bosnia and Herzegovina was founded. It consists of two equal entities: the Republic of Srpska and the Federation of Bosnia and Herzegovina. According to the Dayton Peace Agreement, international supervision has been established by the Office of the High Representative (OHR). The OHR has been given the greatest authority in the interpretation of the civil aspects of the peace agreement, which anticipates the authority of appointing and recalling of the Bosnia and Herzegovina officials at all levels of power, as well as making decisions and passing laws.

The 3.5-year war caused a social and economic breakdown in Bosnia and Herzegovina. The emergence of the war resulted in a lowering of industrial production and the demise of the market economy because of the disintegration of the federal state, which caused important changes in market function. An estimate is that in this period, early in the war, industrial production was 10% of prewar levels, and unemployment was between 60% and 90%. The currency collapsed, and exchange was based on a combination of barter and deutschmarks. Significant industrial capacities were destroyed during the war, which caused criminal groups to take on a leading role as market suppliers. This resulted in the disintegration of the social structure and the state's legitimacy over a long period of time (Kaldor, 2001; United Nations Development Programme, 2002).

The conflicts that have taken place in this region since the early 1990s have resulted in millions of refugees and displaced persons who are vulnerable targets for organized criminal groups. The female refugees in particular are often alone and without their family members, and as a result they became targets for sexual abuse. Their inability to integrate legally in host communities or return to their countries of origin often leads female refugees and children into the hands of the traffickers. Bosnia and Herzegovina has been politically unstable during the postwar period. Laws have been made to control traffickers, but regional conflicts still exist, and the lack of cooperation between entities in suppressing organized crime has been high. The Bosnia and Herzegovina border has been insufficiently controlled, and because of that has become attractive to organized criminal groups looking to exploit the weaknesses of the "soft" border to smuggle narcotics, weapons, and people. The high profits available and the low risk of detention and minor penalties exacted have made trafficking in human beings for the purpose of prostitution very attractive in Bosnia and Herzegovina.

10.5   The Heritage of a Clandestine Smuggling Economy

The war and the postwar economy have significantly shaped Bosnia and Herzegovina society in the postwar period. The market supply, which is now mainly based on smuggling, has developed a strong smuggling environment and created well-organized smuggling networks. Those conditions also created fertile grounds for a clandestine economy based on the smuggling of goods and services (Ebbe, 1999, 2003). The types of goods used for trade are irrelevant—only the profit generated by those criminal activities is important. The Arizona market (in Bosnia) could be taken as an example. That area was established by the North Atlantic Treaty Organization as a zone of separation among Serb, Muslim, and Croat forces after peace was established in 1996. Now it covers an area of 35 hectares and before Bosnia and Herzegovina authorities took control had become a smuggling paradise where alcohol and cigarettes (on which taxes are not paid), drugs, stolen vehicles, weapons, and prostitutes could be found. The development of this market is a clear example of a situation in which it is impossible for authorities to regulate the flow of goods across its borders. As many as 25,000 customers visit the market in a single week, and the Bosnian government lost an estimated $30 million in tax revenue every year from goods sold there.

In 2000 the Arizona market was reportedly a "staging post for bringing in illegal immigrants, prostitutes and drugs from Asia and the ex-Soviet block to Western Europe. Criminal gangs running protection rackets [oversaw] the site" (Andreas, 2003). The situation in the Arizona market has changed since then, as Bosnia and Herzegovina authorities managed to take control over the market.

The breakdown of the economic system in postwar Bosnia and Herzegovina created room for illegal market supply. The profits that have been made through illegal activities have been large and have enabled rapid growth of the financial power and social influence of organized smuggling groups. The clandestine economy found in postwar Bosnia and Herzegovina also had multiple negative effects on the region. Well-organized smuggling networks had been created and effectively smuggled various types of goods across the state border. They exploited the weaknesses of "the soft" border and also exploited the high level of corruption and low level of accountability of customs officers and police. The state thus suffered huge damages resulting from unpaid customs duties and taxes, which caused state revenue to lower. As a result, the availability of funding for the state to finance its law-enforcement forces has been doubtlessly reduced, particularly taking into account the finances needed to purchase high-tech equipment and put into implementation specialized training. In addition, low state revenue has caused the state's law enforcement personnel to be poorly paid, which has made them vulnerable to various forms of corruption and misuse of their authority.

Another consequence of the war and the postwar illegal economy has been the creation of well-organized groups with ample resources to carry out illegal activities, such as the manpower needed to supervise and track shipments, as well as a network of contacts and acquaintances using corrupted government agents in case something goes "wrong." These groups have represented an additional burden to the state's law enforcement's efforts to detect and obtain proof of the activities of organized smuggling groups. The methods used to traffic human beings across the state border have, in the main, been similar to the methods used to smuggle other goods.

10.6   International Peacekeeping Force— Raising Demand for the Sex Industry

As a result of the signing of the Dayton Peace Agreement in 1995, in accordance with Annex 1 of the peace accord, 76,000 peacekeepers were stationed in Bosnia and Herzegovina, as well as numerous staff of other international organizations and agencies.[1] Over time, that number has gone down as the situation in Bosnia and Herzegovina became more stable and secure and the possibility of a new conflict was significantly reduced. In 2003, the number of peacekeepers was 12,000, with the possibility of a further reduction taking place in 2004 and the replacement of the Stabilisation Force in Bosnia and Herzegovina by the European Union. However, the placing of peacekeeping forces in Bosnia and Herzegovina encouraged the sex industry there, especially in the early years after the war.[2] The sex industry appeared to be a good business, especially in a country such as Bosnia and Herzegovina—a country that was one of less developed republics in the former Yugoslavia—whose manufacturing industries were destroyed during the war and in which the production of goods was stopped. In the period after the war, it was crucial that the peace be maintained and the possibility of a new outbreak of conflict be eliminated. In the meantime, traffickers of human beings smoothly captured individuals from all segments of Bosnia and Herzegovina society.

At this time, the so-called night bars were the most common places to find forced prostitution. Such bars were arising literarily every day along separation lines and roads and in cities and villages. These new business opportunities arose rapidly in the war-torn society, in which the legal economy was replaced with supplies—and suppliers—of illegal goods. Even people without a criminal history who had only good business opportunities in mind owned the nightclubs. As a result, the women involved became very attractive "commodities" for international clients located in Bosnia and Herzegovina (Nikolić Ristanović, 2005). A lack of state responsibility concerning the involvement of members of the peacekeeping force in trafficking doubtlessly contributed to the problem. The United Nations Mission to Bosnia and Herzegovina (UNMIBH) has denied any participation of its personnel in trafficking but acknowledges that several members of its staff have been let go for sexual misconduct. However, no critical remarks were made on their personal records (Limanowska, 2002).

10.7 Poverty as an Eden for Recruitment

The high poverty rate in Bosnia and Herzegovina presents the threat that it will become a country of origin of human trafficking to an even larger extent than it is now. The poverty found in Bosnia and Herzegovina is not limited to a certain segment of the population but is widespread. According to official statistical data, unemployment in the country, on average, is at 40%.

Increased poverty levels represent a risk that many of the unemployed will be potential victims of human trafficking. Poverty strengthens the wish to leave the ghetto, which then results in stronger desire for emigration that can further lead to accepting false business offers abroad and entering the world of human trafficking. Statistical data point out that the female population, in comparison to the male population, in matters of employment, is at a disadvantage. Of the 607,443 registered workers found in Bosnia and Herzegovina overall (United Nations Development Programme, 2002), 226,212 (37%) are women (United Nations Development Programme, 2002). The International Organization for Migrations and the local nongovernmental organizations (NGOs) keep records of the women from Bosnia and Herzegovina who have been victims of human trafficking in other countries as well as within Bosnia and Herzegovina. There are no precise data available, but local NGOs claim that there are cases of women from Bosnia and Herzegovina who were victims of human trafficking in Italy, Germany, and even Israel.

10.8   Lack of Political Will to Fight Organized Crime

The lack of political will felt in Bosnia and Herzegovina for a long time, which increased in the postwar lawlessness, encourages trafficking in human beings. However, that lawlessness is now being replaced by the building of collaboration between Bosnia and Herzegovina law enforcement agencies and the creation of new Bosnia and Herzegovina state institutions for enforcing the law, by the foundation of the State Court of Bosnia and Herzegovina, by the reform of the judiciary system, and by the adoption and implementation of the State Action Plan for Prevention of Human Trafficking. Further, Bosnia and Herzegovina is now participating in regional and international initiatives against organized crime, especially within Stability Pace (a benchmark for bringing peace and normalcy to the region) in Southeast Europe. In addition, previously mentioned activities represent a strategic legal and political framework for running a successful campaign against organized crime in Bosnia and Herzegovina and the region. The political will behind this framework is an essential element of the enforcement of antitrafficking activities. In addition, political will is greatly important to the development of an institutional capacity for suppressing organized crime. In contrast, a lack of political will contributes to the strengthening of the criminal network and leads to the undermining of public institutions, which in turn contributes to political instability and has long-term negative political implications. Furthermore, a lack of political will presents an enormous obstruction to the progress of society's transition.

Organized crime has had a huge negative effect on postwar stability and development in Bosnia and Herzegovina, as well as on the integration of Bosnia and Herzegovina in the European Union and the North Atlantic Treaty Organisation. Euro-Atlantic military, political, economic, and cultural integration is the strategic objective of Bosnia and Herzegovina, in which Bosnia and Herzegovina sees itself secure in the political and economical future. Organized crime is a problem not only for Bosnia and Herzegovina, with its negative implications for that country's society, but it exerts great influence on European stability overall.

The membership of Bosnia and Herzegovina in the European Union is of great importance for the continuing development of the nation. For Bosnia and Herzegovina to become a member of the European Union, certain conditions must be fulfilled. The Council of Europe, in its feasibility study, outlined 16 conditions that Bosnia and Herzegovina needs to fulfill including signing the Agreement on Accession and Stabilization with the European Union. Other conditions Bosnia and Herzegovina needs to fulfill include creating and executing a strategy for fighting organized crime and corruption. Human trafficking can have a negative effect on the international status of a country and can cause serious political consequences for those in power. In 2002 and 2003, Bosnia and Herzegovina was on the list of countries released by the United States whose governments did not make enough of an effort at stopping human trafficking. Such a negative report can have very bad consequences that, in turn, can result in a withdrawal of international financial assistance offered to the public institutions of Bosnia and Herzegovina.[3]

10.9 International Implications of Trafficking in Human Beings

Trafficking in women for prostitution became a serious problem in Bosnia and Herzegovina after the signing of the Dayton Peace Agreement and the deployment of peace stabilization forces. In the prewar period, this kind of crime was not present in Bosnia and Herzegovina to the degree to which it is now, according to official statistics and available sources. The issue emerged during the war but because of the circumstances, information and official statistics were inadequate and did not truly show the scope of the problem. Overall, circumstances in postwar Bosnia and Herzegovina made the region a fertile ground for the criminal abuse of women and children. The social disorganization that existed allowed international and local criminal groups to efficiently abuse the weaknesses of the system and to exploit the state's inability to confront the menace in a proper manner.

The trafficking of women in Bosnia and Herzegovina has gone through several phases in terms of the extent of the phenomenon as well as the reaction of the government and nongovernmental sectors to the problem. The first phase started just after the war. Its main characteristics were the huge growth of the criminal groups and the wide expansion of the sex industry. This phase was also characterized by the lack of clear understanding of the government sector, civil society, and the public of what human trafficking involves.

The arrival of girls from East European countries to Bosnia and Herzegovina was seen as the inception of prostitution, which by traditional attitudes of the local population brings a negative social connotation. At the same time, in the criminal legislation system, no criminal law existed with regard to human trafficking, although there were some legal provisions that, conditionally, could be applied to such trafficking.

In this phase of human trafficking in Bosnia and Herzegovina, the public, domestic, and international communities had no visible reaction to the problem. Also in this period, no ethical code of conduct and responsibility for peacekeeping personnel and members of international organizations existed. In addition, this phase of trafficking was characterized by the involvement of local police officers in human trafficking, whether as owners of brothels or bodyguards or as those who issued residential permits or provided the logistics for the transportation of the trafficked women (Human Rights Watch, 2002).

The next phase began in 1998, when United Nations Office of High Commissioner for Human Rights (OHCHR) created its first action plan against human trafficking. Also in that period, the first media reports were published and the NGOs began dealing with this issue. Nevertheless, in the field no significant changes were made. For example, in 2000, international organizations made an assessment that in Bosnia and Herzegovina, there were approximately 3000 women who were involved in prostitution. Of those women, 45% were connected in some way to the Republic of Srpska. According to United Nations Mission to Bosnia and Herzegovina reports, approximately 25%–30% of the women working in local bars and nightclubs were trafficking victims (Limanowska, 2003).

The next phase in human trafficking in Bosnia and Herzegovina included the final months of 2000, when the involvement of International Police Force (Interpol) personnel in women trafficking caused a scandal. The scandal resulted in the repatriation of International Police Force members (Human Rights Watch, 2002). After this event, response to trafficking became more serious than ever before, and ethical codes for international missions personnel were established. In addition, for the first time, the culpability of the local police who were involved in trafficking was established. This phase was also characterized by the creation of a well-defined police strategy through the implementation of the Special Trafficking Operations Program, which resulted in the closure of the vast majority of the nightclubs. However, this program also forced prostitution out of public places and into private houses, hotels, motels, and so on—places to which police could not easily gain access.

The following phase was characterized by a lack of information and an overview of the trafficking situation, which led to changes being made in the *modus operandi* of traffickers. The traffickers' change in tactics in turn brought about a change in the operational practices of the law enforcement agents, requiring more sophisticated methods of detection and data exchange at both the internal and regional levels. Moreover, this phase saw the increased victimization of local women and children brought from the neighboring countries of former Yugoslavia—primarily Serbia. In addition, this period was characterized by the breakdown of one of the biggest women trafficking chains in Bosnia and Herzegovina and by criminal proceedings being brought by the State Court of Bosnia and Herzegovina against the main actors from this criminal group. This case represented a test for the judiciary in Bosnia and Herzegovina and was a symbolic beginning for the rule of law in Bosnia and Herzegovina and also sent a message to other active criminal groups.

10.10   Government Response

Under the joint leadership of the Ministry of Human Rights and Refugees and the Ministry of European Integration, the working group has developed a comprehensive NPA to combat trafficking. This NPA was adopted by the Council of Ministers in December 2001. It focuses on the following goals for Bosnia and Herzegovina: establishment of a committee responsible for the implementation of the NPA; increase in border control and law enforcement; support of the victims of trafficking; building of safe and secure shelters that will provide medical, legal, and psychological support; providing victims with language and interpretation services and educational materials; beginning legal reform; promoting legal harmonization between the entities and the Brčko District; and educating and raising the awareness of all citizens.

In March 2002, the Bosnia and Herzegovina Council of Ministers created a state commission charged with the implementation of the Bosnia and Herzegovina National Action Plan to combat human trafficking. According to a commission document, four state ministries and five ministries from each entity, along with the State Border Service, were charged with implementing the NPA. As of 2003, the new state Ministries of Security and Justice, along with the State Information and Protection Agency, are also expected to be involved with the NPA. Financial investigators in Bosnia and Herzegovina, most of whom come under the authority of the Finance Ministry, have also played an increasing role in the law enforcement actions taken against traffickers.

In April 2002, the Chairman of the Council, the Entity Prime Ministers, and the Mayor of Brčko signed a Memorandum of Understanding to create Bosnia and Herzegovina's first nationwide, interagency, organized crime task force. It comprises prosecutors, police officers, and financial investigators from all the participating groups and the Brčko District, as well as members of the State Information and Protection Agency.

Bosnia and Herzegovina maintains links with regional law enforcement partners via a ministerial working group brokered in 2001 by the United Nations Mission in Bosnia and Herzegovina and the Southeast European Cooperative Initiative Center in Bucharest. In cooperation with the Southeast European Cooperative Initiative,[4] Bosnia and Herzegovina established a National Focal Point in Sarajevo's Interpol office. Bosnia and Herzegovina also assigned a full-time liaison officer to the Southeast European Cooperative Initiative Center. However, the officer reportedly returned home in late 2002 after the Bosnia and Herzegovina government failed to pay his expenses.

The State Commission and the Ministry of Human Rights and refugees have both worked closely with the International Organization for Migrations and local NGOs, and since collaborating on the National Action Plan, the commission also has worked with NGOs on several major initiatives, the most important of which is a joint initiative between the Bosnia and Herzegovina government, the International Organization for Migrations, and local NGOs to set up a network of shelters and safe houses throughout the country for victims of trafficking.

10.11   Assessment of Local Law Enforcement Capacities

A basic assessment of the situation, based on experience gained by the International Police Force and the European Police Mission, identifies the following problems (EUPM, 2003):

- No or little ownership by the local police of the fight against human trafficking because the International Police Force officers organized and executed the raids and investigations;
- Lack of a standardized police structure at all levels to tackle human trafficking as part of organized crime;
- Inefficient training and professional knowledge with regard to human trafficking and to identifying with and hearing the victims;
- Failing ethics and values—and even indifference and ignorance—concerning the trafficking problem within the local enforcement agencies, the national community, and even the internationals residing in Bosnia and Herzegovina;
- No cooperation and intelligence sharing between the local police forces;
- No proactive intelligence gathering and no use of new investigation techniques;
- No cooperation with international police institutions;
- No cooperation with the judicial authorities, resulting in superficial investigations;
- Lack of proactive engagement and prevention campaigns in which valuable information about the trafficking problem can be obtained;
- No help line or professional contact points for trafficking victims;
- Failing cooperation between the judicial authorities, the local police, and the social organizations in providing assistance, transport, shelter, a cool-down period, and a remedy for the victims;
- Absence of professional and individual hearing rooms for trafficking and sexual offenses victims; and
- Lack of basic logistic needs provided for the antitrafficking teams of the local police when investigating.

The European Police Mission also has launched Fight Against Human Trafficking, an intensive antitrafficking program in Bosnia and Herzegovina, the goals of which include improving the investigation capabilities of local law enforcement agencies. The program also includes training in new investigation techniques created to legal, democratic, controlled, and internationally accepted standards, including both mobile and static use of informants, technical surveillance, financial investigation, undercover agents, interception of communications, witness protection, and forensic investigation. The Fight Against Human Trafficking plan also includes the training of local police officers to tackle trafficking in accordance with the instructions given by the Stability Pact and to identify traffickers in line with the Palermo Protocol.

Fight Against Human Trafficking anticipates cooperation and an exchange of information between Bosnia and Herzegovina local enforcement agencies and all police partners concerned: the State Information and Protection Agency Strike Force, the Southeast European Cooperative Initiative, Interpol, the Stability Pact, the European Police Office, the Stabilisation Force in Bosnia and Herzegovina, the Military Police, and the judicial authorities. Moreover, the plan anticipates logistic proposals that include establishing a computer network and compatible software to exchange information and provide reliable situation reports as a basis for further operational actions (raids, etc.).

10.12   Legislation

Until recently, Bosnia and Herzegovina did not have in place an explicit prohibition on trafficking in persons for the purpose of prostitution. Republicka Srpska's criminal code,[5] which was enacted in October 2000, provides many provisions that could be used to prosecute traffickers. In the most recent revision of the criminal code, the Republicka Srpska adopted an explicit prohibition on trafficking in persons for the purpose of prostitution. In addition, the Bosnia and Herzegovina State Criminal Code, enacted on January 24, 2003, specifically prohibits trafficking in persons and mandates up to a 10-year sentence for those convicted of this crime. This provision is consistent with the United Nations Protocol on Human Trafficking. The Bosnia and Herzegovina Criminal Procedure Code, also enacted on January 24, 2003, includes important tools for combatting all organized crime, including human trafficking: witness immunity, plea-bargaining, asset forfeiture, and so on. Finally, Tier labor regulations have limited abuses of residence permits, which enabled traffickers to falsely document victims as legal workers.

10.13   International Legal Standards in the Field of Trafficking

Bosnia and Herzegovina has signed and ratified International Labour Organization Convention 182, prohibiting and indicating immediate action for eliminating the worst forms of child labor. It has also signed and ratified the Sale of Children Protocol supplementing the Rights of the Child Convention. Bosnia and Herzegovina also has signed and ratified (in March 2002) the Protocol to Prevent, Suppress, and Punish Trafficking in Persons, especially Women and Children, supplementing the United Nations Convention Against Transnational Organized Crime.

In legal terms, as it has now signed and ratified these crucial international conventions, Bosnia and Herzegovina is now mostly in compliance with international legal standards. However, the suppression of trafficking in human beings in Bosnia and Herzegovina is more a problem in practice than a legislative problem (Mrvić-Petrović, 2003).

10.14   Role of NGO Sector in Anti-Trafficking Efforts

On March 9, 2000, the local NGO signed an agreement for the foundation of Ring, an antitrafficking network. On that occasion, the network adopted a platform that defines its main goals and activities as:

- Promotion of human rights of trafficking victims and nondiscriminatory treatment of victims, with regard to the obligation of state to respect and enforce international human rights standards, as stipulated in international agreements;
- Cooperation with local and related international agencies and organizations in the field of antitrafficking efforts and prevention and assistance to trafficking victims;
- Establishment of safe houses, providing legal, medical, psychological, and financial services, as well as providing assistance regarding safe and voluntary repatriation of the victims;
- A campaign aimed at raising awareness; and
- Cooperation with similar networks or organizations in the region.

Trafficking in women was taboo in Bosnia-Herzegovina for a long time. Therefore, the foundation of Ring holds an important place in the nation's antitrafficking efforts. Ring has had many successes in dealing with trafficking before the public or government institutions, in its education campaign, in raising awareness, and in providing psychosocial assistance to victims. The local NGOs have a limited capacity because of their lack of sustainable founding. To date, the Stability Pact for Southeast Europe has provided the main funding for Ring's activities.

Ring members were also actively engaged in the creation of the National Action Plan for the prevention of trafficking in human beings in Bosnia and Herzegovina, and recently, Ring has focused on the improvement of communications between governmental and nongovernmental actors engaged in combating trafficking. Through Ring's initiative, for the first time, key local actors convened to openly discuss the issue of trafficking.

In the fight against trafficking in women and children, a partnership and common strategy between the governmental and nongovernmental sectors is crucial. At times, NGOs can provide better service and expertise than the public sectors, and it is important that they continue to build their antitrafficking capabilities and increase their role in Bosnia and Herzegovina in the future. In this regard, positive changes take place in the Bosnia Herzegovina region.

10.15 Conclusion

The issue of trafficking in human beings in Bosnia and Herzegovina raises many questions. Whether the extent of this phenomenon will diminish or increase depends directly on a variety of related factors, such as the ability of traffickers to exploit political instability, the insufficient efficiency of the judiciary, "soft" borders, and pervasive corruption. Addressing these factors while simultaneously raising institutional capacities to efficiently confront organized crime, will be essential for Bosnia and Herzegovina as it combats both traffickers and the misery for which they are responsible.

The absence of official statistics does not mean that trafficking is not expanding. The causes of human trafficking are rooted in the social structure of the contemporary world, and such problems are not easily solved. It is reasonable to anticipate that trafficking is expected to be a long-term problem in Bosnia and Herzegovina and the rest of the world. Its continued existence depends on the balance of global and local factors that compound the problem. The complexity of the problem is increased by the fact that many countries can be countries of origin, destination, or transit. Bosnia and Herzegovina remains a country of destination and transit and, lately, of origin for trafficking victims. This phenomenon deserves special treatment and a strategy that is up to the task of confronting it, as well as the use of all available social resources to eliminate the problem.

Notes

1. Since 1995 there have been a large number of international actors present in Bosnia and Herzegovina, representing the government, international agencies, and nongovernmental organizations. The following have a mandate under the Dayton Peace Agreement: the Office of High Representative; the United Nations Mission in Bosnia and Herzegovina; the United Nations Mission in Bosnia and Herzegovina, mandated by the Security Council; the International Police Force; the United Nations High Commissioner for Human Rights; the Stabilisation Force in Bosnia and Herzegovina Stabilization Force of the Partnership for Peace; and the Organization for Security and Cooperation in Europe (The General Framework Agreement for Peace in Bosnia and Herzegovina, Paris, December 14, 1995).

2. There is no doubt that a correlation exists between the phenomenon of trafficking in women and the settlement of a peacekeeping force in Bosnia and Herzegovina. However, it would be wrong and groundless to observe the settlement of the peacekeeping force as a primary cause of the phenomenon. Trafficking in women exists in the other parts of the Balkans, as well as in the other regions in the world, where peacekeepers are not present. For information on State Border Service, State Investigation and Protection Agency, see the U.S. Trafficking Victims Protection Act of 2000, which deals with, in accordance with documents, government resistance to approve help (excluding humanitarian aid and certain assistance concerning development) from international financial institutions, especially the International Monetary Fund and multilateral banks for development, such as the World Bank.

3. Regional Centre for Combating Trans/Border Crime, Bucharest, Romania, see http://www.secicenter.org.

4. Pursuant to the earlier criminal legislation, the police undercover operation was illegal and technical surveillance was not permitted, so proactive intelligence did not play a sufficient role in police operations. The legal institution of witness protection did not exist in either domestic legislation or police practice. The establishment of new investigating mechanisms presents the possiblity of the reconstruction of the police organization and the creation of a new way of operation for the state's crime suppression efforts. With regard to the aspect of trafficking in women, application of the new operative methods presents the only possiblity for success in the investigation of trafficking networks, particularly in the current situation, where most of the night bars have been closed down and prostitution is taking place in private apartments and similar places to which police have no access.

5. Republika Srpska amended its criminal code in October 2000, becoming the first of the entities in Bosnia and Herzegovina to incorporate explicit provisions criminalizing trafficking in human beings.

References

P. Andreas, *Criminalized Conflict in Bosnia*, paper presented at Clandestine Political Economy of War and Peace: Insights from the Balkans, Thomas J. Watson Center for International Studies, Brown University, May 6, 2003.

O.N.I. Ebbe, The political-criminal nexus "slicing Nigerian national cake: The Nigerian case," *Trends in Organized Crime*, 1999, 4(3): 29–59.

O.N.I. Ebbe, Slicing Nigeria's "National cake," In: *Menace to Society: Political-Criminal Collaborations around the World*, ed. Roy Godson, Transaction, New Brunswick, 2003.

O.N.I. Ebbe, *Global Trafficking in Women: The Role of International Law*, presented at the Oxford Round Table, March 26–31, 2006.

European Union Police Mission, *Human Trafficking*, Annual Report, 2003.

Europol, Crime assessment—Trafficking of human beings in European Union, Annual Report, Europol, 2001.

D.M. Hughes, The "Natasha" trade: The transnational shadow market of trafficking in women, *Journal of International Affairs*, 2000, 53(2): 625–651.

Human Rights Watch, Hopes betrayed, trafficking of women and girls to post conflict Bosnia and Herzegovina for forced prostitution, Local Police Involvement in Trafficking, 2002.

International Organization for Migration, *Trafficking of Women into the EU: Characteristics, Trends and Policy Issues,* presented at the European Union Conference on Trafficking in Women, Vienna, June 10–11, 1996.

M. Kaldor, *New and Old Wars*, Stanford University Press, Berkeley, 2001.

E. Kelly, *Journeys of Jeopardy: A Review of Research on Trafficking in Women and Children in Europe*, IOM, Geneva, 2002.

E. Kelly and L. Regan, *Stopping Traffic: Exploring the Extent of, and Responses to, Trafficking in Women for Sexual Exploitation in the UK,* Policing and Reducing Crime Unit, Police Research Series Home Office, 2000.

B. Limanowska, *Trafficking in Human Beings in South East Europe*, United Nations Development Programme, 2003.

N. Mrvić-Petrović, *Implementation of International Standards in the Field of Suppression of Trafficking in Human Beings in Bosnia and Herzegovina Legislation*, Pravni Savjetnik, Mart, Sarajevo, 2003.

V. Nikolić Ristanović, Trgovina ženama u cilju seksualne eksploatacije: Uticaj rata, militarizma I globalizacije u Istočnoj Evropi, Globalizacija.com, časopia za političku teoriju I istraživanja globalizacije, razvoja, rodnosti, http://www.globalizacika.com/srpski/s_home.htm.

A. O'Neill Richard, *International Trafficking in Women to the United States: A Contemporary Manifestation of Slavery and Organized Crime,* DCI Exceptional Intelligence Analyst Program, Center for the Study of Intelligence, 2000.

L. Shelley, *Trafficking in Women: The Business Model Approach, Transnational Crime and Corruption Center*, Washington, 2002.

United Nations Development Programme, *Status of Women in the Republic of Moldova,* United Nations Development Programme, 2002.

Trafficking in Women for the Sex Industry in Moldova[1]

11

D. SCHARIE TAVCER

Contents

11.1   Introduction

By examining current research and governmental publications, we have gathered some staggering statistics concerning the number of women trafficked around the world for the purpose of the sex industry. The United Nations estimates that 4 million people are trafficked each year around the world either by choice or as a result of coercion by violence, the threat of violence, the abuse of authority, debt bondage, or deception (Caldwell et al., 1997; Wijers and Lap-Chew, 1997). The International Organization for Migration (IOM) indicates that 500,000 women are trafficked annually, mostly from Eastern

Europe and the former Soviet Union to Western Europe (Kelly, 2002). These women constitute a new and growing supply of labor for the international sex industry (McDonald et al., 2000). Furthermore, research performed by non-governmental organizations (NGOs) indicates that the number of women involved may be even higher. Since the early 1990s, the wave of women trafficked from Central and Eastern European countries to Western countries has grown to where it now constitutes one-fourth of the trade throughout the world (Richard, 1999, 2000).

The study of human trafficking in Moldova is of particular importance because Moldova is a post-Soviet transition country and is an origination country for women who have been trafficked as a result of, among other reasons, unstable economic conditions and the absence of the rule of law. Since its independence, Moldova has remained a country in which women's rights are not acknowledged, the feminization of poverty defines women's life decisions, corruption reigns, and the government remains reluctant to acknowledge its role in the prevention and prosecution of trafficking in women.

11.2   Nature and Extent of Trafficking from Eastern Europe to Other Parts of the World

Trafficking in women for the purpose of sexual slavery and exploitation knows no global boundaries and exists in all corners of the globe. The U.S. State Department estimates that at least 700,000 persons, especially women and children, are trafficked each year across international borders. Within Europe, different organizations offer varying estimates of the number of women trafficked for sexual exploitation annually, from between 100,000 and 200,000 (Bassiouni, 2001) to 500,000 (International Organization for Migration, 1996, as cited in Kelly and Regan, 2000), and the organizations involved suggest that the number may be even higher. Unfortunately, some of these agencies lack resources, initiative, or agreement on the definition of trafficking. Some NGOs lack sound data collection methods or rely solely on the official statistics, recorded only when women are brought to the attention of the authorities through arrest, prosecution, deportation, victim assistance, or witness protection. NGOs' statistics are a direct result of their efforts to protect and care for trafficked women survivors, which includes those who voluntarily seek help in addition to those brought to their attention by official sources. Academics tend to use statistics gathered from both NGOs and official records for their research. As a consequence, figures vary and are one-sided. Therefore, it is necessary to be careful using either the statistics provided by government sources or those provided by the NGOs.

According to the Swedish NGO Kvinna Till Kvinna, an estimated 500,000 women from all over the world are trafficked each year to Western Europe alone. A large proportion of these women come from the former Soviet block countries (or Newly Independent States [NIS]). In 1997, an estimated 175,000 women and girls were trafficked from Central East European countries and NIS to Western Europe. Furthermore, 120,000 women and children are trafficked annually into the European Union, mostly through the Balkans. Despite the fact that these figures may be exaggerated, there is ample evidence indicating that a substantial number of women are being trafficked and sexually exploited within Europe.

The trafficking of women for the sex industry in Europe has experienced a boom of productivity and exploitation since the collapse of the communist system in the former Soviet block and elsewhere in Eastern Europe. As a result of the resulting shift in the political climate and economy (from a socialist to a capitalist system), levels of unemployment and poverty have skyrocketed, the rule of law has collapsed, and inappropriate judicial systems have allowed the black market economy and corruption to flourish. The smuggling of goods, arms, and people; corrupt state employees; organized crime groups; and an acceptance of illegal ways to earn money have unfortunately become the new norm in this region.

According to a United Nations and International Labor Organization conference held in 2001, up to 6000 women and children from Eastern Europe are brought to Britain, France, Switzerland, and the Netherlands each year by organized crime groups (Choudhury, 2002). These women are coming from cultures in which girls are not as desirable as boys and are not afforded equal opportunities for education or work, and where the selling of a young virgin (girl) is a method of bringing the family money for food and shelter (Johnson, 2002). Such causes of trafficking in women and children appear more prominently in certain regions than in others.

11.3   Countries of Origin

In addition to trafficking resulting from these factors, there exists a system of trafficking in women who are promised lucrative employment opportunities in Western European countries and who find themselves sold into slavery-like conditions and held as virtual prisoners in cafés or brothels. Ninety percent of foreign migrant sex workers in the Balkan countries are victims of trafficking, and at least 50,000 women are taken out of Russia each year and made slaves abroad (Caldwell at al., 1997). For instance, in Israel, which is the main market for Russian prostitutes, 46% of prostitutes originated from Moldova, 25% from the Ukraine, and 13% from Russia and the Central Asian Republics (Novostei, 2002). An estimated 20–30 women and girls return to

Moldova each month from being trafficked abroad, and most of them are coming back from the Former Yugoslav Republic of Macedonia, Serbia, Bosnia and Herzegovina, Kosovo, and Albania. In addition, the largest group of women trafficked to Western Europe through and from the Balkans are Moldovan, Albanian, Romanian, and Ukrainian nationals (IOM, 2001a).

Nearby countries in South Central Europe, along with Turkey, seem to have the highest number of illegal Moldovan immigrants. The United Nations Children's Fund reported that in 2000 and 2001, Turkey had by far the highest number of deportations of Moldovans, with 6610, with Germany (654), Greece (317), and Italy (232) following, suggesting that not all were consenting migrants. The Interagency Referral System Project in 2000 found that of its 125 referrals, 71 (46.7%) cases were from Moldova (IOM, 2000). An IOM study in the Balkans for 1999 and 2000 (IOM, 2001a), reporting on a combined study from agencies that assist trafficked women in the region, offered that of 5887 cases, 7% originated from Moldova, and of those assisted by IOM (697 cases), the majority (46%) were from Moldova.

11.4   Transit and Destination Countries

The crime of trafficking in women for forced prostitution experienced a surge in the late 1990s. The Balkans and the neighboring regions appear to have become a predominant region of transit and destination for trafficked women in the wake of the humanitarian crises and wars. With the additional presence of international forces and their families, international currency, and copious spending, demand on the sex industry increased.

In a study by Caldwell et al. (1997), 60%–80% of women trafficked to Germany and one-fifth of all female dancer visas issued by Switzerland during 1997 were for Russian women. Scanlan's study (2002) found that, where Moldovan family members abroad were female, the destination countries were primarily Turkey, Greece, and Italy, and male members of the family were primarily found in Russia. Other destination countries for trafficked women included Belgium, the Czech Republic, France, Germany, Ireland, Israel, Romania, the Ukraine, and the United Kingdom. In effect, a cornucopia of trafficking destinations exists. La Strada asserted that in 2001, there were 10,000 Moldovan women rescued from various European countries (Revenco, 2002).[2]

Furthermore, even when their families were working in Russia or Ukraine, potential migrants overwhelmingly wish to go to the West rather than the East. The view that better paid or more suitable work is available in Western Europe was confirmed by Scanlan's interviews of trafficked victims.

In 2003, Strathclyde Police and immigration authorities in Glasgow, Scotland, carried out a number of raids on saunas in the area, which resulted in several women being detained for questioning for entering the country illegally. The women came from various countries including Moldova, Romania, Kosovo, Yugoslavia, Thailand, and Poland (Henderson, 2003). The Transnational AIDS/STD Prevention among Migrant Prostitutes in Europe Project determined the percentages of immigrant women among prostitutes in several European countries. Immigrants made up 90% of the prostitutes in Italy, 85% in Austria, 68% in the Netherlands, 62% in northern Germany, 50% in Spain, 45% in Belgium, 32% in southern Germany, and 25% in Norway and Sweden.[3] It is evident that not all of the women traveled to these countries willingly. Instead some were being trafficked. Reports such as these attest to the fact that many women are exploited in all parts of Europe.

11.5   Definitions and Perspectives

Trafficking does not occur in a vacuum (Robinson, 2002). It is a crime that is the result of various and combined social situations and circumstances, legal systems, and people and their needs. Trafficking is not a single event but a series of consecutive acts and circumstances implicating a wide range of actors.

Trafficking has been defined by international, regional, municipal, and nongovernmental organizations, in addition to definitions that can be taken from varying ideologies. Some consider it a violation of a woman's human rights or another form of violence against women, forced to be a modern-day slave experiencing intimidation, coercion, debt-bondage, limited freedom and independence, passport confiscation, violence, objectification, and second-class citizenship.

Others consider trafficking to be an issue of migration, in that the woman has illegally crossed borders without a proper permit or visa or has stayed beyond her visa's limits; in effect, they say, she has victimized the state. This perspective has been adopted by several governments, which consider the state to be the victim instead of the woman who was trafficked and exploited. Proponents of this point of view use phrases such as illegal entries, false or expired visas, abuse of state resources, and illegal workers. The state, therefore, puts its criminal justice efforts toward closing borders, reducing illegal immigration and the number of work permits, and arresting and prosecuting women caught violating the state law.

For others, it is simply an issue of prostitution. These individuals do not separate the trafficking of women for sexual exploitation from their assumption that prostitution is the woman's main purpose in making herself available for trafficking, when in actual fact some of the women are coerced, bought and sold, or are initially willing participants who are then exploited. However, different prostitution laws and enforcement and regulation practices make it very difficult to come to cross-border agreement on definitions of trafficking and implementation of conventions or protocols and countertrafficking efforts. Some states apply a prohibitionist approach (prostitution is prohibited and clients are punished); others practice legalization or regulation (prostitution and the exploitation of the prostitution of persons of full age is not punishable); and others apply an abolitionist approach (prostitution is not an offense but is exploitation), thereby complicating research, discourse, and legal efforts.

Still others consider trafficking to be largely a problem of organized crime. This approach stems mainly from governments or international bodies seeking a solution to the financial and legal victimization of its institutions and states. It considers trafficking of women one of the many types of criminal activities carried out by organized criminal networks, in addition to drug trafficking, weapons trafficking, violence, and gambling, which cost the state a lot of money in prosecutions alone.

11.6   Varying Definitions

There is no common definition used by all the international and national agencies, governmental and nongovernmental organizations, and regional and local police forces involved with the various components of trafficking in women and children (Coomaraswamy, 2000). Several of these agencies use the United Nation's convention and subsequent protocol, yet within the global effort surrounding the issue, a unified ideology is lacking.

One woman's story of being trafficked is strikingly similar to the stories of the many thousands of other women who have been trafficked from one country to another and forced into prostitution. Sometimes some of these women are willing to go with the trafficker to seek new jobs and new lives, sometimes they are coerced or kidnapped, and sometimes they go with the belief that they will work in the sex industry, although not as a sex slave or slave laborer. Regardless of which scenario pertains to any of the women trafficked each year, trafficking for sexual exploitation involves certain key elements that define it as such: the use of coercion or deceit to obtain and transport women; deceit about the woman's intended destination or employment purpose and circumstances; confiscation of her travel papers or identity documents; physical, emotional, or sexual abuse or the threat of such; and legal or illegal crossing of borders with recruiters or traffickers in tow.

Trafficking for sexual exploitation differs from smuggling in the sense that smuggling involves a person who goes willingly or voluntarily, and sometimes even knowing the dangers ahead. The definitions of trafficking in women vary for various reasons—political, ideological, or judicial. Each state has its own, valid reasons for choosing a definition that matches its needs and goals. Yet in an attempt to form a worldwide combination of resources to combat and prevent the trafficking in women for sexual exploitation, a unified definition needs to be in place. As such, with varying definitions existing among varying countries and among the agencies within those countries, investigative and prosecutorial efforts, prevention and information campaigns, and deportation and reintegration efforts lack cohesion. In effect, these are the obstacles blocking effective cross-border cooperation. Such conditions influence the accuracy of the data compiled on trafficking (IOM, 2001a) and the means and methods used to study the crime and assist its victims. Compounding this inadequacy is the lack of a holistic approach to addressing the problem—not only through the failure to find a unified definition but also through failing to consider all sides of the crime.

Apart from its lack of a unified definition, varying perspectives, and the criticisms surrounding those definitions or perspectives, the trafficking of women for the purpose of sexual exploitation does enjoy working definition. The United Nations 1949 Convention for the Suppression of the Traffic in Persons and the Exploitation of the Prostitution of Others[4] stands as the sole international treaty on trafficking and the source of the working definition (Coomaraswamy, 2000). Along with the UN's Palermo protocol, it is the most commonly applied tool used to define trafficking (see Chapter 1). Although outdated, the convention arises out of a prohibitionist approach to prostitution and trafficking. It seeks to criminalize acts and third parties associated with prostitution, though not prostitution itself, but lacks a specific focus on trafficking for sexual exploitation. Instead, it encompasses all forms of trafficking.

11.7   Factors Contributing to Trafficking

Depending on the region studied, some factors reveal themselves to be more relevant than others. For example, war in the Balkans, powerful and integrated organized crime networks in Asia, and cultural practices in West Africa, including sending young girls to be reared elsewhere, may all be considered factors that facilitate or sustain trafficking. Such factors can push people into the hands of exploitive traffickers or pull them toward certain countries.

Predominant in the current fight against trafficking are legal measures. Although causal factors are acknowledged as being relevant in understanding trafficking, they are not often considered. Nevertheless, any crime-solving equation must include the (proactive) study of the causal factors that lead to the trafficking of women and not solely the legal (reactive) efforts implemented to curb its growth or deter the offenders.

11.8   Push and Pull (Causal) Factors

Women leave their homes for many different reasons. One of the consequences of the changes within the NIS has been the opening of doors to a theoretically "better life" in the West (Caldwell et al., 1997). In search of job opportunities—and education—to help support their families, young women today are ready to travel abroad (Henderson, 2003). The feminizations of poverty, declining public health, and new forms of organized crime have all increased the number of women and girls being victims of prostitution and trafficking.

The reasons behind a woman leaving her country can be described, first as a push, in terms of their influence on her decision (poverty, no job, escaping war or familial violence), and second as a pull that can draw her knowingly or unwillingly to another country (demands of the sex industry, organized crime networks, corrupt officials, perceived prosperity, or porous borders). Such factors are believed to be at the root of trafficking. Without these factors, women are not willing to leave their countries and consequently find themselves vulnerable to exploitation.

11.9   Causal Factors in Moldova

Moldova is a relatively new country, having proclaimed its sovereignty in 1990 and gaining its independence from the Soviet Union on August 27, 1991. Despite the benefits of this independence, almost one-quarter of the population now lives below the poverty line. Women account for nearly two-thirds of all unemployed people nationwide, but this rate is as high as 85% or 90% in some regions of the Russian Federation of Moldova (Caldwell et al., 1997). In 1996, 87% of Russia's employed urban residents whose monthly income was less than 100,000 rubles (US$21) were women (Caldwell et al., 1997).

In a speech commemorating the 20th anniversary of the Convention on the Elimination of All Forms of Discrimination against Women, Deputy Secretary-General Louise Fréchette recognized how violence and discrimination against women pushes them to society's margins and that most countries affected with trafficking have experienced severe economic and social decline. Unemployment, inflation, income differentials, and poverty have increased, and as a result of conflict and economic change, living conditions and access to services have all deteriorated.

Trafficking is an issue encompassing varying perspectives, legislative issues, and social-political concerns. Therefore, it is difficult, if not impossible, to diminish the bevy of interrelated factors that point toward a specific list of push and pull factors influencing women in the dynamics of trafficking (poverty, violence, corruption, demand of the sex industry, criminal networks, and so on). Push and pull factors, however, are validated within the literature of trafficking (Hughes, 1999; Kelly and Regan, 2000; IOM, 2001b), making the study and analysis of such factors a worthy venture.

11.10 Economics

In the stricter sense, the feminization of poverty refers to the fact that women, despite supporting themselves or their families, are becoming the majority of the world's poor (Goldberg, 1990). Despite their rising level of education (soviet precollapse), today's women are employed in jobs that are below their level of skill and that result in lower rates of pay (McAndrew and Peers, 1981; Morgan, 1984, as cited in Kremen, 1990), representing 68% in 1997 of the total number of unemployed persons in Moldova and earning 60%–70% of men's average salary (International Helsinki Federation for Human Rights, 2000).

The feminization of poverty stems from a complex set of circumstances. It is important, first of all, to recognize that although women are increasingly part of the labor force, much of the work they do is unpaid (housekeeping, housewifery, child care, elder care). Furthermore, such work keeps women from supplementing their earnings through overtime pay or bonuses (Goldberg, 1990). In some societies, husbands are still perceived as the family's breadwinners and women as the housekeepers and child minders, regardless of feminist advancements and democratization. In addition, some societies are hesitant to accept new forms of gender roles, and thus the cyclical nature of the feminization of poverty continues.

Increasing poverty in Moldova is depriving many people of the means to sustain themselves. Using a minimum poverty threshold of 120 lei (US$11.50) per month, it was determined that 58% of the population was living below the poverty line in 1998 (United Nations Children's Fund, 2000).[5] Social support networks have been cut, everything from education to healthcare has been taken over by the government, and the dimensions of poverty in Moldova are higher than in NIS and central and eastern Europe (CEE) countries in transition (United Nations, 2000).

Bystydzienski (1989) reported that when Russian women were interviewed about divorce, they "express[ed] confidence that a divorced woman and a single parent could manage well in their society" (Kremen, 1990). However, in this study, the majority of women betrayed a reluctance behind their confidence about such a lifestyle (e.g., "can a working mother establish close relations with her children [the] same as a mother who does not work?" Eight women answered "no," and two answered "don't know." Another question was, "In times of job shortages, should men have the priority of jobs?" Eight of the women answered "yes," and two did not answer the question. When asked, "Are men better workers?" five women answered "yes," one answered "no," and four answered "don't know"; International Helsinki Federation for Human Rights, 2000).

Several years have passed since Bystydzienski's study, and the Soviet Union is no longer in existence. A fresh, more thorough interview process in this study would have elicited greater response and an in-depth commentary on the issue. However, even now the issue remains pertinent—the loss of jobs among Moldovan women was three times that of men in the late 1990s (United Nations, 2000), and so was its perceived acceptance. Scanlan (2002) also supported such reports, in that over 70% of trafficking victims described their material situation, before being trafficked, as either poor or very poor, and 85% of the victims claimed to have gone abroad for work. Up to 1 million persons from a population of only 4.5 million in Moldova are estimated to be currently abroad either for work or as a result of being trafficked.

11.11   Violence

Domestic violence is not a new phenomenon in Moldova, but reported incidents have increased within the last decade. Research has shown that the level of education of the perpetrators is relatively even across all levels, and the prejudice that violence is more often present among uneducated people has not been confirmed. As a form of dominance, male violence against women does not relate to the education of the victim or the perpetrator but, rather, to gender status alone.

The Moldovan legal framework does not address domestic violence specifically, but the Criminal Code provides for the punishment of violence against a person as a general offense. As a general rule, women do not report incidents of domestic violence to the police, and the reasons for this relate largely to societal assumptions of domestic violence, police apathy, and lack of adequate support systems or resources. Violent behavior is often "inherited" by men from their older male relatives through social learning and culturally accepted beliefs and stereotypes. Police officers, most of them male, often accept the excuse used by the perpetrators that the wife's attitude had provoked them. Figures suggest that 30% of all abused women share the information with a family member or friend but only 9% visit a doctor. Younger and divorced women, however, are more likely to speak to a friend about abusive behavior perpetrated by the husband or partner. Most of the women who have been trafficked from Moldova claim that the reasons they chose to leave their country did not necessarily include seeking a better life somewhere else but did include escaping the terrible life they had at home.

Officially reported cases of sexual abuse are almost nonexistent. In an attempt to gain a more reliable picture of sexual abuse, a survey conducted on physical violence included questions about women being forced to have sexual intercourse. The results of the survey showed that physical violence is often associated with sexual violence. On the whole, 4% of the women interviewed indicated that they had been forced into sexual intercourse at some point. Article 102 of the Penal Code punishes sexual intercourse involving the use of force with deprivation of liberty from 3 to 7 years. The penalty is higher if the perpetrator had committed a similar crime before, the crime was committed by a group of persons, the victim was a minor, or the crime resulted in severe consequences to the victim (International Helsinki Federation for Human Rights, 2000). What constitutes severe consequences is not clear. In addition, an investigation can only be initiated once the victim has filed an official complaint and provided forensic and other types of evidence (placing the burden of proof on the victim). Most astounding is the fact that if the victim agrees to marry the perpetrator, the legal proceedings are then dropped. Obviously such a system does not support the legal and human rights of victims of violence.

11.12   Social and Economic Rights

The lack of financial resources and poor infrastructure in Moldova represent serious obstacles to finding solutions to education and poverty, which affect approximately 80% of the population. As more and more families drop below the poverty line, practical access to education for their children becomes very difficult. The number of homeless children, most of whom are girls, has increased significantly compared to the Soviet era, and 1.7% of all children in Moldova receive no education at all or dropped out of school. In this context, the number of girls who drop out of school or do not complete more than a primary school education has decreased. The traditional gender stereotypes related to career development exert an even stronger influence on society. Girls and women are socialized to be less assertive and encouraged to take up gender-specific occupations and to have a successful marriage and family life. Moreover, the education system in Moldova has received less and less money from the state in recent years. The consequences of these cutbacks are more visible in rural areas, where lack of financial resources has caused the closure of many schools because electricity or heating cannot be guaranteed. At the same time, many people living in rural areas do not receive their wages for more than 6 months or so each year, and whatever they produce is used merely to feed their families—not to pay for excess costs such as schooling.

Access to employment has significantly decreased in Moldova in recent years, forcing most of the population to seek work abroad. Reportedly between 600,000 and 1 million persons have left the country to find work abroad. The economic crisis, caused mainly by restructuring and privatization, profoundly and adversely affected women in particular. According to the Archive of the Department of Statistics, the rate of unemployment in 1998 for women was 17.8%, compared with 10.2% for men. This figure for women represents a significant increase since 1994, when it was only 8.9%. Industrial sectors, such as light industry, which traditionally employed about 80%–85% women, were the hardest hit. The country's incomplete transition to a market economy has merely increased levels of poverty. Although economic stability is not assured by the open market, periodic inflation and mass unemployment significantly affect the structure of the active population, and particularly the women's situation within the economy. Figures for 1999 show the proportion of unemployed women (63%) to be significantly higher than that of men (37%).

As a general rule, women occupy jobs requiring a lower level of professional skills and qualifications than men. The average income for women is also lower, representing 60%–70% of the average salary for men. From a legal point of view, men and women have equal rights to vocational education and retraining, but in practice many state-owned enterprises were either liquidated or privatized, and no attention was paid to the need for retraining personnel. As a result, training activities, such as courses on modern business skills, are attended only by those who can afford to pay for them. Women face especially difficult employment problems when they try to return to work after taking maternity leave.

In additional, women have had to perform a huge amount of domestic work in Moldova because of the very low level of access to services that would help them with housekeeping and childcare. In many cases, elder parental care is necessary (for they, too, are without work), and many families move in together to conserve living costs. Combined with stereotypical gender roles and attitudes, all of these issues allow women little time to dedicate to professional development, and they soon find themselves in a vicious circle that prevents them from improving their living standards and economic status.

11.13   Corruption and Organized Crime

With the state-run agencies having little or no money, many civil servants are not getting paid for several months at a time. This includes teachers, police, and border patrol officers, who also have families to feed and lives to support. With organized criminal groups having strong ties throughout

Europe and the financial means to continue in their lucrative practices, such underpaid employees are susceptible to bribes and corruption. Organized criminal groups have a strong hold on many Eastern European cities, easily forcing women into prostitution. This type of trafficking requires border guards to look the other way and not to ask for travel documents, which is achieved by offering them immediate cash to look the other way. This is an easy way for the border patrol officers to earn money and sustain their families.

11.14   Strategies to Combat and Prevent Trafficking

Prostitution is illegal, but the crime of trafficking of women for sexual enterprise is not recognized under Moldovan law. The government has expressed its belief that the trafficking of women for the sex industries is not a phenomenon that affects Moldova, regardless of the number of Moldovans who leave the country on a regular basis. This blindness does not assist agencies that attempt to assist trafficked survivors, nor does it assist in preventing and prosecuting such human trafficking.

When the state is motivated to fight trafficking, laws are enacted and legislation ratified to facilitate criminal justice system cooperation, and research is conducted to highlight the causes of trafficking. All of this can contribute to reducing the number of women trafficked for the purpose of sexual enterprise, but without a solid legal base, judicial responsibilities, and governmental accountability, attempts to fight this form of trafficking are futile.

Acknowledgement of the crime must be the starting point in fighting against trafficking. Attention to the causal factors involved and the stories of the women who have been affected by trafficking also must be considered when devising prevention and prosecution measures. In addition to the various perspectives and amounts of research available discussing and supporting causal factors of trafficking of women for sexual exploitation, each woman's experience, in particular, from certain countries versus others, must be understood. Each country and its issues concerning women (unemployment, inequality, laws against violence, advocacy, attitudes, etc.) must be taken into account, because it is those specific environments and experiences that influence a woman's decision to leave her home country to work abroad in unhealthy or illegal environments.

Finally, cooperation with other governments, financial support for victims, cross-border police support, and judicial cooperation will all help victim assistance and reintegration programs.

11.15   Effective Approaches

At present in Moldova, nongovernmental agencies seem to be doing most of the advocacy and educational work regarding the trafficking of women. Agencies such as International Center for Women Rights Protection and Promotion, La Strada, work diligently on the issue of trafficking in women. La Strada Moldova forms one part of the La Strada Network, which comprises nine organizations implementing the La Strada Programme of Prevention of Traffic in Women in Central and Eastern Europe.[6] La Strada Moldova works to educate people about the dangers of traveling abroad for work and about the realities of prostitution and café employment, to prevent trafficking of women, to facilitate media contact and political lobbying, to assist in the safe return of trafficked women, and to provide social assistance and the reintegration of women who have been trafficked and returned home.

The International Organization for Migration[7] is an intergovernmental body with offices worldwide that assists people in migrating safely. The International Organization for Migration is also involved in education and prevention campaigns concerning the trafficking of women and works to assist in the safe return of trafficked women to their home countries or to third countries for the purpose of resettlement.

Within each of this agency's programs are units that advocate the legal creation of funding for telephone hotlines, information media campaigns, programs to support education, and victim assistance measures such as community reintegration, resettlement, educational training, and medical and psychological care. Unfortunately for countries such as Moldova, limited acknowledgement of the problem from its national government makes funding of these programs a constant battle. Support is sought elsewhere, and along with the Stability Pact for South Eastern Europe[8] and other European bodies and national governments, such as those in Belgium and the Netherlands, such programs persevere as Eastern Europe melts its borders with a growing influence from the European Union.

Notes

1. The contents of this chapter result from a summary of research conducted toward the writer's doctoral thesis and the published work of the International Helsinki Federation for Human Rights, "Women 2000: An Investigation into the Status of Women's Rights in Central and South-Eastern Europe and the Newly Independent States."
2. The figure was accumulated as a result of La Strada cooperation with various other nongovernmental organizations and shelters across Europe.
3. Transnational AIDS/STD Prevention among Migrant Prostitutes in Europe Project, http://www.europap.net/links/tampep.htm.

4. United Nations Convention for the Suppression of the Traffic in Persons and of the Exploitation of the Prostitution of Others Approved by General Assembly resolution 317(IV) of 2 December 1949 *entry into force* 25 July 1951, in accordance with article 24. Special Committee of the United Nations 6 October 2000 The Protocol to Suppress and Punish Trafficking in Persons, Especially Women and Children supplementing the United Nations Convention against Transnational Organized Crime.
5. Assessment done by independent experts from the Center of Market Problems in 2000 for the United Nations in Moldova.
6. http://www.ecn.cz/lastrada.
7. http://www.iom.int.
8. http://www.stabilitypact.org/trafficking/default.asp.

References

C. Bassiouni, *Investigating International Trafficking in Women and Children for Commercial Sexual Exploitation Phase 1: The Americas*, International Human Rights Law Institute, DePaul University, Chicago, Illinois, 2001.

J.M. Bystydzienski, Women and socialism: A comparative study of women in Poland and the USSR, *SIGNS*, 1989 14: 668–684.

G. Caldwell, et al., Crime and servitude: An expose of the traffic in women for prostitution from the Newly Independent States, presented at the Trafficking of NIS Women Abroad Conference, Moscow, Russia, November 3–5, 1997.

G. Caldwell, S. Galster, and N. Steinzor, *Crime and Servitude: An Expose of the Trafficking of Newly Independent States,* Global Survival Network, Washington, DC, 1997.

B. Choudhury, Police "losing battle" against sex trade: Thousands of women are forced into Britain's sex trade, *BBC Social Affairs Stop-Traffic Digest*, 2002, 1: 622.

R. Coomaraswamy, *Integration of the Human Rights of Women and the Gender Perspective: Violence Against Women*, Report of the Special Rapporteur on Violence Against Women, Its Causes and Consequences, *Commission on Human Rights resolution* 1977/44, E/CN.4/2000/68 February 29, 2000.

G. Goldberg and E. Kremen, The feminization of poverty: Discovered in America. In: *The Feminization of Poverty: Only in America?* ed. G.S. Goldberg and E. Kremen, Praeger, 1990, pp. 2–15.

A. Henderson, Time to put the brakes on sex trade, *Stop-Traffic Digest*, 2003.

D. Hughes, Introduction. In: *Making the Harm Visible Global Sexual Exploitation of Women and Girls Speaking Out and Providing Services*, ed. D. Hughes and C. Roche, 1999.

International Helsinki Federation for Human Rights, Moldova. In: *Women 2000: An Investigation into the Status of Women's Rights in Central and South-Eastern Europe and the Newly Independent States*, ed. R. Weber and N. Watson, International Helsinki Federation for Human Rights and International Helsinki Federation Research Foundation, Vienna, 2000.

International Organization for Migration, *Trafficking of Women into the EU: Characteristics, Trends and Policy Issues,* presented at the European Union Conference on Trafficking in Women, Vienna, June 10–11, 1996.

International Organization for Migration, New IOM figures on the global scale of trafficking, *Trafficking in Migrants Quarterly Bulletin*, 2001a, 23.

International Organization for Migration, *Victims of Trafficking in the Balkans: A Study of Trafficking in Women and Children for Sexual Exploitation To, Through and From the Balkan Region*, International Organization for Migration, Austria, 2001b.

International Organization for Migration, *Trafficking in Women and Children for Sexual Exploitation, Republic of Moldova*, International Organization for Migration, Chisinau, 2000 and 2002.

International Organization for Migration and International Catholic Migration Commission, *Research Report on Third Country National Trafficking Victims in Albania*. International Organization for Migration, Albania, 2000.

D. Johnson, Trafficking of women into the European Union, *New England International and Comparative Law Annual*, 2002, 5.

E. Kelly, *Journeys of Jeopardy: A Review of Research on Trafficking in Women and Children in Europe*, IOM, Geneva, 2002.

E. Kelly and L. Regan, *Stopping Traffic: Exploring the Extent of, and Responses to, Trafficking in Women for Sexual Exploitation in the UK*, Policing and Reducing Crime Unit, Police Research Series Home Office, 2000.

E. Kremen, Socialism: An escape from poverty? Women in European Russia. In: *The Feminization of Poverty: Only in America?* ed. G.S. Goldberg and E. Kremen, Praeger, New York, 1990, pp. 157–181.

M. McAndrew and J. Peers, The New Soviet woman—Model or myth? *CHANGE* January 1981 International Reports. Women and Society. London, 1981.

L. McDonald, E. Moore, and N. Timoshkina, *Migrant Sex Workers from Eastern Europe and the Former Soviet Union: The Canadian Case*, Centre for Applied Social Research, University of Toronto, Toronto, 2000.

R. Morgan, *Sisterhood is Global*, Anchor Press/Doubleday, Garden City, NJ, 1984.

M. Novostei, Slavery in Russia, What the Papers Say Agency, *Stop-Traffic Digest*, 2002, 1:584.

A. Richard O'Neill, *International Trafficking in Women to the United States: A Contemporary Manifestation of Slavery and Organized Crime*, U.S. State Department, Washington, DC, 1999.

A. Revenco, Presented at NGO Briefing on Women's Rights, February 4, 2002, Vienna, Austria.

A.O. Richard, International trafficking in women to the United States: A contemporary manifestation of slavery and organized crime, U.S. Department of State Bureau of Intelligence and Research, Center for the Study of Intelligence, 1999. Retrieved November 1, 2002, from http://www.cia/gov/csi/monograph/women/trafficking.pdf.

M. Robinson, The High Commissioner for Human Rights for the Council of Europe panel discussion: Combating trafficking in human beings—A European Convention? *Stop-Traffic Digest*, 2002, 1:541.

S. Scanlan, Report on trafficking from Moldova: Irregular labour markets and restrictive migration policies in Western Europe, International Labour Organization, 2002.

United Nations, *Common Country Assessment. Republic of Moldova*, United Nations, Moldova, 2000.

United Nations Children Fund, *The Situation of Children and Women in the Republic of Moldova, 2000–2001; Assessment and Analysis*, UNCF, Moldova, 2001.

M. Wijers and L. Lap-Chew, *Trafficking in Women, Forced Labor and Slavery-Like Practices in Marriage, Domestic Labor and Prostitution*, Global Association Against Trafficking in Women and Foundation Against Trafficking in Women, 1997.

Trafficking in Human Beings: Training and Services in American Law Enforcement Agencies

12

DEBORAH G. WILSON,
WILLIAM F. WALSH,
SHERILYN KLEUBER

Contents

12.1 Introduction

Trafficking in human beings is a modern form of slavery that is one of the fastest growing forms of crime throughout the world. Over the past year, approximately 1–2 million men, women, and children, worldwide, were transported, sold, and held against their will in unsafe and abusive conditions (International Organization for Migration, 2003). The most recent U.S.

145

Department of State estimate indicates that although between 700,000 and 1 million women and children are trafficked each year across the globe, 50,000 of them are imported into the United States (Richard, 1999; Hughes, 1999; Kelly, 2002; Miko, 2000). The United States has become a major importer of sex slaves (Landesman, 2003). However, these numbers are only estimates, because human trafficking is a hidden transnational crime that occurs in private homes or behind the façade of legitimate business (Braun, 2003).

In the past decade, human rights, women's rights, migration, and child advocacy organizations have repeatedly attempted to bring attention to the complex and troubling issue of human trafficking. The International Organization for Migration, Human Rights Watch, Amnesty International, Global Survival Network, Global Alliance Against Trafficking Women, United Nations Development Fund for Women, United Nations Children's Fund, and ECPAT are among the organizations that have provided leadership in addressing this crime. These organizations have been instrumental in providing services needed in combatting trafficking, organizing repatriation programs, conducting massive information campaigns to educate women and children about trafficking, and organizing education and job training.

Through research and public awareness campaigns conducted by several global nongovernmental organizations and worldwide governmental initiatives, a variety of proactive resolutions and legislation has been created and implemented for the purpose of criminalizing and ultimately preventing trafficking in human beings. Although statutes have existed for decades in several countries to prevent and criminalize such offenses as slavery, prostitution, and kidnapping, not until the last 5 years have international legislative efforts been focused on the specific criminal elements of human trafficking and the need to provide victim support services.

The Protocol to Prevent, Suppress, and Punish Trafficking in Persons, Especially Women and Children, supplementing the United Nations Convention Against Transnational Organized Crime, has been the most significant advance seen, in terms of international political and legal instruments, on the issue (International Organization for Migration, 2002). More than 100 countries have signed the protocol since its ratification in October 2000. By mandate of the protocol, countries are required to criminalize participation in an organized crime group, laundering of the proceeds of crime, and public sector corruption (defined in the United Nations convention). The criminalization obligation served as a tool to address both the lack of uniformity in national legislation and international cooperation and the serious impediments that exist to effective antitrafficking measures (Gallagher, 2001). The convention also presents a range of measures to be adopted by the states to effect coordination between authorities and encourage effective law enforcement strategies such as the formation of joint investigative entities and the provision of training and legal assistance to law enforcement. States are also required to provide assistance and protection to victims and witnesses of trafficking (Gallagher, 2001).

More recently, the United States joined the global initiative to fight trafficking by creating federal victim assistance and trafficking prevention legislation. Recent Department of State research identified the central trafficking routes and cities in the United States (Landesman, 2003). The Trafficking Victims Protection Act of 2000, P.L. 106-386, was enacted by Congress in October 2000. Its purpose is to prevent human trafficking, to protect victims of human trafficking, and to prosecute traffickers (Braun, 2003).

In the United States, policing is a local government function, and thus it is the police officers on the beat who are usually the first officials to become aware of human trafficking. However, there exists a diverse and fractionalized law enforcement environment in the United States, with approximately 17,784 full-time agencies in existence. This complex body of police agencies involves a variety of city, suburban, county, rural, and state police agencies, all of which adds to the complexity of forming a national effort to address the problem of human trafficking. This chapter reviews existing policy and legislative efforts of the United States and delineates law enforcement's responsibilities and its response to the issue at the local level.

12.2   The United States Response

In the late 1990s, the issue of trafficking finally made its way to the congressional floor. Introduced in 1999 by Representative Chris Smith of New Jersey, the Victims of Trafficking and Violence Protection Act (VTVPA) became law in October 2000. This law supplements existing laws that apply to human trafficking, such as the 13th Amendment, the Mann Act, and Sections 1581 and 1584 of Title 18, which criminalize peonage and involuntary servitude. In addition to the aforementioned laws that apply to human trafficking, the VTVPA formally criminalizes sex trafficking in adults and children, as well as the unlawful confiscation of a victim's documents (VTVPA P.L. 106-386, 2000). This legislation supplemented existing statutes applicable in many trafficking cases such as human smuggling, kidnapping, prostitution, organized crimes, racketeering, and money laundering.

The U.S. Department of Justice, in conjunction with the Departments of State, Labor, and Health and Human Services, has assumed the primary responsibility in addressing human trafficking in the United States. Together, these agencies established the Trafficking in Persons and Worker Exploitation Task Force. The task force provides a toll-free complaint line where personnel handle initial reports of trafficking and then refer these reports to federal investigators and prosecutors (U.S. Department of Justice, 2002). Trafficking cases are prosecuted by the Criminal Section of the Civil Rights

Division, Department of Justice, which also enforces slavery and peonage statutes. According to the Trafficking in Persons National Security Presidential Directive, the Department of Justice prosecuted 76 traffickers in 2001. As of 2005, there are approximately 125 open trafficking investigations in this agency.

As mandated in the VTVPA, in February 2000, a cabinet-level Interagency Task Force to Monitor and Combat Trafficking in Persons was established by President George W. Bush. This interagency task force has delegated a number of responsibilities: to "measure and evaluate progress of the U.S. and other countries in the areas of trafficking, prevention and protection"; "expand interagency procedures to collect and organize data"; "engage in efforts to facilitate cooperation among countries of origin, transit, and destination"; "examine the role of the international 'sex tourism' industry in trafficking"; and "engage in consultation and advocacy with governmental and non-governmental organizations (VTVPA P.L.106-386, 2000, §105)". Authorized by the task force, the Office to Monitor and Combat Trafficking was established within the Department of State in 2001. The office is intended to assist the task force in collecting data, conducting research, and consulting with nongovernmental organizations and trafficking victims. In addition, the office produces the *Annual Trafficking in Persons Report*, also mandated by the act. This report provides information on the current state of trafficking and includes an individual report on each country in the world for which relevant data is available. Each country is ranked according to the effort it has made within that year to address and prevent trafficking; countries are placed in one of three tiers. In accordance with the act, "countries whose governments fully comply with the Act's minimum standards for the elimination of trafficking are placed in Tier 1. Countries whose governments do not fully comply with those standards are placed in Tier 2, if they are making significant efforts to bring themselves into compliance with the standards, or in Tier 3, if they are not." Tier 3 countries risk the withdrawal of U.S. nonhumanitarian aid (U.S. Department of State, 2002).

The VTVPA also requires an array of services and protection for victims of severe forms of trafficking. The act defines "severe form of trafficking in persons" as:

(a) sex trafficking in which a commercial sex act is induced by force, fraud, or coercion, or in which the person induced to perform such act has not attained 18 years of age; or

(b) the recruitment, harboring, transportation, provision, or obtaining of a person for labor or services, through the use of force, fraud, or coercion for the purpose of subjection to involuntary servitude, peonage, debt bondage, or slavery.

This definition differs from the general definition of trafficking given in the United Nations Protocol (see chapter 1) in that, to be a victim of a severe form of trafficking, one must have endured physical abuse or physical restraint or threat of serious harm from a trafficker or exploiter (VTVPA P.L. 106-386, 2000).

In 2002, the U.S. federal government allocated $10 million to fund service providers and programs designed to assist and support victims of severe forms of trafficking. In February 2003, 12 grants were awarded to victim service providers by the Office for Victims of Crime (U.S. Department of State, 2003). In addition, the Office on Violence Against Women has designated $1 million to provide technical assistance to grantees on human trafficking. Office on Violence Against Women funding "will support training for law enforcement on the investigation and prosecution of trafficking and training for attorneys and advocates on the legal rights of trafficking victims" (U.S. Department of State, 2003).

Current research concerning trafficking prevention and the law enforcement response in the United States is quite limited. Most research focuses on the need to train and reform law enforcement in countries of origin and destination outside the United States (Richard, 1999; Bertone, 2000). Arguments focus on government complacency and police corruption in these countries (Caldwell et al., 1997; Holmes and Berta, 2002). There is a limited amount of literature that does present the steps taken by U.S. federal law enforcement agencies to interdict trafficking and prosecute cases. However, this literature discusses neither the role of local law enforcement in combating human trafficking in the United States nor their responses to and views on human trafficking in the United States.

The Office on Violence Against Women created a funding source for training law enforcement in issues and strategies related to human trafficking. However, this initiative is limited and includes agencies other than law enforcement, such as prosecutors and victims advocates. As such, the International Association of Chiefs of Police (IACP) has become the leading voice for the need to address human trafficking at the state and local law enforcement levels. At the past two IACP annual conferences, roundtable discussions have been held on human trafficking.[1]

In October 2002, the IACP's Police Response to Violence Against Women Project implemented a brief survey entitled, "Police Response to Human Trafficking." The purpose of the survey was to determine whether a department had participated in any human trafficking–related investigations, whether officers had been trained to address issues related to human trafficking, and whether the department would be interested in receiving training on human trafficking. This survey was posted on the IACP Web site, distributed at the 2002 IACP Annual Conference in October, mailed with the IACP newsletters, and provided when any agencies requested any information from the

IACP.[2] The IACP also printed a one-page informational flyer to encourage state and local law enforcement officers to seek information about human trafficking from the federal law enforcement agencies in their areas, and they include the two brochures created by the U.S. Departments of Justice, State, Labor, and Health and Human Services when agencies ask the IACP for information related to human trafficking.[3]

Aside from the recent efforts of the IACP, however, little has been done to educate and solicit the assistance of local level law enforcement. Although the Federal Bureau of Investigation and the Immigration and Naturalization Service have requested the assistance of some municipal police departments in specific human trafficking investigations, little is known about what local law enforcement agencies know about trafficking and about what training initiatives exist on this topic for these agencies.

According to De Baca and Tisi (2002), local police officers are likely to encounter the victims and perpetrators of human trafficking before federal agencies became aware of the situation. The local police are the front line of law enforcement and must be engaged in activities integrated with those of the federal law enforcement agencies. De Baca and Tisi (2002) recommend that local police departments seek out federal law enforcement offices near them to set up working groups to investigate and prosecute human trafficking. Collaboration with others is key to fighting this crime (De Baca and Tisi, 2002).

12.3   Methods

This study is exploratory in nature and seeks to address the local law enforcement response to trafficking in human beings in the United States. It was conducted as a means of raising issues and prompting future research rather than developing conclusive findings. It is viewed as a first step in the development of empirical information concerning this issue and includes an assessment of the following:

- attitudes and perception of the nature and extent of human trafficking in the United States,
- training of law enforcement personnel on issues related to human trafficking, and
- investigative activities of law enforcement related to human trafficking.

Information on local law enforcement perceptions of trafficking and related means of addressing trafficking was collected through the distribution of a mailed survey sent to selected local law enforcement agencies throughout the United States.

12.4   Survey Distribution and Sample

The sample included all municipal and county police departments with jurisdictions of 150,000 or more in population and was drawn from the National Public Safety Information Bureau Directory Data Set for 2001–2002. The final number of agencies included in the sample was 163. These departments were selected as part of the targeted sample for a number of reasons. First, the departments, although not necessarily representative of the population of police agencies in the United States, serviced more than 50% of the U.S. population and therefore have a significant influence on crime prevention as measured by number of individuals served. Second, these agencies, as a result of the size of the population served, as well as the size of the agency, were viewed as leaders within law enforcement in the United States and therefore are more likely to have exposure to and an awareness of a wider range of crime issues than some smaller agencies. Third, these agencies, because of the size of their population, geographic location, and accessibility, were likely to be trafficking destinations or sites that were part of the transit pathway of traffickers and to have had experience with trafficking cases.

The surveys were addressed to the senior manager of the department (i.e., chief, deputy chief, sheriff, superintendent, or commissioner). Cover letters were personalized to the specific manager and signed by the director of the Southern Police Institute. The inclusion of a cover letter signed by the director was used as a means of establishing credibility for the survey through its linkage with one of the preeminent police executive development programs in the United States—that of the Southern Police Institute. This enhanced credibility was seen as a means to increase the response rate and comprehensiveness of survey responses.

The cover letters and surveys were sent together with a stamped return envelope addressed to the Southern Police Institute at the University of Louisville. Respondents were asked to return the survey via mail to the researcher. Most surveys were returned through mail, though some were returned via fax.

In an effort to secure an adequate response rate, follow-up postcards were mailed to each of the 163 agencies approximately 4 weeks after the survey. An early assessment of the respondent pool indicated a substantially lower response rate from agencies located in the eastern portion of the United States. In an effort to increase responses from this region, this area was targeted for follow-up phone calls. Every department in the eastern region that had not returned a survey was contacted approximately 8 weeks after the initial mailing of the survey.

Of the 163 municipal and county police departments surveyed, approximately 85 completed and returned the survey. This final response rate for the survey was approximately 51%.

Of the 163 departments solicited for the original sample, approximately 86% ($n = 138$) were identified in the National Public Safety Information Bureau Directory as municipal departments, and 15% ($n = 25$) were identified as county departments. Among those returning completed and useable surveys, 76% ($n = 63$) were municipal departments, and 19% ($n = 16$) were county departments.[4]

The survey instrument used for data collection contained a number of items designed to gather information on the perception of trafficking and on the related services and training provided to individuals within the law enforcement agency. In addition, some limited information on the agency was collected. Agency information asked for included the number of sworn and civilian personnel and the type of department (i.e., municipal, county, etc.).

Two sets of attitudinal questions were included in the survey. The first set, consisting of seven questions, addressed police agency attitudes toward trafficking. Each question was closed-ended, using a 4-point Likert scale (i.e., strongly agree, agree, disagree, and strongly disagree). Respondents were asked to identify the response item that best reflected the position of the department regarding the following:

- whether human trafficking was currently an issue for local police departments,
- whether human trafficking would be an issue in the future,
- where, geographically, human trafficking was an issue, and
- which law enforcement agency was responsible for addressing human trafficking.

The second group of questions were designed to measure attitude and were also closed-ended, using the same 4-point Likert scale. These four questions were intended to measure agency beliefs about the perpetrators of human trafficking. Respondents were asked to what extent their department agreed that human trafficking is perpetrated by transnational organized crime networks, national organized crime networks, local organized crime networks, and individuals without organized crime connections.

Questionnaire items addressing training were both forced choice and open-ended. The forced choice questions were dichotomous (i.e., yes or no). Respondents were asked whether officers in the department received training on human trafficking, domestic violence issues, and immigration issues, both in the academy and during in-service training. In an open-ended question labeled "hours," respondents were asked to provide the approximate number of hours and type of training the officers received. To determine who conducted the training in human trafficking, this closed-ended multiple response item was used four times, as it was applicable to training received specifically by patrol officers, supervisors, detectives, and managers or command staff.

Six closed-ended dichotomous response items were used to determine whether the responding department had any of the following: personnel assigned to deal with human trafficking, a written policy to guide officers who may encounter trafficking, policies to aid officer response to human trafficking, and policies and services to address the needs of victims of human trafficking. A series of open-ended questions followed each of the six questions to determine dates of policy implementation, list the respective policies and services in existence, and provide additional commentary.

Finally, respondents were asked three dichotomous, closed-ended questions. These questions were: "Has your department investigated any human trafficking cases in the past 3 years?"; "Has your department made any arrests in the past 3 years concerning human trafficking?" and "Would you mind if we followed this questionnaire with a phone call?"

12.5   Postsurvey Interviews

For the purpose of obtaining additional information related to survey responses, phone interviews were conducted with several of the survey respondents following the receipt and review of their completed survey. Departments were selected for interview if they indicated a follow-up call was welcomed, if they had investigated any human trafficking cases in the last 3 years, and if their department had made any arrests in the last 3 years concerning human trafficking.

Interviews were conducted with officers representing 11 of 19 departments, or 58% of this specific group. Most interviews were conducted with the survey respondents, although some were conducted with the person who assisted the respondent in completing the questionnaire (see appendix A for the interview questions).

12.6   Findings

The findings from this survey provided information about the perceptions of local law enforcement concerning trafficking in human beings. The findings, although providing new information, raised more questions and indicated that more in-depth information was needed to guide policy development and that law enforcement initiatives were needed to address this crime.

Table 12.1 Departmental Attitudes Regarding Human Trafficking

Human Trafficking is	Agree (n)	Disagree (n)	Missing (n)	Total (n)
Currently an issue for local police agencies	35% (29)	61% (51)	4% (3)	100% (83)
A significant issue for our department	12% (10)	86% (71)	2% (2)	100% (83)
A problem within our jurisdiction	18% (15)	80% (66)	2% (2)	100% (83)
A problem within the state	40% (33)	53% (44)	7% (6)	100% (83)
A problem within our region of the United States	46% (38)	47% (39)	7% (6)	100% (83)
Best addressed by federal law enforcement	72% (60)	25% (21)	2% (2)	100% (83)

12.7 Attitudes Toward Human Trafficking

Seven items were included in the survey to measure departmental perceptions concerning human trafficking. These items were designed to identify where, geographically, a department believed human trafficking was an issue, whether or not human trafficking would be an issue in the future, and who was in the best position to address human trafficking. Table 12.1 contains the findings for six of these seven survey items. As shown in Table 12.1, almost half of the police agencies (46%) believe that trafficking in human beings is "a problem within their region of the United States," and 40% believe that trafficking in human beings is a "problem within their state." However, although 35% of the agencies view trafficking as a "problem for local law enforcement agencies," only 18% believe it is a problem within their own jurisdiction, and only 12% believe that it is a significant issue for their department.

The perceptions are that, although trafficking might be a problem for other law enforcement agencies, it is not considered to be a problem for the reporting agency itself. Consistent with the attitude that this is not really a local law enforcement problem (61%), the majority of agencies (72%) believe that trafficking in human beings is "best addressed by federal law enforcement."

12.8 Perception of Human Trafficking Perpetrators

Four items are included in the survey to assess departmental perceptions of the types of perpetrators of human trafficking operations. Table 12.2 represents the findings of this assessment. Most of the respondents (75%) agree that human trafficking is perpetrated by transnational organized crime

Table 12.2   Law Enforcement Perceptions of Human Trafficking Perpetrators

Human Trafficking is Perpetrated by	Agree (n)	Disagree (n)	Missing	Total (n)
Transnational organized crime networks	75% (62)	7% (6)	18% (15)	100% (83)
Large national organized crime networks	64% (53)	17% (14)	19% (16)	100% (83)
Local organized crime networks	41% (34)	41% (34)	18% (15)	100% (83)
Individuals without organized crime connections	39% (32)	43% (36)	18% (15)	100% (83)

networks, and 64% agree that large national organized crime networks are the perpetrators of human trafficking operations. In contrast, only 41% of departments believe that local organized crime networks perpetrate human trafficking, and only 39% reported the belief that individuals without organized crime connections are perpetrators of human trafficking operations.

These findings indicate that the local law enforcement perception of the perpetrators of human trafficking is limited and may be more reflective of a sensationalized, media representation than reality. The local law enforcement agencies are more likely to report that trafficking was committed by transnational organized crime than by other forms of criminal organizations or by individuals without organized crime connections.

12.9   Training in Human Trafficking and Related Issues

Several items were included in the survey to determine whether departments conducted or received training related to trafficking in human beings. The training activities were then assessed for four distinct groups of officers: patrol officers, supervisors, detectives, and management or command staff. Overall, only seven agencies (8%) reported that they had conducted or received training in human trafficking. Though the numbers are limited, the percentages of agencies reporting some training on human trafficking do not reflect variations in the prevalence of training based on the rank of officers. Patrol officers (8%), supervisors (7%), detectives (7%), and managers (6%) are reported to have participated in training in equal proportions.

Very few departments received human trafficking training. However, the majority of the departments (96%) do receive training in domestic violence, and a slight majority (55%) have participated in training on immigration laws and issues. Although both of these areas are related to trafficking in human beings, the vast majority of agencies in this sample (94%) had not participated in any specialized training related to this crime.

The average number of domestic violence training hours received by 80 departments reporting participation in this type of training is 18, and the average number of training hours received in the 46 departments reporting immigration training is 4.4. Of the seven departments participating in human trafficking training, the average length of training is 2.5 hours.

12.10 Investigations and Arrests

Approximately 23% of the agencies reported having conducted at least one investigation related to human trafficking in the last 3 years, and 17% reported having made at least one arrest related to this crime. Of the 19 departments that reported engaging in an investigation of human trafficking, 14 (74%) also reported making an arrest related to the investigation. Interestingly, the majority of departments engaged in human trafficking arrests (63%) and other arrests (64%) had not participated in training related to this crime.

12.11 Human Trafficking Personnel and Policies

Agency personnel were asked to respond to questions concerning units or personnel devoted to addressing the crime of trafficking in human beings. Only 4% of the departments indicated that they had personnel assigned to deal exclusively with issues involving human trafficking. However, 37% acknowledged that the department has personnel or a unit whose duties include addressing human trafficking issues or cases.

Various vice, organized crime, crimes against persons, and child exploitation divisions, as well as detective bureaus, are most frequently listed as the units responsible for addressing human trafficking issues. Although 37% of the departments that completed the survey acknowledged the presence of a unit whose responsibilities include human trafficking, 62% do not—these respondents were not aware of a unit in their agency that was capable of addressing issues of human trafficking.

The agencies were also asked whether or not they had written policies related to trafficking in human beings. The majority of the agencies (98%) did not have a written policy specifically addressing human trafficking, though 27% of the agencies have policies that do not specifically address human trafficking. Among these agencies, the majority indicated that policies pertaining to domestic violence, prostitution, and kidnapping can be used to respond to human trafficking. Seventy-one percent of the departments indicated that they do not have any polices that could aid officer response to human trafficking.

Considering the potentially numerous state and federal crimes that often accompany human trafficking (e.g., sexual assault, kidnapping, prostitution, pimping and pandering, drug trafficking, money laundering, forgery, and fraud), most departments should have an understanding of the wide applicability of current policies to human trafficking. At the present time, the data reflect little direct responsibility for the issue and few specific policies to address human trafficking. It is difficult to address a crime that is as complex as human trafficking without some guidance from policies.

Although the majority of agencies (96%) do not have a policy that specifically addresses the needs of human trafficking victims, 46% of the agencies reported that they did have several policies that could assist officers in addressing the needs of the victims of human trafficking. Most of these law enforcement agencies have conducted domestic violence and sexual assault training, and officers are aware of related victim services. Departments noted their ability to offer the social services that are afforded to all crime victims, specifically those provided by victim assistance units; for example, several departments that had conducted investigations referred to using Children of the Night, located in Los Angeles, to assist juvenile prostitutes.

12.12   Exposure to and Perceptions of Human Trafficking

The variance in attitudes toward human trafficking demonstrates a need to further assess factors and experiences that may influence departmental perceptions of the issue. Training and Investigation/Arrest activities were assessed, in relation to attitudes toward human trafficking, in an effort to determine whether or not these factors were related. Although the small number of departments (seven) actually participating in training in issues related to human trafficking invalidates tests of significance, the exploratory nature of the current research provides for the inclusion of these findings. Agencies that had participated in training in human trafficking are more likely to agree with the following statements than those agencies that had not participated in the training:

- Human trafficking is a problem within the region of the United States[5];
- Human trafficking is a problem within the state[6];
- Human trafficking is a problem within the jurisdiction[7];
- Human trafficking is currently a problem for local law enforcement[8]; and
- Human trafficking will be an issue in the future for local law enforcement.[9]

Table 12.3   Training and Attitude Toward Human Trafficking

Agree that Trafficking is a	With Training	With No Training
Problem within region	71%	47%
Problem within state	86%	39%
Problem within jurisdiction	71%	14%
Problem for local police	86%	32%
Future problem for local police	100%	53%

It was also apparent that those agencies involved in training related to human trafficking have a more realistic perception of the perpetrators of the crime. Specifically, more agencies participating in this training reported the belief that organized crime could be perpetrated by local crime networks (71%) and individuals without organized crime connections (57%) than those agencies not participating in training. Among those agencies not participating in training, only 48% believed that trafficking in human beings is perpetrated by local crime networks, and 46% responded that trafficking is perpetrated by individuals without organized crime connections.

Similar to the increased awareness that seemed to follow from participation in training, those agencies reporting participation in an investigation or making an arrest related to trafficking in human beings are more likely to agree with the following statements than their counterparts who had not participated in investigations and arrests related to trafficking in human beings (see Table 12.3):

- Human trafficking was a problem within the state;
- Human trafficking was currently an issue for local law enforcement; and
- Human trafficking would be a problem in the future for local law enforcement.

As noted in the findings related to participation in training and perceptions of the nature of the perpetrators of human trafficking, participation in investigations and arrests related to human trafficking expanded perceptions of the potential perpetrators of this crime. Specifically, those agencies that had participated in training are as likely to believe that human trafficking is perpetrated by transnational organized crime groups (89%) and that human trafficking is perpetrated by national organized crime groups (77%) as are representatives from agencies that had not participated in training (92% transnational organized crime groups and 80% national organized crime groups). However, those who participated in training are more likely to agree that human trafficking could involve perpetrators with local organized crime connections (72%) than those who had not participated in the training (41%). Similarly, those who had participated in the training are also more likely than those who had not participated in training to agree that human trafficking can be committed by individuals without organized crime connections (67% vs. 39%).

12.13 Conclusions and Recommendations

Local law enforcement officers in the United States will most likely be the first officers to come in contact with victims of human trafficking because of the nature of their functions. However, the findings of this research indicate that they are ill prepared to recognize human trafficking victims or investigate this emerging crime problem. Recent analysis of this subject indicates that these victims are hiding in plain sight but that local police usually do not know trafficking when they see it. Furthermore, the operating attitude of police agencies in the United States is that women who sell their bodies do so by choice and that undocumented foreign women are both prostitutes and trespassers into the United States (Landesman, 2003).

Our findings indicate that local police agencies view trafficking as a problem "elsewhere" and for "other" law enforcement agencies. Consistent with the attitudes that this was not really a local law enforcement problem (61%), the majority of the agencies (72%) believe that trafficking in human beings is "best addressed by federal law enforcement."

These findings indicate that the local law enforcement perception of the perpetrators of human trafficking is limited and may be more reflective of a sensationalized media portrayal than of reality, in that local law enforcement agencies are more likely to report that this crime was committed by transnational organized crime than by other forms of criminal organizations or by individuals without organized crime connections. Most law enforcement agencies are unaware of the true nature of the trafficking.

Related to the lack of knowledge about the crime of trafficking, the findings indicate that the majority of the responding departments did not have specific policy, procedures, or training addressing human trafficking. Of the 19 departments that investigated human trafficking, 14 also made arrests. Interestingly, the majority of departments engaged in human trafficking arrests (63%) and other arrests (64%) had not participated in training related to this crime. At present, these data reflect little direct responsibility for the issue of human trafficking.

Trafficking is a global issue, and although some progress has been made, U.S. local law enforcement agencies should join the global community and actively participate in the interdiction and prevention of trafficking in human beings. Specifically, local law enforcement should establish policies, procedures, and training related to trafficking in human beings.

Law enforcement executive leadership establishes agency direction through policy and procedures, which are then reinforced through training. Only after the U.S. police departments make the interdiction and prevention of human trafficking a priority and provide their officers with accurate information concerning the nature and characteristics of this crime will police officers understand the severity and implications of trafficking and the critical role they play in addressing this crime.

Local law enforcement needs to take ownership of this problem; however, the nature of trafficking and its victims also creates a need to form varied partnerships in strategies to address this crime. Local and federal law enforcement, victim support groups, local and federal prosecutors, and social service representatives need to formulate coalitions, task forces, and coordinated community responses to provide the most effective way to address this crime and to assist the victims of this crime. Several specialized national agencies such as the Coalition to Abolish Slavery and Trafficking can be called on to assist in identifying the participants in these coalitions as well as providing materials and support for training and policy development.

Trafficking is an international problem, and the United States will continue to be a major point of destination for these victims. We cannot afford to have local law enforcement intentionally or inadvertently ignoring this problem. However, the promotion of involvement in initiatives to address trafficking in human beings must begin with leadership in law enforcement. It must begin with the commitment of the chief executive officers to set the tone and develop strategic initiatives for their agencies. This will not happen until these leaders have a clear view and a more realistic understanding of the nature and consequences of this crime as well as the significant role that local law enforcement can play in crime control and in the reduction of human trafficking.

Appendix A

Interview Questions

Departmental/officer experience with trafficking investigations:

- How does your department/unit first encounter trafficking operations?
- When are human trafficking operations encountered?
- What types of trafficking operations has your department encountered?
- What are the demographics of the trafficking victims?
- Who are the perpetrators of trafficking in the cases encountered by your unit/department?
- What other crimes are typically affiliated with human trafficking?

How the department addresses human trafficking:

- Who (in the department) is responsible for investigating human trafficking?
- Is the department involved with any other law enforcement agencies for the purpose of addressing human trafficking operations?
- Does the department have or participate in a task force to address human trafficking?
- What departmental policies address officer response to human trafficking?
- Does the department have officers/staff available to translate language should the service be needed in a human trafficking investigation?
- Does the department provide or receive training specific to human trafficking?
- What are the best tactics for addressing and preventing human trafficking?

Notes

1. N. Turn, personal communication, February 5, 2003.
2. Ibid.
3. Ibid
4. The remainder (5%, $n = 5$) were merged city/county agencies and were combined with the city agencies for the purpose of the analysis.
5. See Table 13.3.
6. Ibid.
7. Ibid.
8. Ibid.
9. Ibid.

References

A.M. Bertone, Sexual trafficking in women: International political economy and the politics of sex, *Gender Issues*, 2000, 18(1): 4–18.

J.M. Braun, The girls next door, *New York Times Magazine*, 2003, 30–75.

G. Caldwell, et al. Crime and servitude: An expose of the traffic in women for prostitution from Newly Independent States, presented at the Trafficking of NIS Women Abroad Conference, Moscow, Russia, November 3–5, 1997.

L. De Baca and A. Tisi, Working together to stop modern-day slavery, *The Police Chief*, 2002, 69(1–12): 78–80.

A. Gallagher, Human rights and the new UN Protocols on trafficking and migrant smuggling: A preliminary analysis, *Human Rights Quarterly*, 2001, 23: 975–1004.

P. Holmes and K. Berta, Comparative matrix on legislation and best practices in preventing and combating trafficking in human beings in EU member states and candidate countries, presented at the European Conference on Preventing and Combating Trafficking in Human Beings: Global Challenges for the 21st Century, 2002.

D. Hughes, Introduction. In: *Making the Harm Visible Global Sexual Exploitation of Women and Girls Speaking Out and Providing Services*, ed. D. Hughes and C. Roche, 1999.

International Organization for Migration, New IOM figures on the global scale of trafficking, *Trafficking in Migrants Quarterly Bulletin*, 2002, 1–6.

International Organization for Migration, Temporary resident permits: A new way to protect victims? *Trafficking in Migrants Quarterly Bulletin*, 2003, 1–2.

E. Kelly, *Journeys of Jeopardy: A Review of Research on Trafficking in Women and Children to Europe*, IOM, Geneva, 2002, 11.

P. Lindesman, Collaborations: The key to combating human trafficking, *The Police Chief*, 2003, 70(2): 28–74.

F.T. Miko, Trafficking in women and children: The U.S. and international response, Congressional Research Service Report 98-649 C, 2000, from http://usinfo. state.gov/topical/global/traffic/crs0510.htm#05.

A.O. Richard, International trafficking in women to the United States: A contemporary manifestation of slavery and organized crime, U.S. Department of State, Bureau of Intelligence and Research, Center for the Study of Intelligence, Washington, DC, 1999. Retrieved November 1, 2002, from http://www.cia/ gov/csi/monograph/women/trafficking.pdf.

U.S. Department of State, Victims of trafficking and violence protection act: Trafficking in persons report, 2002. http://www.state.gov/documents/organization/10815.pdf.

U.S. Department of State, Accomplishments in the fight to prevent trafficking in persons, 2003. http://www.state.gov/g/tip/rls/fs/17968pf.htm.

The Challenges of Trafficking in Women and Children in Sierra Leone

13

BRIMA ACHA KAMARA

Contents

13.1   Introduction

This chapter explores the relationship between the nature and extent of the criminal exploitation of women and children in Sierra Leone and the extent to which the Sierra Leone Police (SLP) have the capacity to address the level of criminality that emerged before, during, and after the most brutal civil war in the country's history. The main thrust of this study is the examination of the political climate that allowed criminal exploitation to develop in the first place.

13.2   Literature Review

The criminal justice system of Sierra Leone has an adequate legal code consisting of constitutional law, statutory law, and common law. Sierra Leone is also a signatory to the Universal Convention of Human Rights. In theory, there are sufficient powers for women and children to be able to seek legal redress through the courts in more or less the same way that victims have access to justice in the developed countries of the west. However, the discriminatory practices associated with customary law have been seen to circumvent that process.

13.3   Law

There are three types of law in Sierra Leone: received, applied, and customary law. Received law, also known as adopted English law, is any legislation enacted before 1880, such as the Offenses Against the Person Act (1861), Malicious Damage Act (1861), Highways Act (1835), and Vagrancy Act (1824). Applied law means that English-enacted legislation does not apply in Sierra Leone unless it has been specifically adopted and passed by Parliament and becomes part of the general law, such as the Larceny Act (1916) and Judges Rules (1912).

13.4   Customary Law and Equality

Customary law governs how the individuals in the chiefdoms go about their everyday lives, especially in relation to land law, inheritance law, and family law. Customary law is only applicable outside Freetown in the three provinces, and it varies according to geographical location. The 1991 Constitution of Sierra Leone (Act No. 6) says that all people should be treated equally (Section 27); however, Section 27 also says that it does not apply to customary law. This means that in these regions, there is legal discrimination against women in the areas of marriage, family, and inheritance.

In the provinces, there is a culture of silence reinforced by secret societies, and many people in these remote villages do not want the SLP to investigate criminal cases involving sexual offenses, sexual abuse, or sexual exploitation. The fallacious belief that customary law takes precedent over common law means that there exist "hidden" crimes that are not reflected in the annual recorded crime statistics. The SLP do not know the extent of criminal exploitation in the provinces.

Public law offenses such as rape and unlawful carnal knowledge should be investigated and dealt with in the criminal courts, but many of the victims' families hold the belief that it is the Paramount Chief who enforces customary law and that they must abide by whatever he or she (if it is in the south of the country) says, meaning that some of the senior police officers in the chiefdoms face many difficulties working with these victims of sexual offenses. This adherence to customary law in some ways supports the criminal exploitation of women and children, and marriage and female circumcision also fall within the realm of customary law.

Universal civil law tends to follow the legal age of consent, which, for a civil marriage, in general, is 18 years. In Sierra Leone, however, the legal age of consent for civil marriage is generally held to be 14 years because of the legal element of unlawful carnal knowledge, for which it is an offense to have sexual intercourse with a child under the age of 14 years (Act of Parliament #28). With regard to rape, statutory law says that it is an offense to have sex with any woman 16 years of age. Thus, a child cannot be raped, and there is a statutory law regarding nonconsenting sex with children between the ages of 14 and 16 years. Customary law, however, says that traditional marriages can take place at any age, and it is common for children to be married off at an early age. Female circumcision is a female initiation ceremony that falls within customary law practices unless an Act of Parliament expressly forbids it, as is the case with the Female Circumcision Act (1984) in Britain.

Two pieces of research have been conducted in this area, with findings indicating that women and children are criminally exploited through forced marriages and through a lack of consent in initiation ceremonies and that, within Muslim marriages, junior wives are used for slave labor. These wives are treated as slaves and are expected to undertake all of the kitchen and domestic duties for the senior wives, and because the main industry in the provinces is agriculture, they are also expected to work on the farms. Farm work is manual labor, and their domestic duties are tedious and unrewarding (Nicol, 2000; Fanthorpe, 2001).

13.5   Human Rights and International Conventions

Human rights are generally accepted principles of fairness and justice or moral rights that belong equally to all people simply because they are human beings. Sierra Leone is a signatory to all of the applicable conventions and covenants, but unfortunately none have been enacted into domestic law. The country's 1991 constitution covers the basic human rights of the people, but for specific rights, the constitution is that they are only advisory. Having said that, one of the conditions for receiving international donor aid is that the program for the beneficiaries complies with international conventions.

Sierra Leone is a party to the following five conventions and covenants:

- International Covenant on Civil and Political Rights,
- International Covenant on Economic, Social, and Cultural Rights,
- Convention on the Elimination of All Forms of Discrimination Against Women,
- Geneva Conventions of 12 August 1949, and the
- African Charter on Human and Peoples' Rights

Sierra Leone also has ratified or confirmed its adherence to the following:

- Convention on the Rights of the Child in 1990, and its Optional Protocol on the Involvement of Children in Armed Conflicts,
- Rome Statute of the International Criminal Court, and
- Convention Against Torture and Other Cruel, Inhuman, and Degrading Treatment or Punishment

These conventions and covenants have been implemented because child protection is a worldwide concern, and according to the United Nations Children's Fund (UNICEF) Child Protection Fact Sheet, children are treated abysmally:

- more than 1 million children worldwide are living in detention as a result of being in conflict with the law;
- about 14 million children under 15 years of age are estimated to have been orphaned as a result of AIDS alone;
- approximately 246 million children work, with about 180 million engaged in the worst forms of child labor;
- an estimated 1.2 million children are trafficked every year;
- 2 million children are believed to be exploited through prostitution and pornography;
- at any given time, over 300,000 child soldiers, some as young as 8 years old, are exploited in armed conflicts in over 30 countries, and more than 2 million children are estimated to have died as a direct result of armed conflicts during the 1990s;
- an estimated 100 million to 130 million women and girls alive today have undergone some form of genital mutilation/cutting; and
- 40 million children below the age of 15 years suffer from abuse and neglect and require health and social care

This catalog of unnecessary suffering inflicted on children is why domestic law should reflect international conventions. Child protection processes are directly linked to criminal law, and in the event of overwhelming circumstantial evidence, the burden of proof should be on a balance of probabilities.

The main reason for this phenomenon in Sierra Leone is a less than satisfactory political climate that does not wish to address public concerns over the high levels of corruption surrounding the diamond and mineral mining industry. Those concerns could have been nipped in the bud by the criminal justice system, but instead they were allowed to magnify to such as extent that it enabled a section of society to rebel with such ferocity that hostilities lasted for a little over 10 years (1991–2002). The atrocities on record are some of the worst known in any civil war. Victims of the war were murdered, raped, maimed, and tortured. Young girls were abducted from their own villages to work in the military camps by day and as sex slaves at night. Young boys were recruited into the Boys Brigade and forced to partake of narcotic drugs. The moment they became addicted to hard drugs, they became the dreaded protagonists of brutality.

In addition, when the peacekeepers of the Economic Community of West African States Monitoring Group and the United Nations Mission in Sierra Leone arrived in Sierra Leone, they too sexually exploited the women and children—males as well as females. Even since the war has been declared over those who escaped to neighboring Guinea were held hostage, and the exploitation continued. When the refugees fled back to the safe havens of United Nations High Commissioner for Refugees camps, registration difficulties meant a shortage of rice for some families—a Save the Children report to UNICEF found that aid workers had abused their positions of trust by negotiating sex from young women and girls in exchange for extra portions of rice.

As in many African states at war, poverty is one of the major components of the conflict. Sierra Leone is only a small country, but it is rich in agriculture, fishing, livestock, and mineral wealth—diamonds is one mineral that is generally thought of when Sierra Leone is mentioned, but it is only one of many. The other minerals found in Sierra Leone are gold, rutile, bauxite, and aluminum, and we are now being told that oil has been found in the inshore coastal waters. Yet as a result of the nation's history of postindependence electoral malpractices, failed governments, and corrupt practices, Sierra Leone became like Disraeli's *Two Nations*—the rich and the poor—and the grinding poverty found there was one driver of the brutal civil war.

The Special Court of Sierra Leone is now about to start hearing the indictments made against alleged war criminals, which will increase our knowledge about the extent of trafficking in women and children in Sierra Leone.

The SLP also have faced the challenges of tackling corruption and child labor. Local Needs Policing, made possible through partnership boards, is addressing the concerns of the people in all parts of the country, and a Family Support Unit has been set up to respond to the growing number of sexual offenses reported. Very recently, an integrated Crime Services Department introduced an organized crime unit to stem the rise in cyber and transnational crimes. In addition, the Community Relations Department is working with UNICEF to combat child labor. An individual who is under the age of 18 years is considered to be a child—adults are registered for electoral purposes at the age of 18 years, though state schooling is provided up to the age of 21 years. However, schools, colleges, and universities all were devastated during the war, and the program to restore the infrastructure needed to rebuild the schools has only been running for approximately 12 months, although compulsory education for all children was reintroduced at the end of 2003 (Education Act). Preschool starts at age 3 years, and at 6 years of age, children enter the primary school system for a period of 9 years. However, such is the parlous state of finance in the Sierra Leone education department that schoolteachers' salaries are still not being paid, there is no equipment available for the schools, and schoolchildren must contribute small amounts to the school. In addition, the children are required to wear school uniforms, and girls must have their hair braided. The outcome of this lack of funds is that the children of the poor are not sent to school.

The general law of Sierra Leone allows a child to be engaged in light work at the age of 13, in full-time work at the age of 15, and in hazardous work at age 18 years, which includes working at night (between 8 p.m. and 6 a.m.).

The end result of some children not attending school is that these children wander the streets looking for any kind of work, and they soon become exposed to criminality—generally in the form of drug abuse and sexual exploitation, either by local adults or by transnational traffickers. Some even voluntarily become prostitutes. Those children who do not turn to the streets may be forced to work by their parents. For example, in Sierra Leone, it is traditional for young children to help fetch water and firewood for their families and perhaps feed the animals. In addition, in the mining areas, children help out in alluvial diamond mines. It has to be accepted that children will skip school to work or will work after the school day is over, but to encourage very young children to work for pennies is overt exploitation. The World Bank and the U.S. Embassy do not allow any of their money to be applied where it is known that child labor is used, as child labor exposes children to health risks. Unfortunately, in Sierra Leone, child labor is increasing.

13.6   Public Order Activities and an Abuse of Human Rights

The police are constitutionally bound to keep the peace and are legally responsible (Public Order Act, Act No. 46 of 1965) for policing all activities relating to public order or outbreaks of disorder; this does not include suppressing dissenting views. However, the police did use this power to control governmental opposition and those who held dissenting opinions. Processions and demonstrations held by opposition parties, students, or persons and groups for which the police held no respect were always turned down.

The effect of this misuse of power by the police was that any spontaneous outburst now tends to take the form of heavy-handed violence toward the police. As a result of the tyrannical attitude of the police and the disdainful treatment some dissidents received from them, some citizens have held their anger—waiting for the right moment to retaliate. Some dissidents were tortured and forced to admit wrongdoings, and many of these innocents were sent to prison. When the rebels released them from prison, the rebels were seen as saviors and the freed prisoners immediately wreaked havoc on the police force and anything else that gave them cause to remember what the police had done to them.

13.7   Special Court

One of the main challenges facing the Special Court is ensuring that its activities are transparent. Substantial security concerns have arisen around the arrests and indictments of the leaders and decision makers of the Revolutionary United Front, Civil Defense Force, and Alliance for Patriotic Reorientation and Construction. Some of these security problems result from the fact that the court is located in Sierra Leone, unlike the United Nations' tribunals for former Yugoslavia and for Rwanda, which are located outside the countries of concern.

13.8   Responding to the Challenge of Addressing Criminal Exploitation

The war in Sierra Leone has had a devastating and permanent effect on the nation's children and their families. Children have been forcibly abducted from their families and held in abominable conditions, mistreated both physically and sexually, and denied basic human needs. They have been forcibly conscripted into the rebel military and paramilitary and forced to commit heinous acts against others, often while drugged and undergoing brutal treatment in the hands of their superiors. Girls were captured as sex slaves to serve as "wives" to combatants, who treated them with the utmost cruelty. Children of all ages were separated from their families, in many cases never to be reunited. Many of them have grown up in abominable conditions both in Sierra Leone and as refugees in neighboring countries.

Women and children were exploited before the war started, and they and other segments of the society became aggrieved and lost faith in the formal criminal justice system. As a means of seeking informal redress, they joined the bandwagon of rebellion—they saw the gun barrel as the only means for them to rectify the powerless state in which they found themselves.

13.9   The Way Forward

The war is now over, but the peace is still fragile. If it is to be sustained, then postconflict development must address the criminal exploitation of the poor, which by its very nature includes the exploitation of women and children. Manpower is short—over 350 police officers were killed in the war, and others have died since—and personnel are needed to keep the peace and support police operations. However, recruitment is ongoing, and it is hoped that revenue to pay the police will be generated from the sale of diamonds, rutile, and agricultural products. Strategies have been directed toward dealing with diamond and mineral mining and strengthening the borders, and a new anti–organized crime unit is addressing the trafficking of people, especially women and children, in and from the nation. Sierra Leone is a known transit route for traffickers from Nigeria to Europe, and trafficking is a high-profile issue for the SLP and the West African security services. Recently, the SLP has renewed its membership with the International Criminal Police Organization, and already missing children, taken out of the country under the false promise that they would get a fresh start in Europe, have been traced.

13.10   Criminal Exploitation

The issues of criminal exploitation of women and children in Sierra Leone include the collusion of parents in forced marriages, begging, and child labor. Since Sierra Leone moved into its postconflict phase, followed by the Disarmament, Demobilization, and Reintegration, initial successes were identified, such as when individuals and groups progressively laid down their arms and volunteered for various training schemes. However, the Reintegration component of the process has not had the level of success that was hoped for at the outset. The excombatants have not been reintegrated into their communities, the internally displaced persons have been reluctant to leave Freetown, and inflation has affected the price of food. One of the restructured parts of the SLP is the Operations Support Division, which is a rapid reaction force, or Special Weapons and Tactics team. However, throughout 2003, using due process of law, the division removed 18,000 internally displaced persons who had refused to leave closed camps. This was done sensitively and without gratuitous violence, and there was no resulting spontaneous breakdown of public order.

One of the social consequences of the lack of reintegration is the number of young people who do not have an extended family network with which to support their own families. Parents are now exploiting their own children. This exploitation can be performed in a number of ways, such as sending young children out to work instead of sending them to school, allowing their girls to be taken out of the country to places such as Lebanon as maids, or forcing them into early, often polygamous, marriages.

In the Kono region, where alluvial diamond mining is the most prolific, the area has been compared to the Gold Rush in the Klondike, and Koidu Town, found in the heart of the mining area, can be likened to Dawson City. Working the diamond mines, or pits, is very arduous, but some parents willingly send their children to dig out the pits and wade in the mud looking through sieves for diamonds. If there is no water at the bottom of the pit, they are forced to dig out the gravel and then carry it on their heads to a water source, where they can wash the gravel through the sieves. Even when the children find diamonds, they are not paid their full wage—the license holder, or his or her agent, subtracts an exorbitant amount for the purchase of the shovel, sieves, and pans, plus the children's food and lodging, and the child gets next to nothing for his or her efforts.

In a country as poor as Sierra Leone, it is inevitable that children will work within the system of Local Needs Policing. Since 2001, Family Support Units have been set up to deal with all manner of offenses relating to women and children. Every staff member has undergone extensive training, including how to handle child protection and domestic violence and sexual offenses (see Appendix A). The units were set up as the war was ending, and although the awful experiences the women and children suffered through have been highlighted above, the SLP now find themselves dealing with more and more women and children who present themselves at police stations with appalling injuries, in shock, or lost. The SLP have also been part of stemming the tide of increased transnational crimes. In Sierra Leone, Lebanese traders have run many of the businesses and commercial imports for almost 150 years. Many Sierra Leonean families work in Lebanese family homes as drivers, cooks, gardeners, nannies, stewards, and so on. One common practice is for parents to collude with their Lebanese employers to send their children, usually daughters, to Lebanon to work as maids. On the surface, this sounds like an ideal opportunity for the teenage children to make good and earn a living wage. Unfortunately, this practice is another component of trafficking in children for the purposes of sex industry.

When these young people arrive in Lebanon, the evidence shows that they become sex slaves to the young men in their sponsor's family. Because of the strict Muslim code that many of these families follow, young Lebanese women are chaperoned and are not allowed to be alone with young men until they are married. The frustrated young men of the family sexually abuse the maids almost as soon as these girls arrive in the household. The girls then find it difficult to come back to Sierra Leone. The Lebanese family will also withhold their passport, and the girls' wages are sent back to Sierra Leone to the girl's family, not paid directly to the maids. It is also known that the girls are sometimes introduced to drugs to help them cope with their shame. Some girls who have returned to Sierra Leone are clearly traumatized by the experience, and many have not recovered. They are seen around the community presenting psychiatric tendencies.

The SLP Community Relations Department is presently focused on child labor. They are working with UNICEF and other nongovernmental organizations to combat child labor, especially where hard manual labor is involved. In the diamondiferous areas, the diamond company has instructed its general duty personnel to be extra vigilant with regard to child labor. Reception centers are being set up for the police to take the children for assessment of why they are working. If it is known that their parents are exploiting them, then their case is investigated. At this point, it must be made clear that this strategy is about tackling child labor using very young children. All parents and guardians are being advised about alternative methods of income generation, such as the availability of microfinancing for agricultural projects.

13.11   Children Are Tomorrow's Workforce, not Today's

During the restructuring process, the SLP were also keen to make sure that funds donated were used ethically. The sincere use of donations support the international acknowledgement that a crime of sexual violence is an attack on the physical integrity of the victim and not an attack on the personal dignity of the victim. The United Nations Special Rapporteur on Violence Against Women, Radhika Coomaraswamy, stated that "systematic and widespread rape and other sexual violence have been a hallmark of the conflict in Sierra Leone" (Coomaraswamy, 2000). The number of rapes increased, and some of the nongovernmental organizations, which worked with commercial sex workers, were expressing concern over the number of women being attacked. An additional concern was the age of the girls who were resorting to commercial sex and who appeared to have no careers.

The SLP recognize that injustice was one of the causes of the civil war and wants to work with the victims of all crimes, especially exploitative crimes, to alleviate any grievances that are still festering. To this extent, it would appear that the victims of crime have more confidence in the SLP, as the number of reported crimes for 2003 has increased. Unfortunately, the attrition rate has also increased, and very few assault cases actually reach the courts. Two reasons have been determined to cause that phenomenon. The first is the cost of a medical examination (more than a month's household expenses), and the second is that there are insufficient court sessions, and the backlog is increasing. The SLP have been in consultation with the director of public prosecution and the attorney general about increasing the number of magistrates and local courts throughout the country, especially in the newly accessible areas.

In a country with so many young excombatants on the streets, juvenile justice needs to be addressed to ensure that cases involving young people are dealt with speedily and competently. The Law Reform Commission must work with all stakeholders in the criminal justice system to address the laws that make job of protecting women who are raped or subjected to crimes of violence very difficult.

Appendix A

Aims and Objectives of the Family Support Unit

Aims:

1. To professionally handle matters relating to sexual abuse, domestic violence, cruelty to children, and physical assault on women, children, and vulnerable groups to stop or minimize the occurrence of such offences in our society.
2. To detect, apprehend, investigate, charge, and prosecute offenders of sexual abuse in court and to make sure they are punished by the law.
3. To sustain partnerships with nongovernmental organizations to upgrade the Family Support Unit by providing office buildings and materials relating to Family Support Unit matters.

Objectives:

1. To raise awareness by sensitizing communities with regard to sexual abuse, domestic violence, child cruelty, and physical assault on women, children, and vulnerable groups.
2. To monitor the judiciary for cases of sexual abuse charged to court and to ensure that such trials are conducted in privacy to protect the integrity of survivors.
3. To ensure that women, children, and vulnerable groups are protected from the violence of such crimes.

4. To ensure that perpetrators of domestic violence know the rights of women and children by counseling them on minor assault or by sending them to court for judicial action for major physical assaults, such as wounding or wounding with intent.

References

R. Coomaraswamy, Integration of the human rights of women and the gender perspective: Violence against women, Report of the special rapporteur on violence against women, its causes and consequences on trafficking in women, women's migration and violence against women, 2000.

D. Fanthorpe, Communities formal and informal justice system. Commissioned by the Department for International Development 2001.

V. Nicol, Promoting gender and equality through reform, 2000. Paper presented to the UN Commission for Peace in Sierra Leone, May.

United Nations Children's Fund, UNICEF fact sheet, http://www.unicef.org, 2000.

The Challenges of Combating Trafficking in Women and Children in Nigeria

14

KEMI ASIWAJU

Contents

14.1   Introduction

Trafficking in human beings is a new genre of transnational crime that is ravaging Nigeria, with women and children being the major victims. This crime has recently received a lot of attention in Nigeria, which, like other African societies, has a history of an extended family system, whereby children may be given away to an aunt, uncle, or other relation to raise. There is also the imbalance in the opportunities for self-actualization available to the men compared with those available to the women. Much attention should be focused on women, mainly because of their vulnerability in a society in which laws are increasingly not protecting women.

This study focuses on seven thematic areas. Section one describes and analyzes the transnational crime of human trafficking and explores the different definitions that have been given to the concept. This is followed by an analysis of the literature to date on the issue of human trafficking. Section two analyzes the historical perspective of human trafficking by examining its earliest forms and tracing its development to the current state of affairs from a legislative perspective. This section also looks at the trafficking routes in Nigeria. Section three analyzes the causes of human trafficking, the push and pull factors involved, and other factors that contribute to the growth of human trafficking in Nigeria. Section four is an excursion into the legal framework for combating human trafficking in Nigeria. This section looks at the period before the enactment of the Trafficking in Persons (Prohibition) Law Enforcement and Administration Act 2003, the challenges faced by the law enforcement officials, the framework in place at the time of the prosecution of human trafficking cases. This section also attempts a brief description of the Trafficking in Persons (Prohibition) Law Enforcement Administration Act 2003. Section five looks into the actions that have been taken so far in combating human trafficking in Nigeria, both nationally and internationally. This section also looks at the bilateral agreements made and subregional initiatives taken in combating human trafficking in Nigeria. Section six considers the roles played by law enforcement officials, as well as the likely challenges they face in the enforcement of the law. This section critically examines the antitrafficking units within the Nigeria Police Force, their success so far, and the challenges of interagency cooperation. The role of the Nigeria Immigration Service also is analyzed. Section seven is the conclusion and provides suggestions and recommendations on the way forward for combating human trafficking in Nigeria.

14.2   Description and Analysis of Human Trafficking

Trafficking in human beings, especially women and children, has recently become a global problem that is affecting different communities and countries. Attempts at finding solutions to the problem have revealed that a multilateral approach should be adopted to combat it. In an apparent response to growing concern for the problems posed by trafficking in human beings, the United Nations Convention on Transnational Organized Crime and its supplementary protocols were drawn up in Palermo, Italy, in December 2000 (Luda, 2005).

Although human trafficking is a worldwide phenomenon, analysis of it has been difficult, and its definition is still a bit unclear because it has elements of migration, criminality, morality, and human rights. According to the United Nations, "trafficking in persons for the purpose of prostitution and servitude is incompatible with the dignity and worth of human persons and endangers the welfare of the individual, the family and the community" (United Nations, Treaty Series 1951, vol. 96. no 1342:270).

According to the International Organization for Migration (IOM), trafficking can be said to occur "when a migrant is illegally engaged (recruited, kidnapped, sold, etc.) and/or moved either within national borders or across international borders by intermediaries (traffickers) who during any part of the process obtain economic and other profit by means of deception, coercion, and/or other forms of exploitation under conditions that violate the fundamental human rights of migrants" (Gaycar, 1999).

The Trafficking in Persons (Prohibition) Law Enforcement and Administration Act 2003 defines trafficking as including "all acts and attempted acts involved in the recruitment, transportation within or across Nigeria borders, purchases, sale, transfer, receipt or harboring of a person involving the use of deception, coercion or debt bondage for the purpose of placing or holding the person whether for or not involuntary servitude (domestic, sexual or reproductive) in force or bonded labor, or in slavery-like conditions."

From the above conditions, the following key elements that inform the trafficking process can be determined:

- Recruitment of persons for trafficking either through voluntary or involuntary means;
- Movement or transportation of recruited persons from country of origin to country of destination;
- Traffickers or intermediaries who engage in recruitment, provision of false traveling documents, transportation and sale of trafficked persons to prostitution brokers; and
- Profit making through sexual and labor exploitation that violates the fundamental human rights of the migrant.

Various persons have written about human trafficking, but they have all written from different perspectives. The moral issues with human trafficking follow.

14.2.1 Moral Problem

Trafficking in human beings has been recognized as an evil that needs to be nipped in the bud. Therefore, actions aimed combating and punishing the parties involved can also involve punishing the trafficked person. This is illustrated by the Edo State Amended Criminal code, which punished the trafficked victims. The former head of the United Nations program to stop sexual trafficking said, "extreme poverty in developing nations exacerbates the problem. A policeman who has not been paid in four months will close his eyes to take a bribe" (Luda, 2005), therefore making it easy for the traffickers to smuggle their victims across porous borders as is the case in Nigeria.

14.2.2 Criminal Problem

To control the problem, severe punishments should be introduced, and attempts should be made to improve international police cooperation, leading to more effective prosecution of offenders. The problem is that in the criminal justice process the interests of women are subordinated to the prosecution interests of the state.

According to Richard (1999), "International trafficking in persons to the United States is a significant problem as well as crime affecting men, women and children." Based on the fact that the elements of the crime are about the same in all parts of the world, it can be inferred that it is also a crime that affects persons in Nigeria as well. Women and children are always the prime targets of the traffickers; they also suffer more harm of a different nature and are less likely to be able to defend themselves. The state is more willing to look at the issue of human trafficking from the criminal perspective, and therefore enact various laws and legislations to combat it.

14.2.3   Migration Problem

Some immigration laws can be considered antiwomen because of the methods used to enforce them. These laws are often aimed at keeping women at home by such actions as demanding the permission of their husbands before they are given passports. Stricter border control measures also prevent women from seeking better opportunities outside their homes. The state says that its paramount interest is keeping out illegal aliens, and so a single woman traveling without a husband has a hard time crossing the borders, but male traffickers can pose as husbands to get trafficked women across international borders.

14.2.4   Human Rights Problem

Forced prostitution is a violation of the human rights of the women involved. It has been argued that prostitution on its own does not violate the human rights of the women but that the conditions under which the women are involved in prostitution—deceit, debt bondage, blackmail, and deprivation of freedom of movement—are the real human rights issues.

Radhika Coomaraswamy (Special Rapporteur on Violence Against Women), in a recent report, highlighted the fact that illegal female migrants are placed in a situation of enhanced vulnerability to violence because of a lack of the independent legal protection that is available to those who are documented immigrants. Therefore, when the undocumented or illegal female migrants want to exercise their freedom of movement, they are put in a vulnerable position with regard to the protection of their human rights. In addition, the overwhelming law-and-order approach that has been adopted by most governments in combating trafficking is often at odds with the protection of human rights.

14.2.5   Labor Issue

The poor legal and social position of women in most societies has put them in a disadvantaged position, evident in their being the primary victims of trafficking. Women worldwide are more likely to be unemployed than men, and when they are employed, they often earn less than men. In effect, there are more women in poverty than men, and this fact makes the women vulnerable to traffickers.

14.3   Historical Perspective of Human Trafficking in Nigeria

International human trafficking cannot be said to be entirely new. Its earliest form was the slave trade, which was formally abolished by an antitrafficking legislation introduced early in the 19th century. Capitalism tolerated slavery at its initial stages, but slavery inevitably had to be eliminated because it was incompatible with the principle of free labor. However, recent studies in different areas, including the history of sexual services (Barry, 1995), have shown that there is a historical continuity of slavery and indentureship in its local, regional, and international forms. This means that despite the abolition of slavery, aspects of slavery, and slave-like conditions, still exist.

Human trafficking, as a new form of slave trade, has really grown over the years, and its effect cannot be overemphasized. Although a reliable figure is hard to come by, it has been estimated that each year, about 45,000–50,000 women and girls are trafficked to the United States alone (McKegancy and Barnard, 1996; Richard, 1999), and up to 1 million women and children worldwide (Mirkinson, 1994). The IOM has estimated that of the 100 million migrants worldwide, about 20 million are refugees, and approximately 30 million are undocumented migrants. Relying on the definition of trafficking as postulated by the IOM, it is estimated that of the 30 million undocumented migrants, 4 million are smuggled or sex trafficked, which practice generates an annual revenue of US$5–7 billion (Gaycar, 1999).

14.4   Trafficking Routes in Nigeria

It has been found that persons recruited from the Edo State in Nigeria are transported through the land border in Lagos and Ogun States to the West African subregion, thereafter moving by road or air, depending on the resources that the traffickers have. Below is an itemized list of the frequently used travel routes in Nigeria:

Air

- Lagos → France → Italy
- Lagos → London → Italy
- Lagos → Netherlands → Italy
- Lagos → Schengen borders → Italy

Land/Sea/Air

- Lagos → Ghana (road) → Italy (by air)
- Lagos → Togo → Morocco → Spain → Italy
- Lagos → Togo → Libya → Italy
- Lagos → Togo → Morocco → Spain → France/Italy
- Lagos → Togo → Burkina Faso → Morocco → Spain → Italy
- Lagos → Togo → Burkina Faso → Mali → France → Italy

- Lagos/Benin City → Katsina/Borno → Chad/Niger → Libya → Spain → Italy
- Lagos/Benin → Chad/Niger → Libya → Italy
- Lagos → Togo → Burkina Faso → Mali → Algeria → Italy
- Lagos → Mali → Algeria → Morocco → Spain → Italy
- Nigeria → Benin → Guinea Conakry → France → Italy
- Nigeria → Chad → Libya → Malta → Italy
- Kano → Sudan → Europe (including Italy)

14.5   Causes of Human Trafficking in Nigeria

The causes of human trafficking can be divided into two broad groups involving either push or pull factors. The push factors can be said to be the situations or circumstances that make women and children vulnerable targets of human traffickers.

14.5.1   Push: Poverty

A high rate of poverty is considered to be one cause of human trafficking. There have been arguments from some quarters to the effect that poverty on its own cannot influence a person to be a victim of human trafficking, but it is clear that the effects of poverty do contribute to human trafficking. Take, for example, women with low levels of education or any form of training, either formal or informal. These circumstances leave women and children with no marketable skills, which means that they have fewer opportunities to earn a living.

14.5.2   Push: Economic Hardship

The introduction of the structural adjustment program in Nigeria brought with it some economic measures that affected the standard of living of everybody in the country in one way or another. The increase in trafficking in human beings has been linked to the implementation of this program. In agreement with this view, Hodgson (1995) stated that the implementation of structural adjustment programs imposed by the World Bank and the International Monetary Fund in different countries have exacerbated and fuelled the rapid growth of trafficking in persons for commercial sex exploitation. The effect of these programs is a massive shrinking of the formal economy, which results in massive retrenchment of workers from the formal sector and inevitably leads to an increased population in the informal economy sector and to an increase in human trafficking.

14.5.3 Pull Factors

There are other factors at work to attract people to the countries of destination—mainly Western European countries. Some of these factors include:

1. The desire of women and children to have a better and brighter future, which they believe to be obtainable in the country of destination.
2. The success of people who had been lured into the exploitative process. For example, in Benin City, it has been found that majority of the girls and women trafficked from the city are responsible for most of the privately owned public transportation businesses in the city.
3. The hope for a better life, good pay, and good living conditions, and a hope that these women and children will be able to escape from their victimization.

14.5.4 Organized Crime

According to the definition given in the 1999 Convention Against Transnational Organized Crime, an organized criminal group is "a structured group of (three) or more persons existing for a period of time and having the aim of committing a serious crime in order to, directly or indirectly, obtain a financial or other material benefit" (Ebbe, 2003). In Nigeria, organized criminal groups can be said to have a loose structure involving three or more persons who have little in common except for their criminal intent.

In Nigeria, the structure of these organizations is such that the victims being recruited are aware that the people recruiting them and the madams or sponsors are working together. This is because in most cases, these recruiters are persons with whom the victims have had one form of contact or the other, such as their uncles, aunties, neighbors, and so on.

The madams or sponsors then make forged passports and visas available for the trafficked victims. These documents can take various forms. It might be that the passport photos of the intending illegal travelers are superimposed into the biodata page of a stolen or borrowed passport containing the visa of a genuine valid traveler. Using this format, the traffickers move as many victims as possible during the lifespan of the visas.

The costs of obtaining the visas are as follows:

- US$1200 to borrow a visa, which means once it is used and the victim gets to her destination, the passport is returned to the trafficker to allow another victim to use it;
- US$1500–2000 to buy a stolen visa;
- US$500–1000 to obtain a "look-alike" visa;
- US$200 to bribe a security official.

14.6   Legal Framework for Combating Trafficking in Nigeria

Before the enactment of the Trafficking in Persons (Prohibition) Law Enforcement and Administration Act 2003, persons arrested in connection with human trafficking offenses were prosecuted under the general criminal legislation that was available in the country—the Criminal Code in the southern part of the country, and the Penal Code in the northern part of the country. Because the legislations were not intended to directly tackle the offenses of human trafficking, the offenders took advantage of loopholes in the legislations to wriggle out of their convictions.

The prosecutors were then faced with the challenge of having to prosecute offenders only under the crime-specific sections of the code. This means that elements of trafficking were identified and the offenders were prosecuted only in regard to the crime identifiable. The Benin judicial division, for example, had about 50 cases go through its lower courts from January 2000 to April 2003. The persons involved were charged under sections 516, 419, and 390 of the criminal code. These sections related to the following offenses: conspiracy (where there was more than one offender), obtaining something capable of being stolen by false pretenses, and intent to defraud and steal, respectively.

Other relevant sections of the criminal code are as follows:

Section 223 provides that any person who—
1. Procures a girl or woman who is under the age of 18 years to have unlawful carnal relationship with any other person or persons, either in Nigeria or elsewhere; or
2. Procures a woman or girl to become a common prostitute, either in Nigeria or elsewhere; or
3. Procures a woman or girl to leave Nigeria with intent that she may become an inmate of a brothel elsewhere; or
4. Procures a woman or girl to leave her usual place of abode in Nigeria with intent that she may, for the purpose of prostitution, become an inmate of a brothel, either in Nigeria or elsewhere, is guilty of a misdemeanor and is liable to imprisonment for 2 years.

A person cannot be convicted of any of the offenses defined in the section on the uncorroborated testimony of one witness. Note that the offender may be arrested without a warrant.

Section 224 provides that any person who—
1. By the threats or intimidation of any kind procures a woman or girl to have unlawful carnal connection with a man either in Nigeria or elsewhere; or

2. By any false pretense procures a woman or girl to have unlawful carnal connection with a man, either in Nigeria or elsewhere; or

3. Administers to a woman or girl, or causes a woman or girl to take any drug or other thing with intent to stupefy or overpower her in order to enable any man whether a particular man or not to have unlawful carnal knowledge of her; is guilty of a misdemeanor, and is liable to imprisonment for two years.

A person cannot be convicted of any of the offenses defined in this section on the uncorroborated testimony of one witness.

Section 225 provides that any person who, with intent that an unmarried girl under the age of 18 years may be unlawfully carnally known by any man, whether a particular man or not, takes her or causes her to be taken out of the custody or protection of her father or mother or other person is guilty of misdemeanor and is liable to imprisonment for 2 years.

Note that it is a defense to a charge of any of the offenses defined in this section to prove that the accused person believed, on reasonable grounds, that the girl was of or above the age of 18 years.

Section 225A deals with persons trading in prostitution and provides as follows:

Subsection 1: Every male person who:

a) Knowingly lives wholly or in part on the earning of prostitution; or

b) In any public place persistently solicits or importunes for immoral purposes; shall be liable to imprisonment for two years, and in the case of a second or subsequent conviction, shall, in addition to any term of imprisonment awarded, be liable to caning.

14.6.1   Penal Code

Section 275

Section 275 of the Penal Code provides that whoever, by means whatsoever, induces a girl under the age of eighteen years to go from any place or do an act with intent that the girl may be, or knowing that it is likely that she will be, forced or seduced to illicit intercourse with another person shall be punished with imprisonment which may extend to ten years and shall also be liable to a fine.

Section 276
Whoever imports into the Federal Capital Territory, Abuja, from a country outside Nigeria, a girl under the age of twenty-one years with intent that she may be, or knowing it to be likely that she will be, forced or seduced to illicit intercourse with another person shall be punished with imprisonment which may extend to ten years and shall be liable to a fine.

Section 281
Whoever, in order to gratify the passions of another person, procures, entices or leads away, even with her consent, a woman or girl for immoral purposes shall be punished with imprisonment which may extend to seven years and shall also be liable to a fine.

14.7   Brief Description of the Trafficking in Persons (Prohibition) Law Enforcement and Administration Act 2003

The Trafficking in Persons (Prohibition) Law Enforcement and Administration Act 2003 prohibits and prescribes punishment for traffickers in persons, particularly women and children. It also provides punishment for related offenses. The act also establishes a National Agency for Prohibition of Traffic in Persons and other related matters, vesting it with the responsibility for the investigation and prosecution of offenders and the counseling and rehabilitation of trafficked persons.

The act further provides for the protection of trafficked persons, informants, and information gathered in the course of investigation in respect to an offense committed or one that is likely to be committed. The National Agency for the Prohibition of Traffic in Persons and other related matters has special powers to cause investigations to be conducted, as stated in Section 5(1) of the Trafficking in Persons (Prohibition) Law Enforcement and Administration Act 2003, into whether any person has committed an offense under the act and with a view to ascertaining whether any person has been involved in offenses as determined by the act.

Section 8(1) of the act also establishes the following units within the agency to enable it to function effectively: the investigation, legal, public enlightenment, and counseling and rehabilitation units. The agency may also establish other units with the approval of the Board. In addition, the agency has the power to set up technical committees and task forces to assist the agency in the performance of its duties and functions under the act.

The act further provides, in Section 9(1), that the investigation unit shall liaise with the police for the prevention and detection of offenses in violation of the provisions of the act, and shall work in collaboration with the immigration service, customs service, and other relevant security agencies.

Section 10 of the act provides that the agency may initiate, develop, or improve specific training programs for the relevant law enforcement agents and other personnel of the agency charged with responsibility for the detection of offenses created by the act. The programs include

- Methods used in the detection and suppression of offenses under the act;
- Information on routes and techniques used by persons involved in offenses under the act, and their appropriate countermeasures;
- Assistance in monitoring the movement of trafficking persons; and
- Dissemination of information about the law against trafficking in persons.

However, after the enactment of the Trafficking in Persons (Prohibition) Law Enforcement and Administration Act 2003, which is a more comprehensive law with regard to combating human trafficking, the rate of prosecution has not been very successful. There have been some recent arrests in different parts of the country that are presently before different judges, but there are challenges being faced by the prosecutors. These challenges include the following.

14.7.1   Threat or Use of Violence

The traffickers frequently use the threat of force, which includes torture and rape, as a means of ensuring the compliance of the victims. There is also the threat of using force on the victims' family members and friends in their countries of origin, which in most cases proves to be a very effective means of exercising control over the victims.

In addition, most of the victims travel using false travel documents, which are taken away from them when they arrive at their destinations. This gives the traffickers an edge when they threaten the victims with one form of threat or the other—particularly threats of deportation or of alerting the security officials or law enforcement officials of the victims' illegal presence in the country. The traffickers also threaten the victims by informing them that they work closely with the police—which most of the victims believe.

14.7.2   Debt Bondage

Some of the victims get involved in borrowing money for family members or friends, or they borrow from the traffickers to pay them to process their travel documents. The situation is compounded when the victim arrives at her destination and finds that she does not have the good job she was promised and that the debt still exists and must be paid back. Most times, the debt is between $1000 and $35,000.

For those who owe debts to family members, they usually believe that they have no alternative than to earn the money before they return to their home country. It is common for the initial debt owed to be inflated by the traffickers through charges for accommodation, food, and interest on the loan.

14.7.3   Emotional Attachment

Some of the traffickers also use any emotional attachment the woman may feel for them as a mechanism for controlling her and coercing her to work as a prostitute against her will. Most times the traffickers act as "boyfriends" to the victims. They usually suggest to their "girlfriends" that they move from one country to another for a better life. They also perpetrate domestic violence against their victims, which ensures that the women stay with the traffickers for a longer period of time.

14.7.4   Lack of Alternatives

The victims of this sort of crime usually do not have any alternative to working for the traffickers because of a combination of the factors stated above. Other factors that add to their situation are that they usually do not have any money, let alone enough money to pay for a return ticket home; they are unfamiliar with the country in which they have found themselves; and they may likely not speak the language and have no one to help them. Therefore, they usually feel that they do not have any alternative but to submit to the will of the trafficker.

In Nigeria, since the enactment of the Trafficking Persons (Prohibition) Law Enforcement and Administration Act 2003, the agency created under the act has been grappling with the minimal funds available to assist it set up its departments and for it to commence operation fully.

Case Study

The Ogun State Command of the Nigeria Immigration Services arrested a suspect in 2000 while he was trying to smuggle some female victims across the Nigeria–Benin Republic border and for not possessing valid travel documents. The destination was supposed to have been Abidjan, Cote d'Ivoire. The victims were aged between 19 and 21 years.

One female, aged 21 years, had a primary school education and was trained as a fashion designer. She was recruited by the brother to another victim, who was already based in Abidjan, Cote d'Ivoire. The victim was promised a good life in Abidjan and agreed to travel despite her mother's objections. She paid an initial deposit of 1000 Naira out of the fee of 3000 Naira billed for the procurement of traveling documents.

A second female, aged 19 years, had secondary school education and was a trained fashion designer, and a third female, aged 19 years, was a primary school dropout and an apprentice hairdresser. She entered into debt bondage of 70,000 Naira. She also paid 400 Naira of 2500 Naira to a witch doctor.

The profile of the trafficker himself showed that he had no formal education and had several agents in different parts of the country. He also employed the services of a voodoo priest, who assisted in initiating the victims. This means that the victims were made to undergo a secrecy ritual that most of them believed to be very powerful. This ensures that the victims do not divulge any information if they are arrested, or else they may face terrible repercussions.

Recently, in Cross River State, there was a case of a 27-year-old man who was apprehended for trafficking in children. The man's initial inventory consisted of 24 children—11 girls and 13 boys, aged between 9 and 21 years. The children were all from the same village in Cross River State and were given to the trafficker by their parents, who claimed they could neither feed the victims nor provide for them. The children were being taken to Ondo State to work on plantations there. The trafficker chartered an 18-seat commercial bus at the cost of N35,000 ($250), and the 24 children were all packed into the bus like sardines. The arrangement was that the very young ones would be given away as house servants and the older—and less fortunate—ones were to be sold to the cocoa plantations to tend the dying embers of postcolonial aristocracy. The trafficker, however, failed to let the victims know that some of the girls also would be forced into prostitution.

The police apprehended two different buses within this period, containing a total of 62 persons. It is believed that for every bus that was intercepted, about 10 others may have passed through. Similar to the situation in the first case study, the educational background of the offender was low; in fact, he said he was a farmer.

The challenges being faced by the law enforcement officials include those depicted in the case studies presented here. For example, because the children are trafficked by virtue of their consent, which was received either from the victims themselves or from their parents, it is difficult for the agents of law enforcement to get the full cooperation of the victims, which is needed if there is going to be a successful prosecution of the cases in courts.

The cooperation that the traffickers get from the victim's family also makes it difficult to prosecute. For example, in October 2004, when the program manager of International Labour Organization/International Programme on the Elimination of Child Labour and a team of journalists visited the traditional departure sites of trafficked victims in Oron, Cross River State, the traditional rulers explained that the parents of the victims actively cooperated with the traffickers. They show off their newly purchased clothes as money from trafficking and brag openly to the other villagers about their new source of income. They even boast about the number of children they have given to the traffickers.

14.8   Actions Taken to Stop Human Trafficking

Because trafficking has been recognized as a crime that has to be combated by the concerted efforts of all persons and countries affected, steps have been taken on the international, regional, and national levels to combat this problem globally. There have been various international legislations and platform of action, training, and technical assistance in form of bilateral agreements between different countries, as exemplified by the cooperation between Nigeria and the Italian government. For example, in 1999, the Nigerian Embassy in Italy, with a Note Verbal No 210/99, formally requested administrative assistance from the Italian Ministry of Foreign Affairs for the development of a plan of action for Nigeria to combat both trafficking in human beings and sexual exploitation and to enhance consultation among the law enforcement agencies of the two countries.

At the subregional level, Libreville 2000 (treaty between Nigeria and Gabon to stop human trafficking between the two countries) was a common platform of action for the development of strategies to fight child trafficking for exploitative labor purposes in West and Central Africa. Some of the initiatives derived from the platform of action included that formulation and enforcement of a legal framework aimed at protecting women and children, training and retraining stakeholders and providing a public enlightenment program, and educating members of the public.

The following year, the Economic Cooperation of West African States (ECOWAS) declaration and plan of action to combat trafficking in persons was also rolled out. These various action plans positively affected the training program organized for the Nigeria Police Force and the Nigeria Immigration Service in the past year. Various organizations have organized some forms of training, seminar, or workshop for law enforcement officials. For example, the United Nations Interregional Crime and Justice Research Institute organized a joint training workshop for the senior officers working in the antitrafficking units of both the Nigeria Immigration Services and the Nigeria Police Force. The IOM, in collaboration with the CLEEN Foundation, also organized a 3-day workshop for some of the police investigators working in the antitrafficking units.

This training has had an effect of the attitude of the law enforcement officers, particularly the police officers, involved in investigating and arresting suspected traffickers. There have been series of arrests, and some cases are already in court for prosecution.

On the national level, an antitrafficking agency was created by the Trafficking in Persons (Prohibition) Law Enforcement and Administration Act 2003. Although the agency is still recruiting staff, it is expected that the staff would be seconded from other parts of the government civil service to enable the departments to function. For example, officers from the antitrafficking units within the Nigeria Police Force and the Nigeria Immigration Service have been seconded to the agency.

14.9   The Role of the Nigerian Law Enforcement Agencies

The Nigeria Police Force has created antitrafficking units (ATUs) in different states throughout the country. The main purpose of these units is to investigate and ensure the effective prosecution of human trafficking cases. However, the ATUs are not well equipped enough for them to perform their functions effectively.

For example, the ATUs do not have effective communication equipment with which to liaise with each other units, including the head office in Abuja. This naturally affects the rate at which information passes to the units. In addition, it is difficult for the ATUs to purchase simple items, such as stationery, which in turn affects the investigation processes. As a result, the units only carry out reactive investigation, and not proactive investigation, which could be aimed at preventing trafficking and at breaking up criminal networks or syndicates.

The units also suffer from the bureaucracy with which the Nigeria Police Force has had to grapple: the central authority and the Inspector General of Police. Permission has to be sought and received before any actions are taken, including going on raids.

For the Nigeria Police Force to respond adequately to combating human trafficking, there is a need for the officers to undergo specialized training that relates to the unit's mission. This means that child psychologists, lawyers, forensic investigators, sociologists, and so on should be encouraged to join the ATUs.

At this time, there are at least three offices that are combating human trafficking: the office of the special assistant to the president on human trafficking, the agency created by the Trafficking in Persons (Prohibition) Law Enforcement and Administration Act 2003, and the ATUs. Unfortunately, so much attention is being paid to the new agency that no one seems to be talking about the ATUs anymore. The aim of all the offices should be to work together, which means harmonizing their budgets and resources so that they do not duplicate efforts and thus can achieve better results.

There is also a need for the special training of judicial officers to avoid them frustrating the efforts of the police officers with legal technicalities. The officers also need to be fully educated on the need for victim protection and rehabilitation and on the need to avoid secondary victimization.

The Nigeria Immigration Service is an arm of the law enforcement unit in the country that should also be considered because this crime deals with human trafficking, which involves the movement of persons either legally or illegally, and the Nigeria Immigration Service is responsible for the implementation of the Economic Cooperation of West African States protocols relating to movement of persons.

It is worth stating that the initial stage lacked collaborative effort among the law enforcement agencies because most of the officers were not fully aware of the need to collaborate to achieve their aim. For there to be an effective presence of the law enforcement officials, particularly the police, in tackling the incidence of human trafficking, the following should be addressed.

14.9.1   Environment Needed to Combat Trafficking

The situation in Nigeria should be such that the citizens cooperate with the police in combating the crime of human trafficking. It has been said that for there to be effective policing, the community/society must cooperate with the police.

14.9.2   Prosecution of Offenders

The police have to take decisive steps toward ensuring that investigations into these crimes are carried out in the best way possible to ensure effective prosecution. Trained and qualified officers should be drafted into the ATUs to ensure that they do a good job. Closely following this point is the need for training and awareness targeted at the judiciary—to halt this crime, the police need their cooperation.

14.9.3   Domestic and International Cooperation
between Law Enforcement Agencies

Situations of cooperation already exist; for example, between the Nigeria Police Force and the Italian government. More of this type of cooperation should be encouraged to ensure that no country is working in isolation. All countries should be working toward a common cause and purpose, because the world has become a global village.

14.9.4   Inadequate Funding of Antitrafficking Activities Targeted at Law Enforcement Agencies, Particularly the Nigeria Police Force and the Nigeria Immigration Service

There is need to develop a standard training program that would form part of the curriculum of the officers in the police training schools and in the immigration training schools. However, because of the lack of adequate funding, it is currently difficult to impossible to design such training programs. These programs would assist in exposing the officers to all the elements of the human trafficking and to the best practices for combating it and for investigating such crimes.

The lack of adequate funding also affects the initiation of proactive investigations in the ATUs. At this time, only reactive investigations are being conducted. In addition, there is a lack of adequate data to enable the officers involved to study the trend in the country as a whole as well as examining this crime in different parts of the country. The lack of data has also affected criminological assessment in the units. Therefore, policies being implemented might not really affect the problems and situations found on the ground.

14.9.5   Lack of Equipment and Facilities, Particularly in the ATUs

The ATUs are very poorly equipped. Basic communication equipment such as telephone lines and standard office equipment such as computers, printers, fax machines, and so on are lacking. All high-tech equipment, such as the computers and fax machines presently found in the Lagos and the Edo units (not in use), were donated by the Italian government. The Italian government also donated the buses used to convey the victims of trafficking from the airport to the ATU office in Lagos. Unfortunately, there is also a lack of adequate facilities for the victims. For example, there is no standard reception center. Instead, there are two cells, formerly used for detainees, with about 40 mattresses on the floor. There are also no adequate sanitary facilities.

The IOM personnel in Lagos are always privy to the arrival of victims in the country, so they make themselves available at the airports. They provide sanitary towels, basic toiletries, and pure water (packaged water). The officers in the unit usually complain that they have to buy the bread for the victims from their personal resources with no hope of being reimbursed.

Because of the extreme lack of equipment and funding, it is no surprise that the officers in the units cannot effectively relay information to one another.

14.10   Conclusion

It is appropriate to say that trafficking in human beings, especially women and children, is a criminal activity that needs to be fully addressed. It would be more effective if the crime were not only combated as a transnational crime but also tackled as a social problem.

That is, if the members of the public or members of the societies in which trafficking thrives are made to see that the dangers that their children and wards face are too grave, and that the traffickers actually exploit the children and their families, they would be motivated to join in the prevention efforts. There have been situations of open confrontation with nongovernmental organizations that try to educate the masses on the evil effects of trafficking and the dangers that the victims face. The consequences of trafficking—such as contracting sexually transmitted diseases or AIDs, physical and psychological abuse, and at times death—should be explained to the masses.

To make trafficking seem unattractive to its potential victims, the government must be ready to itself provide opportunities that would give potential victims a better life. This requires the cooperation of members of the public and for them to see the issue as a menace and not as an issue to boast about.

The fact that women and children are vulnerable groups in society and lack adequate protection of their rights within the state contributes to the rate at which trafficking in women and children has been increasing in Nigeria. There is a need for the Nigerian president to sign the Children's Rights Bill into law.

There is also a dire need for a comprehensive and critical evaluation of the ATUs to get a clear analysis of the needs of the units, which will help us present a plan to stakeholders that would provide a form of support to the units in carrying out their duties. In addition strong support of the ATUs will ensure that they are well enough equipped to collaborate with other agencies in combating human trafficking in Nigeria.

References

K. Barry, *The Prostitution of Sexuality: The Global Exploitation of Women*, New York University Press, New York, 1995.

O.N.I. Ebbe, Slicing Nigeria's "national cake," In: *Menace to Society: Political-Criminal Collaborations around the World*, ed. Roy Godson, Transaction, New Brunswick, 2003.

A. Gaycar, Trafficking in Human Beings, presented at the International Conference of Migration, Culture and Crime, Israel, July 7, 1999.

D. Hodgson, Combating the organized sexual exploitation of Asian children: Recent developments and prospects, *International Journal of Law and the Family*, 1995, 9(1): 23–53

Human Rights Watch, *The Human Rights Watch Global Report on Women's Rights*,
    Human Rights Watch, New York, 1995.
S. Luda, Human trafficking: UN expert on trafficking in persons end visit to Leba-
    non, presented to the World Press, 2005.
N. McKegancy and M. Barnard, *Sex Work on the Street: Prostitutes and Their Clients*,
    Open University Press, Buckingham, 1996.
J. Mirkinson, *Red Light, Green Light; the Global Trafficking in Women,* Breakthrough,
    Prairie Fire Organizing Committee, Washington, DC, 1994.
A.O. Richard, International trafficking in women to the United States: A contemporary
    manifestation of slavery and organized crime, U.S. Department of State Bureau
    of Intelligence and Research, Center for the Studies of Intelligence, 1999.

Operational Perspective on Trafficking in Women and Children in the United Kingdom

15

WILLIAM HUGHES

Contents

15.1 Introduction

This chapter looks specifically at the operational response in the United Kingdom to the criminal enterprises involved in trafficking of women and children. Although it sets an overall context for the issue, this chapter largely provides an operational perspective.

In common with its European partners, the United Kingdom believes that there has been a rise in the trafficking of women and children over the past few years. What is unclear is the scale of the rise and the current level of activity. Much of the information acquired to date has been patchy and anecdotal.

In 2000, a Home Office study, "Stopping Traffic: Exploring the Extent of, and Responses to, Trafficking in Women for Sexual Exploitation in the UK," concluded that there were no accurate estimates available either nationally or internationally. The authors identified 71 women known to have been trafficked into prostitution in the United Kingdom in 1998 but added that there was a hidden trafficking problem several times greater than they were able to document with certainty. They were, however, able to estimate that the scale of trafficking of women into and within the United Kingdom lay within the range of 142 and 1420 women per year.

The issue of trafficking of children to the United Kingdom came to prominence in the mid-1990s, when an investigation focused on unaccompanied children arriving from West Africa who were thought to be in transit to other European countries. Monitoring of the routes used highlighted a small but steady flow of children to the United Kingdom. This case aside, there are no reliable data showing that trafficking in children is a significant issue in the United Kingdom.

In London, police noticed a rise in foreign nationals involved in off-street prostitution. A snapshot survey carried out in 1999 indicated that in some sectors of the vice trade, notably off-street prostitution, foreign nationals made up a significant majority of the prostitutes. Recent intelligence confirms this result.

More recently, a successful operation against a trafficking ring offered insight into the potential scale of the problem. The arrest of the main trafficker in one organization uncovered an operation that had trafficked 60 women into the United Kingdom from Eastern Europe, mainly from the rural parts of Moldova and Romania.

Assessments are currently underway to provide an updated profile of this sector in the United Kingdom and to fill the gaps in the intelligence picture. Among the obstacles faced are:

- Underreporting of the offense by those encountering trafficked victims because of a lack of awareness of the problem;
- Lack of reporting by victims themselves for fear of reprisal by traffickers; and
- Confusion in identifying those trafficked from those who have willingly been facilitated and from those children who have arrived unaccompanied for immigration purposes. Understanding these distinctions is crucial to establishing the true nature and scale of the problem. Wrongly classifying individuals can lead to an inappropriate level of response.

Despite these gaps, the organized trafficking of women and children is now recognized as a major threat to the United Kingdom. The 2003 U.K. threat assessment places organized immigration crime high on the list of major threats and identifies human trafficking as arguably the most acute threat within this category because of the continuing exploitation involved and the frequent use of intimidation and violence in the commission of this crime.

15.2   Nature of Trafficking in Women and Children in the United Kingdom

Operations and assessments undertaken point to sexual exploitation as the predominant type of trafficking taking place in the United Kingdom, although other purposes have been encountered. The increase of foreign nationals identified in the off-street prostitution trade in London is beginning to spread to other major metropolitan areas. Although Eastern European nationals have figured heavily in trafficking and prostitution operations to date, the actual spread of nationalities is extensive. Those encountered include nationals of Albania, Bulgaria, China, Croatia, Lithuania, Latvia, Moldova, Nigeria, Pakistan, Romania, Russia, Somalia, Sri Lanka, Thailand, Turkey, and Vietnam.

It is not uncommon to identify women who have previously worked in the vice trade in other countries before their arrival in the United Kingdom. The movement of women across national boundaries and from the vice trade perhaps gives a glimpse of the level of organization involved.

The recent dismantlement of a London-based trafficking ring offers a clearer picture of how the traffickers operate. The main trafficker recruited girls from rural areas in Moldova and Romania and lured them to United Kingdom with promises of employment and money. Once in the United Kingdom, the girls were supplied to brothels to begin paying off the debts incurred by bringing them to the United Kingdom. The trafficker even married one of the girls to secure her earning potential, but she was required to work at the brothel on her wedding night. It was claimed that assault and rape was used to ensure that the trafficked women met their target incomes. The full extent of the trafficker's income has yet to be established, but several bank accounts found already indicate an income of in excess of £1m. His activities came to light when two of the women he trafficked escaped from his control.

Although sexual exploitation is the most common form of human trafficking encountered in the United Kingdom, other forms do exist. The use of women and children to partake in street crime such as aggressive begging and pickpocketing is not a new phenomenon. However, only anecdotal information indicates that women are being trafficked to the United Kingdom to provide this service for criminal enterprises.

Labor exploitation is yet another form of trafficking that affects women, children, and men. There has been little evidence of serious and organized criminal activity in this field beyond the organized use of illegal labor in service industries such as hotels and catering. However, labor exploitation is an area that will be covered by legislation.

Perhaps the most pernicious example of human trafficking to come to light so far in the United Kingdom involves an ongoing investigation into the discovery of a child's dismembered torso in the River Thames. The assertion that the child was brought to the United Kingdom from West Africa as part of a ritual sacrifice is being seriously pursued by the investigation team.

Worldwide, trafficking routes are numerous and include the United Kingdom as a transit point as well as a final destination for trafficked women and children. Traffickers are well resourced and flexible and are able to change their travel routes and *modus operandi* quickly in response to increased measures taken against them. Circuitous air routings to avoid enforcement measures are commonplace, and the deception of visa staff—or the immigration officer on arrival—is a favored method of traffickers bringing small but regular numbers of women and children to the United Kingdom. Concealment in vehicles, the preferred tactic of the volume smuggler, is also used.

15.3 Contributors to Human Trafficking

The trafficking of women and children is not a new phenomenon. What has changed over recent years is the scale of the crime in terms of the number of individuals involved and the sheer geographical spread of the problem. Trafficking has become a global phenomenon fed, in part, by an increasing demand within commercial vice trades. There are many reasons—some causal and some that facilitate this practice—many of which are linked:

- Availability of cheap travel and the opening of previously closed borders have led to an increase in the geographical spread of trafficking;
- Poverty and deprivation still provide the economic spur to trafficking. It is here that distinctions between trafficking and smuggling merge— the desire for economic betterment (not necessarily for the victim but for the extended family) remains a powerful push factor;
- Victims' poor education and lack of awareness can enable the trafficker to deceive victims with the lure of a better life;
- The involvement of organized crime, driven by profit, means that the victim becomes a commodity;
- Globalization of business allows criminal enterprises to operate internationally;
- Technological advances—the development of the Internet and other communications systems enables traffickers to respond quickly to demands;
- Weaknesses in legislation and procedures that enable traffickers to operate in jurisdictions where they can not be prosecuted and, if they are caught, provide little deterrent in terms of penalties;
- Lack of international cooperation between source, transit, and destination countries negates both individual and nongovernmental organization efforts;
- Lack of domestic cooperation between law enforcement agencies can lead to the problem falling through the gaps with no clear lines of responsibility and accountability;

- Lack of resources coupled with insufficient priority accorded to tackling the problem can lead to any available capability being used on other problems;
- An increase in irregular migration can provide a screen for the activities of traffickers, making it more difficult to distinguish the victim of trafficking from a smuggled migrant;
- Political/religious upheaval is another driver whereby a vulnerable population will take risks to escape their current predicament; and
- Mass population movements bring with them differing demands and provide further opportunities for criminal gangs to exploit their victims.

15.4   Strategies to Counter Human Trafficking

It appears clear that any response to counter trafficking in human beings requires a strategy that includes

- A strong legislative footing;
- Support to victims;
- A multiagency operational response that relies on intelligence-led policing;
- Preventative and reduction strategies; and
- Strong overseas partnerships.

The United Kingdom has developed a multiagency and multilateral approach that addresses each of the above five areas.

The United Kingdom is a signatory to the United Nations Protocol on Trafficking that supplements the United Nations Convention on Transnational Organized Crime. A subsequent European Union (EU) Framework Decision covered trafficking for sexual and labor exploitation and was adopted in July 2002. It commits EU member states to introducing criminal sanctions covering trafficking for sexual and labor exploitation within 2 years of its adoption. The framework decision also sets EU-wide maximum penalties of 8 years imprisonment for these offenses.

The Nationality and Immigration Act 2002 introduced a stopgap offense of trafficking for the purpose of controlling a person in prostitution with a maximum penalty of 14 years. This offense came into force on February 10, 2003. More comprehensive offenses for trafficking into, within, or out of the United Kingdom for the purposes of sexual exploitation have subsequently been included in the Sexual Offenses Act 2003 with a 14-year maximum penalty. This inclusion is expected to come into force in 2005. In addition, the offense of trafficking for the purpose of exploitation, including forced labor and organ removal, is included in the Asylum and Immigration Bill currently before parliament.

One of the main challenges in combating human trafficking lies in providing support to victims. Traffickers can secure the noncooperation of victims toward law enforcement with threats of violence, reprisals against their families back home, or exposing their often-illegal residence status.

The United Kingdom has been pursuing various options to ensure that victims of trafficking are properly supported. This includes looking at assistance to allow them to escape their circumstances and, in certain cases, to help law enforcement in the fight against organized criminals. When they are willing to come forward to the authorities, special arrangements for their protection may be made. It is also considered whether it would be appropriate to allow them to remain in the United Kingdom.

The U.K. government is working with the International Organization for Migration to establish a return policy for victims who are not entitled to remain or who wish to return to their country of origin. This will help ensure that those who return home are helped to reintegrate into their own communities.

In addition, a scheme for adult victims of trafficking has been introduced involving the use of a voluntary organization with considerable experience of providing specialist housing to victims of domestic violence and other vulnerable women.

Recognizing those who may have been trafficked is an essential element of any strategy. The United Kingdom has recently published a trafficking toolkit that provides a best practice guide for immigration officers, police, and others who potentially may come in contact with victims of trafficking. In particular, it seeks to raise awareness of the difference between trafficking and smuggling and to help those involved treat victims fairly.

However, providing refuge to trafficking victims and legitimizing their immigration status may not be sufficient to persuade victims to provide evidence against the traffickers. The United Kingdom is considering whether it is possible to develop a victimless strategy to investigating human trafficking. That is, a strategy that does not rely on the evidence of victims to prosecute or disrupt the traffickers. The basis of such an approach lies in intelligence-led policing and proactive, rather than reactive, investigations. Disruption also forms part of the strategy—finding the weak spot in an organization to target and using the widest possible range of legislative and administrative tools to do so. These tools may include financial investigation, asset seizure, and the use of administrative immigration powers.

The United Kingdom also has developed and implemented a National Intelligence Model, providing a model for intelligence-led policing across law enforcement. At the heart of the system is a series of analytical products that enable the setting of priorities through a tasking and coordinating process. It also provides for policing to be focused at different levels from local issues up to serious and organized international crime. All U.K. law enforcement agencies are adopting the system, thereby increasing linkage and commonality of approach.

In 2000 the United Kingdom developed a multiagency operational response to tackle organized immigration crime. Known as REFLEX, this multiagency approach brings together law enforcement, the intelligence community, and government departments under a common strategy and shared objectives. It is chaired by the director general of the National Crime Squad, the operational police organization responsible for spearheading the fight against serious and organized crime.

REFLEX is responsible for tackling all aspects of organized immigration crime. Its overall aim is to reduce the harm caused by serious and organized criminality involved in people smuggling and human trafficking by

- Raising the risks that the criminals must take;
- Rendering their illegal businesses unprofitable; and
- Reducing their opportunities to exploit communities.

Led by intelligence, REFLEX operational and preventative measures target those crime groups involved in

- The volume facilitation of illegal migrants;
- Human trafficking (in particular the trafficking of women and children); and
- Running the criminal infrastructures that serve both to facilitate illegal entry and to exploit the illegal population once in the United Kingdom.

Building on the National Intelligence Model, REFLEX has developed systems in which agencies share intelligence on traffickers, jointly consider the best tactics for disruption, and decide who is best placed to carry out the operation. The strength of such an approach lies in the varied backgrounds, expertise, and resources that different agencies bring to the table. It requires individual agenda and culture to be set aside, which is an achievable outcome providing that all agencies share in the success of operations.

This cooperation extends to joint operational teams, in which police officers work alongside immigration officers. This is an innovative approach considering that immigration officers in the United Kingdom are civil servants and are not taken from a police background.

Wherever they operate, traffickers are motivated by profit. Identifying and seizing assets, disrupting the underground money flows, and making it unprofitable for the gangs to operate form a major plank of the U.K.'s approach. However, the realization of profits from organized immigration crime does not always rely on selling a commodity at the end of the process.

Effective action requires the successful blend of existing expertise with new thinking and tactics.

Targeting trafficking feed into the U.K.'s wider strategy on asset recovery that aims at

- Making greater use of the investigation of criminal assets in the fight against crime;
- Recovering money that has been made from crime or that is intended for use in crime;
- Preventing criminals and their associates from laundering the proceeds of criminal conduct and detecting and penalizing such laundering where it occurs; and
- Using the proceeds recovered for the benefit of the community.

Financial investigators are therefore being allocated to immigration crime teams, and a central REFLEX money-laundering unit targets sophisticated illegal money flows that support trafficking and other forms of organized immigration crime.

However, REFLEX is not only about developing operations against traffickers and facilitators. Under its banner, a number of overseas partnerships have been developed leading to systems and procedures being introduced or strengthened to help tackle trafficking at its sources or along the transit routes. This in turn serves to reduce opportunities that the traffickers can exploit.

A particularly good example has been REFLEX Romania, in which a partnership with colleagues in Romania has developed a unit based in Bucharest to disrupt illegal migration and trafficking flows from and through Romania and its neighboring countries. The creation of a central intelligence unit has led to a significant number of arrests and disruptions. During its first phase of operational activity, 105 criminal groups operating in this sector were identified, 48 were disrupted, and 90 individuals were arrested in relation to immigration or trafficking offenses.

A slightly different focus was used in partnership working with Italian, Serbian, and Montenegrin colleagues. The main achievements in this project, known as IMMPACT 2, has been to build strategic working relationships with Serbian and Montenegrin colleagues and to provide specialist training on passenger analysis, forgery, and antitrafficking measures, the latter delivered in conjunction with the IOM.

Under REFLEX, the United Kingdom continues to develop overseas partnerships, with projects in Bulgaria and Macedonia also currently underway. In addition, a network of overseas liaison officers specializing in organized immigration crime, including human trafficking, has been introduced to develop and sustain joint working with overseas partners.

15.5   Issues of Interest

This chapter outlines the United Kingdom's operational approach to tackling human trafficking. It does so from the perspective of considering human trafficking as part of the threat faced by serious and organized immigration crime.

Most countries now agree that we face a significant threat from criminal gangs that are involved in human smuggling and trafficking and that are increasingly sophisticated, well funded, and flexible. Organized immigration crime is a big business, and though it has brought new criminal groups to the forefront, it has also seen other groups switch from other commodities with routes, safe houses, and transportation that can all be used and from which acquired skills in forgery, counterfeiting, and money laundering can all be transferred. Although there are gangs who offer and operate an end-to-end service, our increasing knowledge reveals many loose alliances providing specialist services to move the human cargo up the chain.

The fight against human trafficking is not being well waged. We have laws, rules, regulations, and procedures to follow, and it can take months—even years—for us to achieve a change in policy. However, flexibility is critical if we are to make any headway. We must exploit any weakness, think laterally to disrupt the traffickers' activities, target their finances, and use an intelligence-led approach. Critically, we must avoid playing into their hands by creating further internal barriers that restrict our actions.

The U.K.'s position is that trafficking in human beings and people smuggling can often provide two strands of an organized immigration crime group and that a joint strategy that recognizes and acknowledges the key distinctions is the most appropriate way forward. Otherwise, there is a danger of a silo mentality developing, with multiple strategies in place that allow traffickers to exploit differences in approach.

The distinctions between the two areas of criminality are clear in a legal sense. Trafficking is more of a victim-focused crime than illegal immigration, and as a result, how victims of trafficking are identified, handled, supported, and if appropriate, returned, does need careful and separate consideration. This is recognized in the Protocol on Trafficking under the United Nations Convention against Transnational Organized Crime.

Trafficking in human beings also encompasses various forms of exploitation. Although human trafficking for sexual exploitation may be considered the most significant current threat to the United Kingdom, trafficking for labor exploitation and other forms of abuse cannot be overlooked. Although intelligence on this latter area is limited, it is nevertheless important to recognize that the source countries for trafficking for labor exploitation may not be the same as those for sexual exploitation.

It has been recognized that human trafficking is not wholly an immigration offense. Although it is true that trafficking does not necessarily have to involve a border crossing, the number of those trafficked within the United Kingdom is likely to be a small proportion of the total number of immigrants. It is more likely that they will have been either smuggled or deception deployed to secure entry.

It is tempting to portray traffickers and human smugglers as belonging to two separate criminal groups, and there are criminal elements that do distinguish one from the other—typically the exploitative elements. However, this presupposes that those involved control the whole process from beginning to end. Certain groups do exist that have the capability to do this. However, it is equally clear that this area of criminal activity is moving beyond the family business operated along strictly ethnic lines. Mixed commodities of several nationalities are increasingly common, as are loose alliances of different criminal groups offering different specialist services. Elements of the trade such as transportation, production of false documentation, harboring at transit points, and so on are being provided by specialists operating as subcontractors to the main traffickers. These criminals are motivated by profit and are unlikely to be concerned about the ultimate fate of the human "commodity." This provides common ground for taking operational action against both sectors.

Although trafficking is considered to be a more heinous crime than smuggling, it is, nevertheless, inappropriate to consider those involved in smuggling as providing a form of legal service. They are serious criminals, motivated by greed, and seek to use the humanitarian issues surrounding migration as a veil for their criminal behavior.

It is also not appropriate to believe that the relationship between a smuggler and a smuggled migrant ends once the person has reached his or her destination country. Unless the migrant has paid in full, in advance, the smuggler will invariably continue to exert control until the balance is paid. In such circumstances, does the smuggler become a trafficker and the migrant a victim of trafficking?

There is a significant difference between a victim who has been trafficked and a migrant who has been smuggled. In legal and procedural terms, they require separate handling once they have been identified. However, in operational terms, especially where proactive intelligence-led investigations are being planned, the status of the human commodity may not be readily identifiable from the outset.

If the recruitment of the trafficked persons is carried out by force, then the situation is clear from the outset. However, many of those who end up as victims of trafficking begin their journey in search of a better life and to provide money for the family they left behind. Either at the outset or at some point in their journey, they are deceived and find themselves working, for example, as a prostitute without any control over their earnings or workload. Indeed, they may have worked in the vice trade in their own country and may have known that they would be doing so in the destination country. Nevertheless, they find themselves being subjected to inhumane treatment. A similar scenario applies to those who are promised work in sectors other than the vice trade.

This blurring of motivation and consent makes it extremely difficult to separate the two issues at the outset of an investigation or even when an investigation is underway. Any operation must be intelligence-led and based on solid crime analysis with a clear strategy to counter identified threats. At the center of this approach should be an operational task group charged with managing activity and ensuring that intelligence flows are maintained. This approach supports the National Intelligence Model that U.K. law enforcement is developing to ensure a more proactive method for preventing and detecting crime.

Human trafficking is a serious organized crime. Operational activity against serious organized crime must focus on the criminal rather than the sector or commodity if it is to stand any chance of matching the flexibility the criminals demonstrate.

The Role of Community Policing in Trafficking in Women and Children in Australia

16

JOHN MURRAY

Contents

16.1 Introduction

The former United Nations (UN) Secretary-General Kofi Annan described trafficking in women for sexual slavery as "one of the most egregious violations of human rights" (Annan, 2000). It is clear, too, that responsible countries are unequivocal in regarding this abhorrent criminal activity as a priority public policy issue. As with any complex sociolegal issue, however, how to deal with the problem invites many different points of view. The provision of severe sentences, although entirely appropriate, by themselves will have minimal effect on the situation, especially given the historically low prosecution rate. Obviously, relentless pursuit of offenders is critical, but a more challenging and responsible approach would expend equal energy on understanding the problem and its source than on taking preventative measures.

In line with this, and consistent with the UN protocol that regards women and children as victims, it is incumbent on a country/society to have a public policy that embraces the rights, privileges, and sensitivities to the plight of the victim and to be committed to the restoration of the victims' place in society. At a more pragmatic level, such a progressive victim support process would be more likely to encourage these trafficked women and children to provide valuable information that may lead to the prosecution of the transnational criminals who ply this trade.

The war on terror (following September 11, 2001) had the propensity to have police return to traditional forms of policing with a consequent reversion to paramilitarism (Murray, 2003). This had the potential to distance the police from the rest of the community and to undervalue the principles of community policing, with their emphasis on prevention. This chapter offers the same caution—that in the current environment, community policing is under threat. The abolition or diminution of community policing as a philosophy will adversely affect investigations into the criminal exploitation of women and children. Put another way, the principles of community policing will be more conducive to dealing with the issue because they rely on strong community relations, creative problem solving, and most important, they draw on the police/community relationship to gauge what is exactly happening in the community.

This research sets out to do the following:

- consider the extent of the problem of criminal exploitation of women and children in Australia;
- examine the relevant policies, laws, and processes;
- evaluate prevention and investigation in the context of community policing and the rights of the victim; and
- conclude that traditional policing models, which are largely confrontational at a community level, are likely to be counterproductive but that community policing provides not just a sound ethical base from which to work but also a more effective solution.

16.2   Australia in Relation to the Rest of the World

The island of Australia is located in the southern hemisphere and is geographically one of the largest countries in the world, only slightly smaller than the United States of America. Papua New Guinea and Indonesia lie to the north, and Australia is bordered by the Indian Ocean on the west and the Pacific Ocean on the east. This isolated location has spared Australia many problems experienced by other countries. It has a population of over 18 million, with more than 75% of its citizens living in the eastern states of New South Wales, Victoria, and Queensland. It is also one of the most urbanized countries in the world, with over 85% of its population living in a major capital city or regional center.

Australia's legal infrastructure is both federal and state/territorial, with the commonwealth and state/territorial governments each having law enforcement responsibilities. Laws enforced by the commonwealth are specified within the Australian Constitution (including immigration, drug importation, money laundering, and people smuggling), and the states/territories have the responsibility for all remaining areas (such as property crimes, violence crimes, personal crimes, and conventional community crimes).

Australia has eight police services comprising around 50,000 personnel. The majority of these officers (approximately 46,000) work for the state and territory police, and the remaining 4000 work with the Australian Federal Police (AFP). These police services are complemented by other commonwealth regulatory and revenue agencies, including the Australian Taxation Office, and the Australian Securities Commission. To facilitate cooperation and focus for the intelligence gathering and investigation of national and international crimes affecting Australia, a number of national and interjurisdictional forums have been established, including the Australian Crime Commission. The commission can use its coercive powers to summon witnesses before it and can also compel the production of documents from people and institutions.

16.3   People Trafficking in Australia

Australia is an attractive destination for traffickers mainly because of its geographic proximity to Southeast Asia, where organized crime groups are known to target women and children for the purpose of sexual servitude (Edwards, 2003). Relating to Thailand, for example, Frances (2003) notes that:

- Initially, Thai women started coming to Australia in the mid-1980s to work in the sex industry and meet the high demand for "exotic" sexual partners;
- Most of these women came from the economically depressed rural areas of north/northeast Thailand;
- Many of these women remitted money to family in Thailand—50% were supporting children as well as siblings, parents, and extended family; and
- Women became vulnerable to extortion from those who contracted them—they were subjected to threats against themselves and their families, and there was a move to chaperone them, which in effect would close them off from outside life.

For many reasons, estimates of the true extent of the incidence and nature of human trafficking for commercial sexual exploitation in Australia today (as in most countries) is impossible to quantify. As a study by the Australian Institute of Criminology found, statistical data provide very few insights, as

- Under Australian law, human trafficking is not a specific offense— therefore, no statistics are kept on it;
- The offenses of slavery, sexual servitude, and deceptive recruiting are relatively new—to date, there have been no successful prosecutions;
- Statistics on assault, sexual assault, kidnapping, and like offenses are recorded by the authorities and are not linked to trafficking; and
- Statistics on the offense of organized human smuggling do not indicate whether the offense involved trafficking (David, 2000:10).

Information from other sources, such as nongovernmental organizations, police, sex workers, and others in the sex industry, provide only a rough estimate of human trafficking for the sex industry. Christopher Payne (2003), a former federal agent working on Operation Papertiger, estimated that in 1995, Sydney had 300 women/girls in sexual servitude. In 2001, Puang Thong Simaplee died in the Villawood Detention Centre. The coroner found no evidence that young women had been enticed into Australia with false identification on the promise that they would be provided with legitimate work only to be exploited and forced to work in brothels.

In 1999, Senator Ian Macdonald told the Senate that "intelligence from Australia and overseas sources confirms, that the problem [sexual servitude in Australia] is a significant one." In September 2003, Dr. Jim Hyde, president of the New South Wales Public Health Association, The Royal Australasian College of Physicians, advised the Parliamentary Joint Committee on the Australian Crime Commission Inquiry into Trafficking in Women for Sexual Servitude that 1000 women are trafficked into Australia each year. Drawing from Project Respect (an organization involved in the rights of trafficked sex workers), Hyde reported that:

- In Melbourne, in one case alone, a trafficker brought in at least 40 Thai women; and
- Government estimates put the gross cash flow to organizers of the Australian sex slavery at Aus$1 million a week—a single trafficker in a Melbourne Municipality has allegedly earned Aus$4.5 million from trafficking for prostitution (Hyde, 2003:1).

In October 2003, Commissioner Keelty of the AFP advised the same inquiry that the AFP had investigated 37 matters since 1999; of these, 15 remained open. Since June 2003, eight arrests relating to sexual slavery, servitude, or deceptive recruiting have been made. The cases are still before the court (Keelty, 2003:3).

16.4   Policies, Laws, and Practices in Australia

Australia has been an active participant in the development of the UN Convention Against Transnational Organized Crime and its supplementary protocols dealing with people smuggling and trafficking. As with other conventions, these new treaties guided the legislature in Australia. Carrington and Hearn (2003:7) summarize the process relative to the Trafficking Protocol:

> The UN Protocol to Prevent, Suppress and Punish Trafficking in Persons, Especially Women and Children (Trafficking Protocol) was adopted by resolution A/RES/55/25 of 15 November 2000 at the 55th session of the UN General Assembly. The Trafficking Protocol opened for signature with the Convention and the other two protocols at a high level diplomatic conference in Palermo, Italy, on 13 December 2000. The Convention and its protocols enter into force as international law, 90 days after the 40th instrument of ratification has been deposited. The Trafficking Protocol represents a significant international attempt to conceptualize trafficking, define trafficking in international law and provide a template for international cooperation to address the global problem. Australia signed the Convention on 13 December 2000, the Smuggling Protocol on 21 December 2001, but its signature of the People Trafficking Protocol was delayed until 11 December 2002.

The process of ratifying these instruments is currently under way.

In Australia, the Criminal Code Amendment (Slavery and Sexual Servitude) Act 1999, defines the statutory offenses of slavery, sexual servitude, and deceptive recruiting, which are federal offenses. "Slavery is defined as occurring when ownership rights are exercised over another person and can arise from a debt incurred or contract entered into by the enslaved person" (Section 270.1). Slave trading also includes "exercising control or direction over or providing finance for the trade" (Section 270.2). Sexual servitude covers situations in which sexual services are provided because of force or threats and in which the person is not free to cease providing those services (Section 270.4). This provision applies regardless of any original consent to sex work. Deceptive recruiting occurs when a woman is deceived into believing that she is going to Australia to work in employment other than prostitution (Section 270.7), but as some observers noted (e.g., Carrington and Hearn, 2003: 9; Hyde, 2003:2), there are some limitations to the legislation because it does not capture the situation in which women agree to work in the sex industry but are deliberately deceived about the conditions of work.

Under the Australian legal system, it is desirable to have complementary commonwealth and state/territorial legislation. The Federal Minister of Justice and Customs has developed a Law Enforcement National Plan of Action through the Australasian Police Ministers' Council in which it was agreed by all state/territory jurisdictions that they would review their relevant laws and practices regarding intelligence and investigations.

In terms of law enforcement, there are three main agencies in Australia. These are the AFP, the Department of Immigration and Multicultural Affairs (DIMA), and the Australian Customs Service. Following is the summary of the activities of these three agencies drawn from a review by the Australian Institute of Criminology (David, 2000:26–33).

16.4.1 AFP

AFP is the principal law enforcement body for the federal government. Its role is to enforce federal criminal law and to protect the commonwealth and national interests from crime in Australia and overseas. It has a prime role in enforcing Part IIIA (Child Sex Tourism) of the Crimes Act 1914 and the Migration Act 1958, which is particularly relevant to the issues of human smuggling and trafficking. The AFP gives special emphasis to countering and investigating AFP activities; initiatives include:

- Investigation of people trafficking and international child sex offenses under the two acts referred to above. A Transnational Sexual Offenses Team was established in December 2002 within the AFP's Transnational Crime Coordination Centre. The Transnational Sexual Offenses Team was established to develop targets, coordinate investigation, and liaise with other agencies in relation to transnational sexual offenses, including child sex tourism, slavery, and sexual servitude. Further developments in October 2003 saw the Transnational Sexual Offenses Team incorporated into a new and larger strike team, the Transnational Sexual Exploitation and Trafficking Team. This new team will have a substantial effect on combating sexual servitude in Australia. The team's inaugural People Trafficking Specialist Investigations Training course was conducted in February and March 2004;
- A Family Liaison Coordination Team providing assistance to the victim in the context of the family and also providing assistance directly to the family and friends of the victims;
- Intelligence gathering in conjunction with state/territory services through the Australian Bureau of Criminal intelligence (now the Australian Crime Commission);
- The maintaining of a National Child Sex Offender System (the Australian National Child Offender Register);
- The use of liaison officers—the AFP has 28 liaison officers in 16 countries around the world, with the network being directed from Canberra, Australia;

- The maintenance of strong internal law enforcement links through Interpol and direct links to many other countries in the region; and
- Cooperative assistance activities in the Asia–Pacific region.

16.4.2 DIMA

The DIMA is tasked with managing the movement of people into and out of Australia. Its mission is to contribute to Australia's economic, social, and international interests through programs directed to the lawful and orderly entry and stay of people, settlement of migrants and refugees and their acquisition of citizenship, and appreciation of the advantages of cultural diversity within a framework of national unity.

Policy initiatives relevant to human smuggling and trafficking include:

- Airline Liaison Officers providing expert advice to airline staff on travel documentation and the identification of inadmissible passengers—at this time, Airline Liaison Officers are attached to Qantas in Singapore, Bangkok, and Hong Kong and to British Airways in Kuala Lumpur;
- Fining airlines for bringing inadmissible passengers to Australia;
- Intelligence gathering on immigration malpractice, using investigation units both in Australia and overseas;
- Creating a movement alert list—a database against which applicants for visas are checked before their issue;
- Examining sponsored travel, using a procedure to check on Australians who may be associated with the travel of unaccompanied minors to Australia;
- Making use of international liaisons and the exchange of information;
- Returning illegal migrants;
- Data matching with other government authorities to assist in the identification of people breaching visa conditions;
- Forming domestic education campaigns aimed at encouraging employers to recruit only people with a legal right to work;
- Forming overseas education campaigns designed to warn people of the risks associated with trying to enter Australia illegally and the penalties involved;
- Forming a refugee and humanitarian program with an obligation to provide protection to people in Australia who come within the UN convention definition of refugee; and
- Forming a women at risk program as a subprogram under the refugee and humanitarian program, aimed at affording protection for vulnerable women for whom resettlement is the only option.

16.4.3   Australian Customs Service

The Australian Customs Service facilitates the legitimate movement of people, goods, vessels, and aircraft across the Australian border while maintaining appropriate compliance with Australian law. This includes processing passengers at entry points and using coastal surveillance to detect and deter unlawful activity. Initiatives include:

- Coastal surveillance of the 37,000-km coastline through coast watch;
- Using waterfront closed circuit television surveillance at 23 seaports;
- Promoting Frontline, a cooperative venture between industry and customs in which Frontline members use their own expertise to identify suspicious activity within their industry;
- Instituting a customs watch to facilitate the gathering of information with a freecall number regarding the reporting of illegal or suspicious land, sea, or air activity;
- Federal and state agencies using a passenger analysis and evaluation system to monitor and respond to travel into and out of Australia by persons of interest;
- Having customs and DIMA officers jointly conduct interviews with selected and undocumented migrants to ascertain information relevant to voyage and vessel;
- Using the Oceania Customs Organization to coordinate the activities of the Pacific region countries; and
- Contributing to cooperative assistance activities such as institutional strengthening programs in multilateral and bilateral forums and including law enforcement training in the areas of investigation, intelligence, and enforcement in passenger processing and border operations environment.

16.5   Whole-Government Approach

On October 13, 2003, the Australian government announced a major initiative to enhance existing efforts to combat people trafficking with the introduction of the Commonwealth Action Plan to Eradicate Trafficking in Persons. The Transnational Sexual Exploitation and Trafficking Team, referred to above, is an integral part of this plan.

The key elements of this plan are:

- Closer links between AFP and DIMA officers in the detection and investigation of trafficking;

- New visa arrangements for people identified as possible trafficking victims;
- Comprehensive victim support measures provided through contracted case management, including appropriate accommodation and living expenses and access for victims to a wide range of social support, legal, medical, and counseling services;
- Enhancement of arrangements, including access to additional support for the victims who may be required to remain in immigration detention;
- Development of a reintegration assistance project for trafficking victims who are returned to key source countries in Southeast Asia;
- Improvements to trafficking legislation;
- Legislative amendments to make telecommunications interception available for Criminal Code offenses of slavery, sexual servitude, deceptive recruiting, and people smuggling with exploitation (passed on October 15, 2003); and
- Ratification of the United Nations Protocol to Prevent, Suppress and Punish Trafficking in Persons, especially Women and Children.

16.6   Dealing with the Problem at a Community Level

The events of September 11, 2001, forced countries around the world to consider how military and civil law enforcement authorities should reconfigure to address the fresh challenges that were presented. With some police services, the changes have been dramatic and have amounted to much more than simply tightening up existing practices. These services have made a distinct move (or return) to paramilitarism, characterized by a more aggressive style of dress and manner (Murray, 2003). In terms of policing philosophy, this tends to indicate a move away from the well-respected community-policing model and back to the reactionary traditional policing model. Where this happens, the inevitable trade-off is that there will be a distancing of the police from the rest of the community, which will pose a real threat to the effective prevention and investigation of sexual servitude.

A return to the traditional model of policing with its paramilitary traits is counterproductive. Gaining the trust and respect of ordinary citizens is difficult for conventional sociolegal matters, but with victims of sexual servitude, unique problems are presented that call for special sensitivities so as to gain trust and respect. It is clear that victims of sexual servitude:

- Have a strong fear or mistrust of authorities because of experiences in their own country;
- Will be reluctant to be cooperative with any authority because of their fear of arrest and deportation due to their false travel documents;

- Will feel fear of retribution at the hands of the traffickers;
- Will feel ashamed and embarrassed;
- Have language problems, and sometimes;
- Are conditioned by a culture that positions them as inferior beings.

A highlight of community policing is that it brings about partnerships in the community and works best when that relationship is structured to encourage information sharing from all parts of the community. This (especially) includes groups that tend to be unwilling to assist the police and that require police to make special efforts to win their trust and respect.

In less informed times, women caught in sexual servitude would tend to be treated variously as a law enforcement headache, an immigration problem, a welfare cost to the state, or merely a victim of violence or breach of contract rather than a person with complex needs (Moyle, 2002). It is now generally agreed that trafficked persons, especially women in prostitution, should be no longer viewed simply as illegal migrants but, rather, as victims of crime. Naturally, therefore, persons subject to sexual servitude must be treated with dignity and respect and should also be informed of their options. Their safety and physical and emotional needs are of primary concern, and details of their servitude should be discussed only when essential. The Family Liaison Coordination Team of the Australian Federal Police adopts this philosophy, which is geared to providing assistance and treatment.

Relative to the prosecution of the offenders, the wisdom of maintaining community policing becomes self-evident. Successful prosecutions depend on information. A community–police relationship that is based on mutual trust is more likely to uncover matters that are helpful in identifying sexual exploitation. A more formal community–police relationship, such as is characteristic of the traditional model of policing, would insist on reports of actual law breaking, whereas a good community–police relationship would encourage the sharing of information about something even a bit unusual. That type of community–police rapport can only be achieved if the community feels comfortable about coming forward with information—no matter how slight they believe the connection to sexual servitude to be. The contribution community policing can make is extremely positive. In terms of prevention, it can allow the community to focus on the importance of notifying early warnings/signs, consistent with the spirit that such cooperation is in everybody's interest.

With serious and demanding issues such as national security in an environment of terrorism, police commissioners could be tempted to move back to a traditional style of policing. However, for issues like terrorism and sexual servitude, it would be quite counterproductive to return to the traditional model of policing. Instead of moving away from community policing, police commissioners should look at its qualities and specifically note how this policing philosophy can be used to their advantage. To abandon or diminish this style of policing would undo all the hard work done over the decades to raise policing to the high level of societal acceptance that it now enjoys.

16.7   Conclusion

There is absolutely no doubt that offenders involved in the trafficking of women and children should be rigorously pursued, despite the investigational difficulties unique to this dreadful crime. At the same time, equal attention must be given to its prevention, together with support programs consistent with these women and children being victims of crime. In Australia, this balance seems to have been struck, and considerable time and effort have been spent on developing programs that are supportive of victims and their families. The study summarizes the law, policies, and procedures adopted by Australian authorities but cautions against what seems to be a shift in policing philosophy in some police services after September 11, 2001, when some police services tended toward returning to a traditional model of policing and moving away from community policing. The latter style of policing is fundamentally based on community consultation and cooperation with the police from the rest of the community. What is important about this in relation to sexual servitude is that information (and in turn evidence) about these activities is less likely to be uncovered with traditional policing—without the help of the community. Some governments have put pressure on police commissioners to adopt (or revert to) the more traditional model in the context of the so-called war on terror. National security, of course, is important, but police commissioners should be alert to the inappropriateness of moving back to traditional policing—to do so would be counterproductive.

References

K. Annan, Address to "Women 2000" special session, says future of planet depends on women, UN Press Release SG/SM/7430, 2000.

K. Carrington and J. Hearn, Trafficking and the Sex Industry: From Impunity to Protection, Current Issues Brief, No. 28 2002-2003, Department of the Parliamentary Library, Canberra, 2003.

F. David, Human Smuggling and Trafficking: An Overview of the Resources at the Federal Level, Australian Institute of Criminology, Canberra, 2000, http://www.imm.gov.au/illegals/apenda.html.

G. Edwards, A trade in human suffering, *Platypus*, 2003, 80: 7.

R. Frances, Australia's trade in sex: A history, presented at the History Council of New South Wales, 2003.

J. Hyde, Submission to the Parliamentary Joint Committee on the Australia
    Crime Commission, Inquiry into Trafficking in Women for Sexual Servi-
    tude, 2003, http://www.aph.gov.au/senate/committee/acc_ctte/index.htm.
M.J. Keelty, Submission to the Parliamentary Joint Committee on the Australia
    Crime Commission. Inquiry into Trafficking in Women for Sexual Servitude,
    2003, http://www.aph.gov.au/senate/committee/acc_ctte/index.htm.
I. Macdonald, Criminal Code Amendment (Slavery Servitude) Bill, Second Reading
    Speech, Senate, Hansard, March 24, 1999.
S. Moyle, Trafficking in women for prostitution, presented at the Stop the Traffic
    Symposium, February 25, 2002.
J. Murray, Policing terrorism: A threat to community policing or just a shift in pri-
    orities? *Police Practice and Research*, 2003, 4(2): 105–118.
C. Payne, Trafficking and sexual servitude in Australia, presented at a Vital Issue
    Seminar, Parliament House, Canberra, August 20, 2003.

Trafficking and Exploitation of Women and Children in Croatia

17

MARIJO ROŠIĆ

Contents

17.1   Introduction

There are some stories of women from Croatia working in the sex industry in Western European countries and of Croatian women responding to newspaper advertisements offering jobs as babysitters or cleaners in Italy, but there has been no confirmation that either Croatian women or children have been trafficked.[1] Therefore, the question is whether or not the criminal exploitation of women and children in Croatia is related to current illegal migration trends, and thus is not influenced by the security situation in the Balkan region. Because of a lack of cooperation on the operational level among the governmental bodies (primarily police and customs services) of the countries of Southeastern Europe, and because of political instability in the region, as well as because of the end of the war, the so-called Balkan Route of organized crime has reopened. In 2002, entrance to the Republic of Croatia was denied to 13,374 foreigners, and in the first 6 months of 2003, it was denied to 6915 foreigners. Because of its limited capacity, in 2002 only 936 foreigners were accommodated in the detention center for illegal migration in Ježevo near Zagreb, and in the first 6 months of 2003, only 231 foreigners were denied entry. The best way to analyze the number of illegal migrants is through the number of misdemeanor charges related to the "avoidance of border control" and "illegal border crossing." In 2000, 24,180 persons were registered as illegal migrants. A year later, this number dropped to 17,038, and in 2002 it dropped to 5415. In 2003, there were 91 registered cases of avoidance of border control and 4220 cases of illegal border crossing. In January 2004, no cases of avoidance of border control were registered.

Furthermore, the number of illegal migrants is rapidly decreasing not only in Croatia but also in neighboring countries. This decrease is a result of the application of severe migration laws in Bosnia and Herzegovina,[2] Serbia, and Montenegro.[3] These measures have been taken by the Ministry of the Interior of the Republic of Croatia in close cooperation with neighboring countries.

In 2002, the number of illegal migrants from Turkey, Iran, and China decreased. However, in the first 6 months of 2003, compared to in 2002, the number of illegal migrants from Serbia and Montenegro decreased by around 60%, even as the number of migrants from China, Albania, and Moldova slightly increased.

Generally speaking, we can talk about the stabilization of safety issues in Southeastern Europe. Croatia is a country of transit for illegal migrants and for potential victims of trafficking. Only to a very limited extent, however, can we conclude that Croatia is a country of destination for foreign women who are victims of sexual exploitation. We do, though, have to mention the appearance of seasonal prostitution at tourist destinations in the country. Trafficked women mostly come from Bosnia and Herzegovina and are sent by bar owners to the Croatian coast during the summer.

17.2   Strategies Implemented Against Trafficking in Human Beings

Data show that the highest number of illegal migrants was reached in 2000. This was the result of:

- Nonexistent or weak cooperation among neighboring countries and in the entire region[4];
- Reopening of the Balkan Route after the war ended;
- Structural changes within the law enforcement caused by the war[5]; and
- The internal political instability of the countries of the region, caused primarily by the poor economic situation, war damages, and a badly led transition.

Under the auspices of the Ministry of Foreign Affairs, an Interministerial Meeting on Trafficking was organized at the beginning of 2001. The Ministry of the Interior (the Border Police Directorate in close cooperation with the Criminal Police Directorate) was chosen to coordinate antitrafficking activities in Croatia. A national coordinator was appointed in July 2001 and was officially confirmed in May 2002. The first draft of the National Plan of Action was finalized in the end of 2001. In May 2002, the Croatian government formed a National Committee for Suppression of Trafficking in Persons with the deputy prime minister as its president and the head of the Governmental Office for Human Rights as the government's antitrafficking coordinator. The Secretariat of the Committee was provided by the Governmental Office for Human Rights. Apart from the representatives of all relevant bodies, the committee comprised all other relevant bodies: the state attorney's office, members of the parliament, one media representative, and two nongovernmental organization (NGO) representatives. The first activity of the national committee was the elaboration of the National Plan of Action, which was adopted by the government in November 2002.

17.3   Legislation

The National Plan of Action urges and requires ratification of the United Nations Convention Against Transnational Organized Crime and its supplementary protocols, regulation of the protection and assistance to trafficked persons according to international standards, and regulation of temporary residence of trafficked persons.

17.4   Assistance and Protection of Victims

These activities include proper identification of the victim (Ministry of the Interior, Office for the Suppression of Corruption and Organized Crime; in cases in which children are involved, officers of the Ministry of Labor and Social Welfare are also included), information about victims' rights (State Prosecutor's Office, Office for Suppression of Corruption and Organized Crime), provisions of safe accommodation for trafficked persons (International Organization for Migration; IOM), legal assistance, psychological assistance and medical care (Ministry of Labour, NGOs, IOM, and Ministry of Health). All these activities should be carried out by the proper governmental bodies, NGOs, and international organizations. It is interesting to note that a contact person from the Ministry of the Interior is constantly at the disposal of the NGOs, working on an emergency call principle. According to the Government of the Republic of Croatia, a reception center and three safe shelters for the victims of trafficking were founded in July 2003, and for a systematic view of the problem of trafficking victims, a centralized database within the government office has also been established.

Trafficked persons should be assisted in readmission to their home countries and should be offered suitable conditions for recovery and reintegration. In practice, these activities include psychological and social assistance, alternative accommodation, special programs for professional and work training, and assistance in finding employment and in gaining economic independence. The National Plan of Action also addresses the issue of options other than foreign women returning to the country of origin, for the protection of victims/witnesses.

17.5   Prevention

The National Plan of Action includes a list of measures, the implementation of which should prevent trafficking. These measures include focusing on social and economic causes of trafficking and warning the general public to be aware of the traffickers. To raise public awareness and to inform the public of the roots of trafficking, the National Committee for the Suppression of Trafficking in Human Beings, together with the IOM, conducted a wide public campaign (billboards, television network advertisements, and leaflets) during which an SOS phone line was also opened.

The IOM, together with the local NGOs, also conducted a research poll of public opinion to determine the level of awareness of citizens in Croatia of the problem of trafficking. The results were published in July 2002 and showed that Croatian citizens, especially the middle-aged generation, were well informed about the problem of trafficking.

17.6   Education

Training programs are being proposed for all professionals dealing with the problems of trafficking (police and customs officers), as well as for special target groups (women and children), and schools are now expected to develop special curricula on trafficking. The regional programs of exchanging knowledge and experience, which are organized for the judiciary, police, and customs personnel but are mostly implemented through the Stability Pact for South East Europe, deserve special mention.[6]

17.7   International Cooperation

The National Plan of Action includes cooperation within the Stability Pact, and more particularly with the Working Group on Trafficking in Human Beings, using bilateral cooperation, regional cooperation, cooperation with European Union countries, cooperation with candidate countries for European Union membership, and cooperation with international policing organizations (Europol and Interpol). Fruitful cooperation has been achieved through the Stability Pact Working Group on Trafficking in Human Beings, in which Croatia has received permanent membership. In addition, Croatia's joint activities with Interpol and Europol were especially intensified through cooperation on common projects and operative actions.[7]

17.8   Existing Antitrafficking Legislation

In accordance with the National Plan of Action, the Republic of Croatia ratified the United Nations Palermo Trafficking Protocol in November 2002. The amendments to the Criminal Code, which criminalized trafficking, should have been adopted in 2003, but they still have not come into force.[8] There are a few articles in the existing Croatian Criminal Code, however, that do cover the crime of trafficking.

Article 175: Establishment of Slavery and Transport of Slaves

Whoever, in violation of the rules of international law, place another in slavery or in a similar status or keeps him in such a status, buys, sells, hands over to another person or mediates in the purchase, sale, handing over of such a person or induces someone else to sell his freedom or the freedom of the person he provides for or takes care of shall be punished by imprisonment for one to ten years. Furthermore, whoever, in violation of the rules of international law, buys, sells, hands over to another person or mediates in the purchase, sale or handing over of a child or a minor for the purposes of adoption, transplantation of organs, exploitation by labor, minors, or for other illicit purposes shall be punished by imprisonment for six months to five years.

Whoever, in violation of the rules of the international law, transports persons who are in position of slavery or in a similar status shall be punished by imprisonment for six months to five years.

This article applies to the most serious cases of trafficking done by enslavement and direct physical force. It cannot be used in cases of recruitment and harboring of trafficked persons, although new amendments to the Criminal Code shall eliminate these inadequacies. They will also include provisions on recruitment, harboring, and some specific situations noticed in practice, such as destroying the victim's identity documents during the commitment of the crime, sexual abuse of the person known to be the victim of trafficking, and so on.

Article 177: Illegal Transfer of Persons Across the State Border

Whoever, for lucrative purposes, illicitly transfers a person or a number of persons across the state border shall be punished for up to three years in prison.

If this criminal offense is done within a group or a criminal organization, the perpetrators shall be punished by imprisonment from one to ten years. An attempt is also subject to punishment.

This offense usually attracts a fine and deportation to the country of origin. This article targets smuggling rather than trafficking, because it does not include elements of force, coercion, or exploitation.

Article 178: International Prostitution

Whoever procures, entices or leads away another person to offer sexual services for profit within a state excluding the one in which such a person has residence or of which he is a citizen shall be punished by imprisonment for three months to three years.

Whoever, by force or threat of use force or deceit, coerces or induces another person to go to the state in which he has no residence or of which he is not a citizen, for the purpose of offering sexual services upon payment, shall be punished by imprisonment for six months to five years.

If the criminal offense is committed against a child or a minor, the perpetrator shall be punished by imprisonment for one to ten years.

This article is focused on cross-border movement of victims and sexual exploitation. Coming amendments will have provisions for longer imprisonment (from 6 months to 5 years).

Article 195: Pandering

Whoever, for profit, organizes or assists another person in offering sexual services shall be punished by imprisonment for three months to three years.

Whoever, for profit, by force or by threat of use force, or by deceit forces or induces another to offer sexual services shall be punished by imprisonment for six months to five years.

If the criminal offense is committed against a juvenile, the perpetrator shall be punished by imprisonment for one to eight years.

If the criminal offense is committed against a child, the perpetrator shall be punished by imprisonment for one to ten years.

The fact as to whether the person who is procured has already been engaged in prostitution is of no relevance to the existence of the criminal offense.

Table 17.1 Number of Criminal Offenses for Each Article

	Year	
Article	2002	2003
175	1	2
177	191	157
178	16	1
195	34	48
196	31	37

Article 196: Abuse of Children or Juveniles in Pornography

Whoever uses a child or juvenile for the purpose of making pictures, audiovisual material or other objects of a pornographic content, or who sells, distributes, or shows such material or induces a child to take part in a pornographic show shall be punished by imprisonment for one to five years.

The amendments have a provision on longer imprisonment—from 1 to 8 years if the offenses are committed via the Internet.

The Law on Misdemeanors also regulates prostitution in its Article 12: A person who engages in prostitution can be fined up to EUR 100 or imprisoned for up to 30 days. Article 7 regulates that the provider or mediator of prostitution can be fined up to EUR 175.

The table shows the number of criminal offenses committed according to the articles mentioned above.

Women and children who are taken into custody as illegal migrants are now screened as potential victims of trafficking. Therefore, many training courses for border police officers on trafficking of human beings have been organized, and some concrete results have been reached.

Illegal migrants are fined approximately US$25 when they are stopped for the first time, and they must leave Croatian territory within 24 hours. If they are stopped for the second time during their illegal crossing, they are detained in the detention centre (Jezevo) near Zagreb, the capital of Croatia. If the detained person is suspected to be underage, the local Social Welfare Centre is informed, and they provide some assistance.

The Ministry of the Interior, in cooperation with the Ministry of Labor, Social Work Department, and the IOM, has developed procedures for victim identification. When in doubt, police contact the IOM, whose representatives interview the potential victims in cooperation with NGO representatives.

In June 2002, the Croatian government signed a Memorandum of Understanding with the IOM for cooperation on antitrafficking activities. Women are identified by the police as the victims of trafficking usually while crossing the border illegally or during the implementation of operative measures (e.g., a bar raid). They are first interviewed by the police and then by IOM representatives.

17.9   International Organizations and NGOs[9]

The IOM identified seven foreign women as victims of trafficking in 2002. A Memorandum of Understanding between the Ministry of the Interior and the IOM allows the Ministry of the Interior to cooperate with the NGOs in assisting the victims. This model of assistance is similar in all other countries of Southeastern Europe. As Croatia is specified as a transit—and not a destination—country, the emphasis of the government's work is on prevention. The IOM cooperates with the NGOs to offer shelter to the victims of trafficking. The work of the IOM is based on several activities: programs of voluntary return for migrants, giving assistance to victims in getting new travel documents, providing financial support, offering reintegration programs, making preliminary interviews with potential victims, and so on.

The Center for Woman Victims of War started to operate an information and assistance help line for trafficking in 2002. During 2003, the help line had a toll-free number accessible from all locations in Croatia. The calls from the Dalmatian coast are answered by the Organization for Integrity and Prosperity, the local NGO in Split. The Center for Woman Victims of War also has a database of all incoming calls, which is sent to the National Action Team and the Ministry of the Interior for analysis.

The Organization for Integrity and Prosperity also maintains a hotline on the Adriatic coast that operates 24 hours a day. In addition, the organization maintains a database about trafficking and registers all incoming calls from the region. They have conducted research on trafficking in 16 schools in Split and Dalmatia to collect information on trafficking among children.

The Organization for Integrity and Prosperity is also working on a manual about the treatment of victims of trafficking. The International Catholic Migration Commission (ICMC) and a local NGO, Ženska soba, cooperating with La Strada, Czech Republic, in providing a series of training sessions for the newly established NGO network Prevention of Trafficking in Croatia (PETRA). In 2003, 13 NGO members attended three training sessions, which included topics on prevention, assistance and protection, working with the media, and maintaining an SOS information and assistance help line. The ICMC provided information, awareness material, and technical assistance for all members of the PETRA network. As a result of the extra support, several NGO members have initiated information and awareness campaigns in schools and local community centers and through local radio spots.

The ICMC also supported the local NGO, the Center for Woman Victims of War, to renovate and secure a shelter for trafficked women and to coordinate training activities for Croatian young people to implement an information and awareness campaign. The ICMC also cooperates with Ženska soba to produce a quarterly newsletter. The newsletter provides information, events, and updates from Croatia and the whole Southeastern European region.

The Center for Social Policy Initiatives (CSPI), a national NGO, also has been included in the joint program initiative of the United Nations High Commissioner for Refugees and the alliance of Save the Children organizations, the Separated Children in Europe Program, since 1997. In 2000, the Separated Children in Europe Program expanded to include the countries of Central Europe. In this context, CSPI produced a national assessment on the situation of separated, vulnerable children in Croatia among the migrant populations.[10]

In cooperation with the Ministry of Labor and Social Welfare, CSPI also established a national task force for the protection of separate children in 2002. The procedure for the treatment of separated children was established in 1997. When the child is identified as separated, the police are obliged to inform the Centre for Social Welfare, and a professional from the local social services department must be present during the interview. After the interview, the Center for Social Work appoints a legal guardian to look after the best interests of the child. The separated children are usually accommodated at the nearest social welfare institution.

According to data from the Ministry of Labor and Social Welfare, 227 separated children were identified in Croatia in 2002. Their countries of origin were Serbia and Montenegro (45), Bosnia and Herzegovina (39), Turkey (38), Romania (21), Albania (17), Macedonia (13), Iraq (4), and China, Moldova, and Bulgaria (2 each). One hundred ninety-four of the children were boys, and 33 were girls.

CSPI also developed a curriculum for the prevention of child trafficking. It includes components on child trafficking, sexual exploitation, child exploitation, child pornography, and the worst forms of child labor. As part of the program, CSPI has made a video on the topic of child trafficking.

17.10 Summary and Conclusion

The main conclusions about Croatia on the problems of trafficking are the following. Croatia is a transit country for victims of trafficking, both children and women, and in some exceptional cases, and only to a limited extent, a country of origin as well as a country of destination for victims of trafficking.

The National Plan of Action supported by the government is comprehensive and presents a very good basis for concrete activities as well as for secondary legislation in the fight against trafficking in human beings. The plan covers a number of very important issues like information about legal rights, the issue of availability of options other than a return to the country of origin of trafficked persons, residence rights, and so on. Amendments to the Criminal Code harmonized with the requirements stressed in the Protocol of

Palermo Convention will allow proper legislation in the fight against human trafficking. These amendments shall soon enter into force.

Finally, the activities of the NGOs in Croatia are of high importance. Cooperation between governmental bodies and NGOs is very good and has achieved specific results and measures (SOS hotline for recording cases of trafficking, assistance during the interview, and so on).

Appendix A

The Republic of Croatia is surrounded by Hungary (in the north), Slovenia (in the west), Serbia and Montenegro (in the east), and Bosnia and Herzegovina and has a population of around 4.4 million people. Before the conflict in former Yugoslavia, Croatia was the most developed and prosperous republic, after Slovenia, with a per capita output around one-third above the Yugoslav average. Although the transitional process in most of other Eastern European countries ran peacefully, Croatia passed through a war from 1991 to 1995. Postwar consequences and the following industrial recession resulted in the country closing 10 years of the transition and experiencing slower reintegration with the European and transatlantic regions. Nevertheless, today Croatia is a country with one of the highest gross domestic products among some of the newly independent states (NIS). Both the former and the newly elected governments (2003) stressed the issue of joining the European Union during the next phase of the union's enlargement in 2007.

The total length of the border of the Republic of Croatia is 3332 km, of which 1012.5 km is river border and 950 km is sea border. Surveillance of the state border falls under the auspices of the Ministry of Interior, Border Police Directorate, and is regulated by the Law on the Surveillance of the State Border (National Gazette No. 173.03), which is in sync with European Union standards.

Notes

1. Trafficking in human beings in Southeastern Europe, report on Croatia for 2003.
2. Implementation of visa regimes for citizen of Iran, Iraq in 2000. Before these measures were implemented, citizens of these states of high immigration risk easily reached Sarajevo and Tuzla airports and continued moving through Croatia and Slovenia to Western Europe countries.
3. Fall of the regime of Slobodan Milošević, implementation of visa regimes for citizens of China.

4. First concrete steps on regional cooperation were made during 2001. Within the police forum initiative of the stability pact, several courses were organized for police officers from Bosnia and Herzegovina, Serbia and Montenegro, Macedonia, Bulgaria, Romania, Moldova (joined in 2002), Albania, and Croatia. Through the activities of the regional task forces, the heads of the criminal police directorates of Bosnia and Herzegovina, Croatia, and Serbia and Montenegro discussed security issues for the first time after the war.

5. For example, control of the state border of the Bosnia and Herzegovina overtook the State Border Service (Državna granična služba) with a totally new governmental body on the federation level. Within the Ministry of the Interior of the Republic of Croatia, a new Border Police Directorate was formed in 2002 because of the necessity of fulfilling the Schengen criteria.

6. Training courses on trafficking organized by the Police Forum Initiative (http://www.stabilitypact.org).

7. Negotiations between Europol and Croatia on signing an operational agreement are ongoing.

8. Amendments were voted on, with the majority of the presented representatives in the parliament (normal majority), and according to the constitutional court decision, it should have been voted on with the majority of all members of the parliament.

9. Trafficking in human beings in Southeastern Europe.

10. Separated children are children outside of their country of origin without either of their parents.

Bibliography

A. Adepoju, Review of research and data on human trafficking in sub-Saharan Africa. In: *Data and Research on Human Trafficking: A Global Survery*, ed. Frank Laczko and Elzvieta Gozdziak. International Organization for Migration, 2005, Geneva, pp. 75–90.

O. Agbu, Corruption and human trafficking: The Nigerian case, *West African Review*, 2003, 15: 18–29.

N. Ahmad, Bangladesh in Karachi: Trafficking and/or migrated for work? Trafficking in women and children from Bangladesh to India and Pakistan, *Nepal News*, 1999, 30.

R. Ahuja, *Social Problems in India*, 2001, Rawat, New Delhi.

P. Andreas, Criminalized conflict in Bosnia, presented at Clandestine Political Economy of War and Peace: Insights from the Balkans, Thomas J. Watson Center for International Studies, Brown University, May 6, 2003.

K. Annan, Address to "Women 2000" special session, says future of planet depends on women. UN Press Release SG/SM/7430, 2000.

T. Arewa, Trauma of abuse, *Daily Times Newspaper*, May 14, 1996.

A.A. Aronowitz, Smuggling and trafficking in human beings: The phenomenon, the markets that drive it and the organizations that promote it, *European Journal on Criminal Policy and Research*, 2001, 9: 163–165.

A.A. Aronowitz, Illegal practices and criminal networks involved in smuggling of Filipinos to Italy, United Nations Global Program Against Trafficking in Human Beings, 2002, United Nations, Vienna.

Australian Crime Commission Act, Sex slavery in Australia, 2005, http://www.news.ninemsn.com...au/article.aspx?id=54134.

N.J. Bahuguna, Toxic war on children, Women's feature service, 2003, http://gateway.proquest.com/openurl?ver=z39.88_.

K. Bales, Expendable people: Slavery in the age of globalization, *Journal of International Affairs*, 2000, 53(2): 461–484.

K. Bales, The social psychology of modern slavery, *Scientific American*, 2002, 286(4): 80–88.

K. Bales, Because she looks like a child. In: *Global Woman: Nannies, Maids, and Sex Workers in the New Economy*, ed. Barbara Ehrenreich and Arlie Russell Hochschild, Henry Holt, New York.

K. Bales and P.T. Robbins, No one shall be held in slavery or servitude: A critical analysis of international slavery agreements and concepts of slavery, *Journal of International Affairs*, 2001, 2(2): 18–37.

K. Barry, *The Prostitution of Sexuality: The Global Exploitation of Women*, 1995, New York University Press, New York.

231

C. Bassiouni, Investigating international trafficking in women and children for commercial sexual exploitation phase 1: The Americas, International Human Rights Law Institute, DePaul University, Chicago, Illinois, 2001.

C. Beccaria, *On Crimes and Punishment*, trans. Edward D. Ingraham, 2nd ed., 1819, Philip H. Nicklin, Philadelphia.

J. Bentham, *A Fragment on Government and an Introduction to the Principles of Morals and Legislation*, 1967, Basil Blackwell, Oxford.

A.M. Bertone, Sexual trafficking in women: International political economy and the politics of sex, *Gender Issues*, 2000, 18(1): 4–18.

Blood Weekly, Environment: Lead poisoning threatens kids in India, 1999, http://proquest.umi.com/pqdweb?index=75&did=000000234331271&SrchMode=1&sid=10&Fmt=3&VInst=PROD&VType=PQD&RQT=309&VName=PQD&TS=1079305641&clientId=29440.

W. Bonger, *Criminality and Economic Conditions*, trans. Henry P. Horton, 1916, Dryden Press, New York.

J.M. Braun, The girls next door, *The New York Times Magazine*, 2004, 30–75.

D. Brennan, Methodological challenges in research with trafficked persons: Tales from the field. In: *Data and Research on Human Trafficking: A Global Survery*, ed. Frank Laczko and Elzvieta Gozdziak. Geneva, International Organization for Migration, 2005, pp. 17–34.

Businessline, Rich reap more than poor from healthcare sops, 2004, http://proquest.umi.com/pqdweb?index=0&did=000000523252701&SrchMode=1&sid=2&Fmt=3&VInst=PROD&VType=PQD&RQT=309&VName=PQD&TS=1079298761&clientId=29440.

J.M. Bystydzienski, Women and socialism: A comparative study of women in Poland and the USSR, *SIGNS*, 1989, 14: 668–684.

G., Caldwell, S. Galster, and N. Steinzor, *Crime & Servitude: An Expose of the Trafficking of Newly Independent States*, 1997, Global Survival Network, Washington, DC.

C. Campbell, *Social Problems*, 1981, Free Press, New York.

K. Carrington and J. Hearn, Trafficking and the sex industry: From impunity to protection, Current Issues Brief No. 28 2002-2003, Department of the Parliamentary Library, Canberra, Australia, 2003.

S. Chakrabarthi, The AIDS mess: Unaided victims, *India Today*, 2002, 27(49).

W. Chambliss and M. Mankoff, *Whose Law? What Order? A Conflict Approach to Criminology*, 1976, Wiley, New York.

B. Choudhury, Police 'losing battle' against sex trade: Thousands of women are forced into Britain's sex trade, *BBC Social Affairs Stop-Traffic Digest*, 2002, 1, 622, August 20, 2002.

H. Chukwu, Trauma of abuse, *Daily Times Newspaper*, May 14, 1996.

M. Clinard, *The Sociology of Deviant Behavior*, 1958, Holt, Rinehart and Winston, New York.

R. Coomaraswamy, for the United Nations Economic and Social Council. United Nations, Commission on Human Rights Fifty-sixth session Agenda 12 (a) of the provisional agenda. Integration of the Human Rights of Women and the Gender Perspective: Violence against women. Report of the Special Rapporteur on violence against women, its causes and consequences, Ms. Radhika

Coomaraswamy, on trafficking in women, women's migration and violence against women, submitted in accordance with Commission on Human Rights resolution 1977/44, E/CN.4/2000/68, February 29, 2000.

R. Coomaraswamy, "Integration of the human rights of women and the gender perspective: Violence against women, report of the special rapporteur on violence against women, its causes and consequences, on trafficking in women, women's migration and violence against women," a report submitted to the Commission on Human Rights Resolution, 1997.

F. David, Human smuggling and trafficking: An overview of the resources at the federal level, Australian Institute of Criminology, Canberra, 2000, http://www.imm.gov.au/illegals/apenda.html.

L. De Baca and A. Tisi, Working together to stop modern-day slavery, *The Police Chief*, 2002, 78–80.

J. Doezema, Loose women or lost women? The re-emergence of white slavery in contemporary discourses of trafficking in women, *Gender Issues*, 2000, 18(1): 23–55.

E. Durkheim, *Division of Labor in Society*, 1964, Free Press, New York.

E. Dutt, State Department reports faults India on human trafficking, *News India Times*, 2003, 34(25).

O.N.I. Ebbe, Political-criminal nexus in Nigeria, *Trends in Organized Crime* 1997, 3(1): 3–10.

O.N.I. Ebbe, The political-criminal nexus "Slicing Nigerian national cake: The Nigerian case," *Trends in Organized Crime*, 1999, 4(3): 29–59.

O.N.I. Ebbe, Slicing Nigeria's "national cake," In: *Menace to Society: Political-Criminal Collaborations around the World*, ed. Roy Godson, 2003, Transaction, New Brunswick.

O.N.I. Ebbe, Global trafficking in women: The role of international law, presented at Oxford Round Table, University of Oxford, Oxford, England, March 26–31, 2006.

G. Edwards, A trade in human suffering, *Platypus*, 2003, 80: 7.

B. Ehrenreich, Maid to order, In: *Global Woman: Nannies, Maids, and Sex Workers in the New Economy*, ed. Barbara Ehrenreich and Arlie Russell Hochschild, 2002, Henry Holt, New York.

L. Esadze, Trafficking in women and children: A case study of Georgia, presented at the 2004 ISPAC of the United Nations Crime Prevention and Criminal Justice Programmes held in Courmeuyer Mont Blanc, Italy, 2004.

R.J. Este, The sexual exploitation: A working guide to the empirical literature content. 2001, 5.

European Law Enforcement Organisation, Crime assessment-trafficking of human beings in European Union, Annual Report, 2001.

European Union Police Mission (EUPM), *Human Trafficking*, Annual Report, 2003.

H. Falk, International environmental health for the pediatrician: Case study of lead poisoning, *Pediatrics*, 2003, 112(1).

D. Fanthorpe, Communities formal and informal justice system. Commissioned by Department for International Development, 2001.

A. Fatima, Development-India: Hub works on education for its children, Global Information Network, 2003.

FOIL, Those that are in bondage: Child labor and IMF strategy in India, 1996, http://
    www.foil.org/economy/labor/chldlbr.html.

Foundation of Women Forum, Trafficking in women for the purpose of sexual
    exploitation, The Swedish Ministry for Foreign Affairs, 1998, http://www.nmi.
    utc.edu/w?NH.DBI.EVKQE.RVnMYV.FDdEQ.CeQVPQW.K.

R. Frances, Australia's trade in sex: A history, delivered as an annual history lecture
    for the History Council of New South Wales, 2003.

Global Alliance Against Traffic in Women, A Proposal to Replace the Convention for
    the Suppression of the Traffic in Persons and of the Exploitation of the Prostitu-
    tion of Others, 1994, Global Alliance Against Trafficking in Women, Utrecht.

A. Gallagher, Human rights and the new UN protocols on trafficking and migrant
    smuggling: A preliminary analysis, *Human Rights Quarterly*, 2001, 23:
    975–1004.

A. Gaycar, Trafficking in human beings, presented at the international conference of
    Migration, Culture and Crime, Israel, July 7, 1999.

D. Ghimire, Life in hell: The true stories of girls rescued from Indian brothels, *ABC
    Nepal,* 1998, 3.

Global Survival Network, *Crime and Servitude*, 1997, Global Survival Network,
    Washington, DC.

G. Goldberg and E. Kremen, The feminization of poverty: Discovered in America.
    In: *The Feminization of Poverty: Only in America?* ed. G.S. Goldberg and E.
    Kremen, 1990, Praeger, pp. 2–15.

B.D. Gushulak and D.W. MacPherson, Health issues associated with the smuggling
    and trafficking of migrants, *Journal of Immigrant Health* 2000, 2(2): 67–78.

M. Haralambos, Sociology: Theme and perspectives, 6th edition, 2004, Harper Col-
    lins Distribution Services, New York.

H. Heikkinen and R. Lohrmann, Involvement of organized crime in the trafficking
    in migrants, 1998, International Organization for Migration, Geneva.

A. Henderson, Time to put the brakes on sex trade, *Stop-Traffic Digest*, April 11, 2003.

N. Heyzer, Combating trafficking in women and children: A gender and human
    rights framework, 2002, Vienna, UN Development Fund for Women (UNI-
    FEM) United Nations.

T. Hirschi, *The Causes of Delinquency*, 1969, University of California Press, Berkeley.

D. Hodgson, Combating the organized sexual exploitation of Asian children: Recent
    developments and prospects, *International Journal of Law and the Family*,
    1995, 9(1): 23–53.

P. Holmes, and K. Berta, Comparative matrix on legislation and best practices in pre-
    venting and combating trafficking in human beings in EU member states and
    candidate countries, presented at the European Conference on Preventing and
    Combating Trafficking in Human Beings: Global Challenges for the 21st Cen-
    tury, 2002, http://belgium.iom.int/STOPConference/ConfDocs/ConfPapers.

W.F. Horn, U.S. Human Service Agency's Responding to Trafficking, 2003, U.S.
    Department of Health and Human Services.

S. Huda, Human trafficking: Expert on trafficking in persons end visit to Lebanon,
    2005, http://www.humantrafficking.org/collaboration/regional/ame/news/
    2005_09/expert_statement.

D.M. Hughes, The Natasha trade—The transnational shadow market of trafficking
    in women, *Journal of International Affairs*, 2000, 25: 18–28.

D. Hughes, Introduction. In: *Making the Harm Visible Global Sexual Exploitation of Women and Girls Speaking Out and Providing Services*, ed. D. Hughes and C. Roche, 1999, http://www.uri.edu/artsci/wms/hughes/mhvint.htm.

Human Rights Watch, *The Human Rights Watch Global Report on Women's Rights*, 1995, Human Rights Watch, New York.

Human Rights Watch, *Owed Justice: Thai Women Trafficked into Debt Bondage in Japan*, 2000, Human Rights Watch, New York.

Human Rights Watch, Hidden in the homes: Abuse of domestic workers with special visas in the US, 2001, http://www.hrw.org/reports/2001/usadom/.

Human Rights Watch, Hopes betrayed, trafficking of women and girls to post-conflict Bosnia and Herzegovina for forced prostitution, Local Police Involvement in Trafficking, 2002.

Human Rights Watch, *Borderline Slavery: Child Trafficking in Togo*, 2002a, United Nations, Human Rights Division.

Human Rights Watch, *The Invisible Exodus: North Koreans in the People's Republic of China*, 2002b, Human Rights Watch, New York.

Human Rights Watch, *Hopes Betrayed: Trafficking of Women and Girls to Post-Conflict Bosnia and Herzegovina for Forced Prostitution*, 2002c, Human Rights Watch, New York.

Human Rights Watch, *Nepali Women Trafficked to India*, 2002d, Human Rights Watch, New York.

Human Rights Watch, *Trafficking of Women and Girls*, 2003, United Nations High Commission for Refugees.

J. Hyde, Submission to the Parliamentary Joint Committee on the Australia Crime Commission, Inquiry into Trafficking in Women for Sexual Servitude, 2003, http://www.aph.gov.au/senate/committee/acc_ctte/index.htm.

K.F. Hyland, The impact of the protocol to prevent, suppress and punish trafficking in persons, especially women and children, Human Rights Briefs, 2001, http://www.wcl.american.edu/pub/humanright/brief/index.htm.

N. Ikeano, Child prostitution: A new social malaise, *Daily Times*, March 20, 1998.

International Labour Organization, Children working in Asia, Africa, *New Nigeria*, November, 14, 1999.

International Labour Organization, Poverty main cause of child labor, *Punch Newspaper*, January 5, 1998.

International Labour Organization, Poverty eradication programme, *New Nigeria*, July 11, 1996.

International Helsinki Federation for Human Rights, Moldova. In: *Women 2000: An Investigation into the Status of Women's Rights in Central and South-Eastern Europe and the Newly Independent States*, ed. R. Weber and N. Watson, 2000, International Helsinki Federation for Human Rights and International Helsinki Federation Research Foundation, Vienna.

International Organization for Migration, Paths of exploitation: Studies on the trafficking of women and children between Cambodia, Thailand, and Vietnam, 1998, International Organization for Migration, Geneva.

International Organization for Migration, Trafficking of women into the EU: characteristics, trends and policy issues, presented at the EU Conference on Trafficking in Women, Vienna, Austria, June 10–11, 1996.

International Organization for Migration, New IOM figures on the global scale of trafficking, *Trafficking in Migrants Quarterly Bulletin*, 2001.

International Organization for Migration, *Trafficking in Women to Italy for Sexual Exploitation*, 2002, International Organization for Migration, Geneva.

International Organization for Migration, New IOM figures on the Global Scale of Trafficking. *Trafficking in Migrants Quarterly Bulletin*, 2001a, 23.

International Organization for Migration, *Victims of Trafficking in the Balkans: A Study of Trafficking in Women and Children for Sexual Exploitation To, Through and From the Balkan Region*, 2001b, International Organization for Migration, Austria.

International Organization for Migration, *Trafficking in Women and Children for Sexual Exploitation, Republic of Moldova*, 2002, International Organization for Migration, Chisinau.

International Organization for Migration and International Catholic Migration Commission, *Research Report on Third Country National Trafficking Victims in Albania*, 2000, International Organization for Migration, Albania.

International Organization for Migration, New IOM figures on the global scale of trafficking, *Trafficking in Migrants Quarterly Bulletin*, 2002, 1–6.

International Organization for Migration, Temporary resident permits: A new way to protect victims? *Trafficking in Migrants Quarterly Bulletin*, 2003, 1–2.

S.L. Ivey and E.J. Kramer, Immigrant women and the emergency department: The juncture with welfare and immigration reform, *Journal of American Medicine Women's Association*, 1998, 53: 94–95.

D. Johnson, Trafficking of women into the European Union, *New England International and Comparative Law Annual*, 2002, 5.

K. Johnson, Sweating it out for nothing, 2003, Women's Feature Service, New Delhi.

T.K. Joshi and K.R. Smith, Occupational health in India, *Occupational Medicine*, 2002, 17(3).

M. Kaldor, *New and Old Wars*, 2001, Stanford University Press, Berkeley, CA.

K. Kamal, Bangladesh Manobadhikar Sangbadik Forum (BMSF), e-mail circulation (April), 2004.

M.J. Keetly, Submission to the Parliamentary Joint Committee on the Australia Crime Commission, Inquiry into Trafficking in Women for Sexual Servitude, 2003, http://www.aph.gov.au/Senate/committee/acc_ctte/index.htm.

E. Kelly, Journeys of jeopardy: A review of research on trafficking in women and children to Europe, *IOM Migration Research Series*, 2002, 11.

E. Kelly, Journeys of jeopardy, A review of research on trafficking in women and children in Europe, 2002.

L. Kelly and L. Regan, *Stopping Traffic: Exploring the Extent of, and Responses to, Trafficking in Women for Sexual Exploitation in the UK*, 2000, Policing and Reducing Crime Unit: Police Research Series Home Office, United Kingdom.

E. Krasmigi, ISN Security Watch, 2005, http://www.humantrafficking.org/collaboration/regional/seur/news/2005_09/combating.htm.

E. Kremen, Socialism: An escape from poverty? Women in European Russia. In: *The Feminization of Poverty: Only in America?* ed. G.S. Goldberg and E. Kremen, 1990, Praeger, pp. 157–181.

V.V. Krishna, N.G. Byju, and S. Amizheniyan, Integrated past management in Indian agriculture: A developing economy perspective, 2003, http://ipmworld.umn.edu/chapters/Krishna.htm.

A. Krishnakumar, Children still at work, 2000, Frontline, Chennai.

F. Laczko and E. Gozdziak, eds., *Data and Research on Human Trafficking: A Global Survey*, 2005, International Organization for Migration, Geneva.

P. Lan, Among women: Migrant domestics and their Taiwanese employers across generations. In: Barbara Ehrenreich *New Economy*, 2002, Henry Holt, New York.

B. Limanowska, Trafficking in human beings in South East Europe, 2003, UNDP.

P. Lindesman, Collaborations: The key to combating human trafficking, *The Police Chief*, 2003, 70(2): 28–74.

S. Luda, Human trafficking: UN expert on trafficking in persons end visit to Lebanon, presented to the world press, 2005.

I. Macdonald, Criminal Code Amendment (Slavery Servitude) Bill, Second Reading Speech, Senate, Hansard, March 24, 1999.

S. Majumdar, Undone by HIV-AIDS, 2003, Women's Feature Service, New Delhi.

S. Malla, Cheliko Betha, 1998, year 2, No. 2, Srawan-Asanj 2055, p. 9.

R. Mathews, C. Reis, and V. Iacopino, Child labor: A matter of health and human rights, *Journal of Ambulatory Care Management*, 2003, 26(2).

M. McAndrew and J. Peers, The New Soviet woman-model or myth? In: *CHANGE*, 1981 International Reports, Women and Society, London.

C. McCaghy, *Crime in America*, 1980, Free Press, New York.

L. McDonald, et al., *Migrant Sex Workers from Eastern Europe and the Former Soviet Union: The Canadian Case*, 2000, Centre for Applied Social Research, University of Toronto, Canada.

Neil McKegancy and M. Barnard, *Sex Work on the Street: Prostitutes and Their Clients*, 1996, Open University Press, Buckingham.

R.K. Merton, *Social Theory and Social Structure*, 1968, Free Press, New York.

F.T. Miko, Trafficking in women and children: The U.S. and international response, 2000, Congressional Research Service Report 98-649 C.

J.R. Miller, United States Senate consent to ratification of UN Protocol on trafficking, Office to Monitor and Combat Trafficking in Persons, 2005, Department of State, Washington, DC.

J. Mirkinson, *Red Light, Green Light; the Global trafficking in Women*, 1994, Breakthrough, Prairie Fire Organizing Committee, Washington, DC.

T. More, *Utopia*, trans. H.B.S. Ogden, 1516 and 1949 Appletone-Century Crofts, New York.

R. Morgan, *Sisterhood is Global*, 1984, Anchor Press/Doubleday, Garden City, NJ.

S. Moyle, Trafficking in women for prostitution, Stop the traffic symposium, February 25, 2002.

N. Mrvić-Petrović, Implementation of international standards in the field of suppression of trafficking in human beings in BiH legislation, 2003, Pravni savjetnik, Mart, Sarajevo.

J. Murray, Policing terrorism: A threat to community policing or just a shift in priorities? *Police Practice and Research*, 2004.

North Atlantic Treaty Organisation, Resolution 323 on trafficking in human beings, 2003, Parliamentary Assembly, Committee on Civil Dimension of Security, NATO.

V. Nicol, Promoting gender and equality through reform, paper presented to the UN Commission for Peace in Sierra Leone, May 2000.

V. Nikolić Ristanović, Trgovina ženama u cilju seksualne eksploatacije: Uticaj rata, militarizma I globalizacije u Istočnoj Evropi, 2005, Globalizacija.com, časopia za političku teoriju I istraživanja globalizacije, razvoja, rodnosti, http://www. globalizacika.com/srpski/s_home.htm.

C.C.P. Nnorom, Socio-economic characteristics of child hawkers in Lagos, Nigeria, presented at the Tunisia African Sociology Conference, December, 8–12, 2003.

M. Novostei, Slavery in Russia. What the Papers Say Agency, *Stop-Traffic Digest*, 2002, 1:584.

G.O. Okereke, The international trade in human beings: A critical look at the causal factor, *Contemporary Criminal Justice Review*, 2005, 21(86): 4–17.

R.S. Parrerias, The care crisis in the Philippines: Children and transnational families in the new global economy. In: *Global Woman: Nannies, Maids, and Sex Workers in the New Economy*, ed. Barbara Ehrenreich and Arlie Russell Hochschild, 2002, Henry Holt, New York.

C. Payne, Trafficking and sexual servitude in Australia, presented at a Vital Issue Seminar, Parliament House, Canberra, August 20, 2003.

A. Popoola, Combating trafficking in human beings through legislation in Africa: Challenges, problems and prospects, presented at the First Pan-African Conference on Human Trafficking, Abuja, Nigeria, 2001.

R. Quinney, *Class, State and Crime: On the Theory and Practice of Criminal Justice*, 1977, David McKay, New York.

A. Ramaswamy, Decade of major gains, dispiriting failures: Crucial issues are stagnating infant mortality rate, quality of basic education, declining sex ratio, *News-India Times,* 2002.

R. Ray, Child labor, child schooling, and their interaction with adult labor: Empirical evidence for Peru and Pakistan, *World Bank Economic Review*, 2000, 14(2).

A. Revenco, *Conference presentation on the situation of trafficking in Moldova*, NGO briefing on women's rights, hosted by the International Helsinki Federation for Human Rights, February 4, 2002, Vienna, Austria.

A.O. Richard, International trafficking in women to the United States: A contemporary manifestation of slavery and organized crime, 2000, DCI Exceptional Intelligence Analyst Program, Center for the Study of Intelligence.

A.O. Richard, International trafficking in women to the United States: A contemporary manifestation of slavery and organized crime, 1999, State Department, Washington, DC.

A.O. Richard, International trafficking in women to the United States: A contemporary manifestation of slavery and organized crime, 1999, U.S. Department of State Bureau of Intelligence and Research, Center for the Study of Intelligence.

A.O. Richard, International trafficking in women to the United States: A contemporary manifestation of slavery and organized crime, U.S. Department of State Bureau of Intelligence and Research, Center for the Studies of Intelligence, 1999, http://www.cia.gov/csi/monograph/women/trafficking.pdf.

M. Robinson, High Commissioner for Human Rights for the Council of Europe panel discussion: Combating trafficking in human beings—A European convention? *Stop-Traffic Digest*, 2002, 1: 541.

G. Sangraula, Cheliko Betha, 1999, year 3, No. 1, Bansakh-Asa 2056, p. 17.

S. Scanlan, Report on trafficking from Moldova: Irregular labour markets and restrictive migration policies in Western Europe, 2002, International Labour Organization.

L. Shelley, Trafficking and smuggling in human beings, presented at Corruption without Security Forces: A Threat to National Security Conference, Garmisch, May 14–18, 2001.

L. Shelley, Trafficking in women: The business model approach, *The Brown Journal of World Affairs*, 2003a, 10(1): 119–131.

L. Shelley, Trade in people in and from the former Soviet Union, *Crime, Law and Social Change*, 2003b, 40(2–3): 231–249.

L. Shelley, *Trafficking in Women: The Business Model Approach*, 2003b, Transnational Crime and Corruption Center, Washington, DC.

P.K. Shetty, Ecological implications of pesticide use in agro-ecosystems in India, 2002, National Institute of Advance Studies, Bangalore, India.

V. Shiva, Monsanto and the mustard seed, *Earth Island Journal,* 2002, 16(4).

I. Sloan, *Child Abuse: Governing Law and Legislation*, 1983, Oceana Publications, New York. 20(1).

B. Sullivan, Trafficking in women: Feminism and new international law, *International Journal of Politics*, 2000, 6(1): 67–91.

S. Suri, Rights-India: Horror stories behind those veils of silk, Global Information Network, 2003, http://gateway.proquest.com/openurl?url_ver=Z39.88-2004&res_dat=xri:pqd&rft_val_fmt=info:ofi/fmt:kev:mtx:journal&genre=article&rft_dat=xri:pqd:did=000000279887801.

G.P. Thapa, Counteractive management of human trafficking in Nepal: The law and its enforcement, unpublished thesis, 2002.

S. Thapa, D. Chhetry, and R.H. Aryal, Poverty, literacy and child labor in Nepal: A district-level analysis: intervention programs aimed at reducing child labor need to focus on both alleviating poverty and increasing literacy, *Asia-Pacific Population Journal*, 1996, 11(3).

M. Torstein, *Child Slavery: Nigerian Human Rights Group Reporting*, 1996, Press Digest, Lagos.

H. Tripathi, *Existing Modality of Criminal Trial System in Nepal: The Lacunal, Challenges and Perspective,* presented in the National Workshop on Criminal Justice in Nepal: Existing Reality and Prospects for Reformation, June 10–12, 1997.

L. Tucker and A. Ganesan, The small hands of slavery: India's bonded child laborers and the World Bank, Multinational Monitor, 1997, http://www.thirdworldtraveler.com/IMF_WB/SmallHands_MNM.html.

G. Tyldum and A. Brunovskis, Describing the unobserved: Methodological challenges in empirical studies on human trafficking. In: *Data and Research on Human Trafficking: A Global Survery*, ed. Frank Laczko and Elzvieta Gozdziak. Geneva, International Organization for Migration, 2005.

United Nations Children's Fund, The Situation of Children and Women in the Republic of Moldova 2000–2001: Assessment and Analysis, 2000, United Nations Children's Fund, Moldova.

United Nations Children's Fund, UNICEF fact sheet, 2000, http://www.unicef.org.

United Nations, *Trafficking in Women and Girls, Report of the Secretary General,* 2000, United Nations, Geneva.

United Nations, *Common Country Assessment. Republic of Moldova*, 2000, UN in
    Moldova, Moldova.
United Nations, Trafficking in human misery, 2001a, http://www.unfpa.org/gender/
    trafficking.htm.
United Nations, *Significant Progress in the Fight against Trafficking in Human Beings
    in West African States*, 2001b, United Nations, Geneva.
United Nations Development Programme, *Status of Women in the Republic of Mol-
    dova*, 2002, United Nations, Geneva.
United States Department of State, Victims of trafficking and violence protection
    act of 2000: Trafficking in persons report 2001, 2001, Department of State,
    Washington, DC.
United States Department of State, Victims of trafficking and violence protection
    act of 2000: Trafficking in persons report 2002, 2002, Department of State,
    Washington, DC.
United States Department of State, Victims of trafficking and violence protection
    act of 2000: Trafficking in persons report 2003, 2003, Department of State,
    Washington, DC.
United States Department of State, Victims of trafficking and violence protection
    act of 2000: Trafficking in persons report 2004, 2004, Department of State,
    Washington, DC.
United States Department of State, Victims of trafficking and violence protection
    act: Trafficking in persons report, 2002, http://www.state.gov/documents/
    organization/10815.pdf.
United States Department of State, Accomplishments in the fight to prevent traffick-
    ing in persons, 2003a, http://www.state.gov/g/tip/rls/fs/17968pf.htm.
D. Venkateswarlu, J. Kasper, R. Mathews, and C. Reis, Child labor in India: A Health
    and Human Rights Perspective, *Lancet*, 2003, 362.
M. Wijers and L. Lap-Chew, *Trafficking in Women, Forced Labor and Slavery-Like
    Practices in Marriage, Domestic Labor and Prostitution*, 1997, Global Association
    Against Trafficking in Women and Foundation Against Trafficking in Women.
S. Zhang and C. Ko-lin, Characteristics of Chinese human smugglers: A cross-
    national study, final report, U.S. Department of Justice Grant #99-IL-CX-
    0028, 2003.

Websites

http://www.ecn.cz/lastrada
http://www.iom.int
http://www.stabilitypact.org/trafficking/default.asp
http://www.worldbank.org
http://www.saveinfo.or.jp/kinyu/yoron/per03.html#04
http://www.unodc.org/unodc/en/trafficking_human_beings.html
http://www.humantrafficking.org/countries/eap/Vietnam/news/2005_08/ht_
    capactiy_building.htm
http://www.traffickinginpersons.com/voices.htm
http://www.news.bbc.co.uk/hi/English/World/Americas/newid_1815000/1815537.
    stm

http://www.captive.org?byandaboutCD/CDdocuments/cddefinitionoftrafficking.
    htm
http://www.unode.org/unodc/en/trafficking_victim_consents.htm
http://www.inet.co.th/org/gaatw/soliderity/action/HRSLetter.htm
http://www.trafficinginpersons.com/about_trafficking.htm
http://www.humantrafficking.org/countries/eap/United_States/news/2005_10us_
    action_un_pro
http://www.usinfor.state.gov/topical/global/traffic/cs0510.htm
http://www.stabilitypact.org
http://www.big5.hauxia.com/ca/mtcz/00116887.html
http://www.gazx.gov.en/text_view.asp?newsID=807
http://www.law.westen.com/ztbd/daguai/31.htm
http://www.bjyouth.com.cn/Bq6/20000527/GB/4261%5ED0527B0214.htm
http://www.dailynews.sina.com.cn/society/2000-09-01/122773.htm
http://www.legaldaily.com.en/gb/content/2002-08/09content_41296.htm
http://www.gazx.gov.cn/text_view.asp?newsID=807
http://www.news.bbc.co.uk/li/chinese/talking_point/newsid_30830801.stm
http://www.en.news.yahoo.com/031217/55/1xr3g.html
The English version could be seen at http://www.gis.net/Chinalaw/lawtranl.htm
http://www.legaldaily.com.cn/gb/content/2000-10/12/content_6518.htm
http://www.trafffickinginpersons.com/restoration.htm
http://www.unodc.org/unodc/en/trafficking_victim_consents.html
http://www.humantrafficking.org/about/trafficking.html
http://www.humantrafficking.org/countries/eap/malaysia/news/2005_07/hrc_
    seeks_crackdown
http://www.humantrafficking.org/countries/eap/australia/news/2005_07/ACSSA_
    trafficking_rep
http://www.optusnet.com.au.13_August_2005
http://www.minermsn.com.au/article.aspx?id=54134

International Police Executive Symposium (IPES)

The International Police Executive Symposium was founded in 1994. The aims and objectives of the IPES are to provide a forum to foster closer relationships among police researchers and practitioners globally, to facilitate cross-cultural, international, and interdisciplinary exchanges for the enrichment of the law enforcement profession, and to encourage discussion and published research on challenging and contemporary topics related to the profession.

One of the most important activities of the IPES is the organization of an annual meeting under the auspices of a police or educational institution. To date, meetings have been hosted by the Canton Police of Geneva, Switzerland (Police Challenges and Strategies, 1994), the International Institute of the Sociology of Law in Onati, Spain (Challenges of Policing Democracies, 1995), Kanagawa University in Yokohama, Japan (Organized Crime, 1996), the Federal Police in Vienna, Austria (International Police Cooperation, 1997), the Dutch Police and Europol in The Hague, The Netherlands (Crime Prevention, 1998), and Andhra Pradesh Police in Hyderabad, India (Policing of Public Order, 1999), and the Center for Public Safety, Northwestern University, Evanston Illinois, USA, (Traffic Policing, 2000). A special meeting was co-hosted by the Bavarian Police Academy of Continuing Education in Ainring, Germany, University of Passau, Germany, and State University of New York, Plattsburgh, USA, to discuss the issues endorsed by the IPES in April 2000. The Police in Poland hosted the next meeting in May, 2001 (Corruption: A threat to World Order), and the last annual meeting was hosted by the Police of Turkey in May, 2002 (Police Education and Training). The Kingdom of Bahrain hosted the annual meeting in October, 2003 (Police and the Community).

The 2004 meeting in May of that year (Criminal Exploitation of Women and Children) took place in British Columbia in Canada, and it was co-hosted by the University College of the Fraser Valley, Abbotsford Police Department, Royal Canadian Mounted Police, the Vancouver Police Department, the Justice Institute of British Columbia, Canadian Police College, and the

International Centre for Criminal Law Reform and Criminal Justice Policy. The last meeting (Challenges of Policing in the 21st Century) took place in September, 2005 in Prague, The Czech Republic. The Turkish National Police hosted the meeting in 2006 (Local Linkages to Global Security and Crime). We have just concluded Fourteenth Annual Meeting in Dubai on April 8-12, 2007 (Urbanization and Security).

The majority of participants of the annual meetings are usually directly involved in the police profession. In addition, scholars and researchers in the field also participate. The meetings comprise both structured and informal sessions to maximize dialogue and exchange of views and information. The executive summary of each meeting is distributed to participants as well as to a wide range of other interested police professionals and scholars. In addition, a book of selected papers from each annual meeting is published through Prentice Hall, Lexington Books, Taylor and Francis Group and other reputed publishers.

Closely associated with the IPES is the *Police Practice and Research: An International Journal (PPR)*. The journal is committed to highlighting current, innovative police practices from all over the world; providing opportunities for exchanges between police practitioners and researchers; reporting the state of public safety internationally; focusing on successful practices that build partnerships between police practitioners and communities, as well as highlighting other successful police practices in relation to maintaining order, enforcing laws and serving the community. For more information visit our website, www.ipes.info.

The IPES is directed by a board of directors representing various countries of the world (listed below). The registered business office is located at 402 East Jackson, Macomb, IL 61455,USA; Registered Agent Douglas J. March; Tel: 309-837-2904; Fax: 309-836-2736; Email: mmdlaw@macomb.com.

IPES Board of Directors

President Dilip Das, 6030 Nott Road, Guilderland, NY 12084, USA, Tel: 318 274 2520, Fax 318 274 3101, Email: dilipkd@aol.com

Vice President Tariq Hassan Al Hassan, P.O. Box 13, Manama, KINGDOM OF BAHRAIN; Tel: (973) 17 756777, Fax: (973) 17 754302 Email: Ropac@batelco.com.bh

Treasurer/Director Jim Lewis, 406 Quail Lane, Ruston, Louisiana 71720, USA, Tel: 318 413-0551

Directors

Rick Sarre, GPO Box 2471, Adelaide, 5001, South AUSTRALIA; Tel: 61 8 84314879 (h), 61 8 83020889, Fax: 61 8 83020512 Email: rick.sarre@unisa.edu.au

Tonita Murray, 73 Murphy Street, Carleton Place, Ontario K7C 2B7 CANADA; Tel: 613 998 0883 (w) Email: tmurray@ca.inter.net

Mark Chen, Professor, Central Police University, Taiwan, mark@mail.cpu.edu.tw

Snezana (Ana) Mijovic-Das, 6030 Nott Road, Guilderland, NY 12084, USA, Tel: 518 452 7845, Fax: 518 456 6790, Email: anamijovic@yahoo.com

Horace Judson, PO Drawer 607, Grambling, LA 71245, Tel 318 274 6117, Fax 318 274 6172, Email, judsonha@gram.edu

Paulo R. Lino, 111 Das Garcas St., Canoas, RS, 92320-830, Brazil; Tel 55 51 8111 1357, Fax 55 51 466 2425 Email: paulino2@terra.com.br

Rune Glomseth, Police Superintendent, Norway Police University, Slemdalsveien5, Oslo, 0369, Norway, E-mail: Rune.Glomseth@phs.no

Mustafa Ozguler, Chief of Police, Ankara, Turkey, E:mail: Mustafaozg@hotmail.com

Maximillian Edelbacher, Riemersgasse 16/E/3, A-1190 Vienna, AUSTRIA; Tel: 43-1-601 74/5710, Fax: 43-1-601 74/5727 Email: edelmax@magnet.at

IPES operates through active support, cooperation and subscriptions of the Institutional Supporters. Our present Institutional Supporters are:

IPES Institutional Supporters

1. Dubai Police Department, (Dr. Mohammed Murad Abdulla, Director), Decision- Making Support Center, P.O. Box 1493, Dubai, United Arab Emirates, Tel 971 4 269 3790, Fax 971 4 262 3233, email: dxbpolrs@emirates.net.ae

2. Bahrain Police, (Lt. General Shaikh Rashed Bin Abdulla Al Khalifa, Minister of the Interior), Manama, P.O. Box 13, Bahrain, The Arabian Gulf, Tel 973 17 270800, Fax 973 17 253 266, e-mail: Colonel Tariq Hassan AL Hassan, Ropac@batelco.com.bh

3. Fayetteville State University, (Dr. David E. Barlow, Professor and Interim Dean), College of Basic and Applied Sciences, 1200 Murchison Road, North Carolina, USA Tel 910-672-1659, Fax 910-672-1103, e-mail: dbarlow@unfscu.edu

4. Athabasca University, (Dr. Curtis Clarke, Coordinator, Criminal Justice Program), 10-26312 TWP. RD 514 Spruce Grove, Alberta, Canada T7Y 1C8 Tel 780-470-4270 , Fax 780-497-3411, e-mail: curtisc@athabascau.ca

5. University of Hull, (Dr Bankole Cole, Director of Undergraduate Programmes, Department of Criminology and Sociological Studies), Cottingham Road, Hull HU6 7RX, UK, e-mail: B.Cole@hull.ac.uk

6. National Institute of Criminology and Forensic Science, (Director, Sharda Prasad, Inspector General of Police) MHA, Outer Ring Road, Sector 3, Rohini, Delhi 110085, India, Tel 91 11 275 25095, Fax 91 11 275 10586, e-mail: prasadsharda@ediffmail.com

7. Grambling State University, (President Horace Judson), PO Drawer 607, Grambling, LA 71245, USA, Tel 318-274-6117, Fax 318-274-6172, USA, e-mail: judsonha@gram.edu
8. University of Central England, (Mike King) Center for Criminal Justice Policy and Research, Birmingham, W. Midlands B42 2SU, UK, Tel 0121 3315163 Fax 0121 3316938, e-mail: Mike.King@ucc.ac.uk
9. Association of Defendologist of Republika Srpska, (Valibor Lalic), Srpska Street 63, 78000 Banja Luka, Bosnia and Herzegovina, Tel and Fax, 387 51 308 914 e-mail: lalicv@teol.net
10. University of Maribor, (Dr. Gorazd Mesko), The Faculty of Criminal Justice and Security, University of Maribor, Kotnikova 8, 1000 Ljubljana, Slovenia, Tel 386 1 300 83 39, Fax 386 1 2302 687, e-mail: mesko.gorazd@siol.net
11. Florida Gulf Coast University, (Charlie Mesloh, Ph.D., Director), Weapons and equipment Research Institute, 10501 FGCU Blvd S., Fort Myers, Fl 33965, USA, Tel 239-590-7761 (office), Fax 239-229-3462 (cellular), e-mail: cmesloh@fgcu.edu, fthompso@fgcu.edu
12. Ohio Association of Chiefs of Police (Todd Wurschmidt), 6277 Riverside Drive, #2N, Dublin, Ohio 43017, USA, Tel. 614 761 0330, Fax 614 718 3216. email todd.wurschmidt@oacp.org
13. Kent State Univ. Police Services (John A. Peach, Chief of Police), P. O. Box 5190, Stockdale Safety Building, Kent, Ohio 44242-0001, Phone#: 330 672 3111, email jpeach@kent.edu
14. Justice Institute of British Columbia Law Enforcement & Regulatory Training Program, (Mark LaLonde, Program Director), 715 McBride Boulevard New Westminster, British Columbia V3 L5 T4, Canada, Tel 604-528-5768 Fax 604-528-5754, e-mail: mlalonde@jibc.bc.ca
15. Abbotsford Police Department, (Ian Mackenzie, Chief Constable), 2838 Justice Way, Abbotsford, British Columbia V2 T3 P5, Canada, Tel 604-864-4809, Fax 604-864-4725, e-mail: imackenzie@abbypd.ca
16. Royal Swaziland Police, (Isaac Mmemo Magagula), PO Box 49, Mbabane, Swaziland, Tel 268-606-2312, Fax 268-404-4545
17. University College of the Fraser Valley, (Dr. Darryl Plecas), Department of Criminology & Criminal Justice, 33844 King Road, Abbotsford, British Columbia V2 S7 M9, Canada, Tel 604-853-7441, Fax 604-853-9990, e-mail: Darryl.plecas@ucfv.ca
18. National Police Academy, Japan, Koichi Kurokawa, Assistant Director, Police Policy Research Center, Zip 183-8558: 3-12-1 Asahi-cho Fuchu-city, Tokyo, E-mail: Tcr01@anpac.jp
19. Canterbury Christ Church University (Claire Shrubsall), Department of Crime and Policing Studies, Northwood Road, Broadstairs, Kent CT10 2WA, UK, Tel 44 (0)1843 609115, Fax 44 (0) 1843 280700, email claire.shrubsall@canterbury.ac.uk
20. Police Standards Unit, (Stephen Cahill), Home Office, 2 Marsham Street, London, SW1P 4DF, UK, Tel 44 207 035 0922, Fax 44 870 336 9015, email Stephen.Cahill@homeoffice.gsi.gov.uk
21. Deputy Commissioner Pacific Region & Commanding Officer "E", RCMP (Gary Bass), 657 West 37th Avenue Vancouver BC V5Z 1K6, Canada, 604-264-2003, Fax 604 264 3547, email gary.bass@rcmp-grc.gc.ca

Index

A

AIDS/HIV, 69, 77, 89, 131
Amnesty International, 27–28, 42, 83
Australia, trafficking case study, 19, 25–26, 207–217
    Australian Federal Police (AFP), 209, 212–213
    community level action, 215–217
    Customs Service, 214
    Department of Immigration and Multicultural Affairs (DIMA), 212–213
    overview of, 207–209
    policies, laws, and practices, 211–212
    whole-government approach, 214–215
Australian Center for the Study of Sexual Assault, 25–26

B

Beccaria, C., 34
Bentham, J., 34
Body parts (human organs), 3, 11
Bosnia and Herzegovina, trafficking case study, 6, 109–124
    Arizona market (example), 114
    background to, 109–110
    conflict in, 113–114
    female refugees, 113
    government response, 120–121
    international implications, 118–119
    international legal standards, 123
    international peacekeeping force, 115–116
    legislation, 122
    local law enforcement capacities, 121–122
    organized crime in, 117–118
    poverty factor, 116
    role of NGO sector in, 123–124

    scope of, 110–112
    smuggling economy, 114–115
    southeastern Europe, 112–113

C

Cambodia, 35–36
Captive Daughters International, 8
Child labor, 8, 21, 168; *see also* India, child labor case study; Nigeria, child labor case study
Child pornography/prostitution, in Japan, 49–50
Child trafficking, 7–13
    orphans concentration areas, 35
    UN Protocol definition, 8
China, trafficking case study
    causes of, 56
    economic background, 56–57
    economic incentive for, 57–58
    government control/regulation of, 62–63
    ignorance of law, 57
    lenient punishment, 57
    nature/extent of, 55
    prostitution business, 58–61
Classical School of Criminology, 34
Coalition Against Trafficking in Women (CATW), 42–43
Committee Against Modern Slavery, 9
Community policing, 208
Constitutional Rights Project Report, 26
Counterfeit marriage, 95–97
Criminal victimization, in Nepal, 98–101
Croatia, trafficking case study, 6, 219–229
    antitrafficking legislation, 223–225
    antitrafficking strategies, 220–221
    assistance/protection of victims, 221–222
    education, 222
    international cooperation, 223